# Mysteries of My Father

# Mysteries of My Father

Thomas Fleming

WILEY

John Wiley & Sons, Inc.

Published by John Wiley & Sons, Inc., Hoboken, New Jersey
Published simultaneously in Canada

Design and composition by Navta Associates, Inc.

For general information about our other products and services, please contact our Customer Care Department within the United States at (800) 762-2974, outside the United States at (317) 572-3993 or fax (317) 572-4002.

Wiley also publishes its books in a variety of electronic formats. Some content that appears in print may not be available in electronic books. For more information about Wiley products, visit our web site at www.wiley.com.

**_Library of Congress Cataloging-in-Publication Data:_**

Fleming, Thomas J.
  Mysteries of my father / Thomas Fleming.
     p. cm.
  ISBN 0-471-65515-5 (cloth: alk. paper)
  1. Fleming, Teddy, 1888-1959. 2. Fleming, Thomas J.—Family. 3. Politicians—New Jersey—Jersey City—Biography. 4. Sheriffs—New Jersey—Hudson County—Biography. 5. Jersey City (N.J.)—Biography. 6. Hague, Frank, 1876-1956. 7. Jersey City (N.J.)— Politics and government—20th century 8. World War, 1914–1918—Biography. 9. Soldiers—United States—Biography. I. Title.
  F144.J553F58 2005
  974.9'2704'092—dc22
                                                                2004015426

Printed in the United States of America

10  9  8  7  6  5  4  3  2  1

# Contents

*Photographs begin on page 165*

# Author's Note

Because it was impossible to recall after the lapse of dozens of years the exact names of many people who appear in the text, I have invented some names to give the narrative a realistic flow. In no instance does this alter the essential truth of the various accounts.

# Acknowledgments

As readers will quickly discover, most of this book is based on memory. Wherever possible I have bolstered the memories with historical research. For their unstinting and enthusiastic help in this task I must thank the staff of the New Jersey Room at the Jersey City Public Library—Director Charles E. Markey and his assistants, Cynthia Harris and Joseph Donnelly. I would also like to thank the former director of the New Jersey Room, Kenneth French, who was a great help when I started work on the book several years ago. Also on my gratitude list are the staff of the Plainfield Public Library and Barbara Petrick, author of a brilliant study of Jersey City's public and parochial schools, who gave generously of her time and advice. Also helpful were Mitchell Yockelson of the Modern Military Records Branch of the National Archives and historian Robert R. Ferrell, who shared with me his files of research on the Argonne. Steven Bernstein and my son, Richard Fleming, pursued many obscurities on the Internet and in libraries on my behalf, saving me hours of travel and labor. Equally warm thanks go to Richard Snow, the editor of *American Heritage*, who in 1991 published an article about my father, and to Martin Tucker, the editor of *Confrontation*, in which I published some early drafts about my mother. My wife, Alice, was invaluable as a counselor as well as a genealogical explorer. As a catalyst whose insights gave the book its form, after many false starts, my editor, Stephen Power, was a constant resource. At least as important was the enthusiasm and support of my literary agent, Ted Chichak.

# 1

# A Message from the Past

Through the blank impersonality of cyberspace whizzed an e-mail to the "Mairie" (City Hall) of Jersey City, New Jersey, a town that sprawls on the Hudson River almost within hailing distance of the Statue of Liberty and New York's shimmering skyline.

My name is Gil Malmasson. I'm a 31 year old Frenchman who lives in a suburb of Paris. I work as a professional photographer but one of my favorite hobbies is metal detecting. A few years ago I was searching near a small American monument in memory of WWI American soldiers who fought in the Argonne Forest. Suddenly I found a gold ring with an onyx stone. Inside was engraved: "FROM MAYOR FRANK HAGUE TO SHERIFF TEDDY FLEMING 1945." I went to the U.S. Embassy in Paris and to U.S. Army headquarters to ask their help in finding the owner. They were unable to assist me. Finally, on the internet I found the page you wrote about Frank Hague and the many years he served as mayor of your city. Can you help me find Sheriff Fleming or his children?

Gene Scanlon, Jersey City's director of communications, forwarded a copy of this e-mail to me in my New York apartment. Gene had graduated a year ahead of me from the local Jesuit high school, St. Peter's Prep. Without him, Gil Malmasson's message might have gone unanswered. No one else in City Hall would have been likely to connect me with the days when Mayor Frank Hague and Sheriff Teddy Fleming strode the corridors of power.

I sat there, staring at the message, not quite able to believe what I was reading. Thirty years had passed since this ring had vanished into loose dirt on a hillside in that blood-soaked French forest. I had gone there to write an article for *American Heritage* magazine on the fiftieth anniversary of the climactic battle of World War I. The ring had slipped off my finger on a cold March day and vanished into loose shale. Now it had come back to me in this extraordinary way. What did it mean?

I was not sure. For the moment I was only certain of one thing. I handed a printout of the e-mail to my wife, Alice, and said, "I want to go back to the Argonne and have him put the ring on my finger exactly where I lost it."

Maybe then I would understand what it meant. But I somehow doubted it. Already I sensed it would take more than a journey to France to understand the many meanings of the man who had accepted that ring and the mayor who gave it to him. They represented something large and imponderable that I had tried to deal with in a half dozen novels. But I had never confronted them as history. Was it time to do that? Inwardly, I flinched from the task that I half knew was being imposed on me. All writing was a mixture of pain and pleasure. In this venture I feared pain would predominate.

Alice and I flew to Paris on Monday, November 25, 1998. A smiling Gil Malmasson met us at Charles de Gaulle Airport. With him were his father, François, a well-known architect, and his brother Marc, a gifted musician. Also on hand were a reporter and photographer from Agence France-Presse, the French news agency, who interviewed us briefly and took pictures. Gil had told the story of the ring to several friends in the media.

The next day, François Malmasson drove Gil and Alice and me to the Argonne. During the 170-mile ride, we talked about how Gil had found the ring. He had begun exploring historic sites with his metal detector when he was a teenager and now had a collection of Roman-Celtic artifacts and other discoveries that was moderately famous among fellow hobbyists.

I asked Gil why had he had gone to so much trouble to locate me. "As a Frenchman I wanted to express my gratitude to the Americans for the help they had given us twice in this century," Gil said. "Without you, France would not be a free country today."

When we reached Varennes, the Argonne's principal town, we discovered that Gil and I were on the front page of *L'Est Républicain*, the regional newspaper published in Verdun. The headline read: LA BAGUE D'ARGONNE. It told the story of the loss and recovery of "the Argonne ring."

Within an hour, a television crew arrived to interview us. I told them how much the restoration of the ring meant to me personally. It had renewed my sense of closeness with my father. As an historian, I was also ready to discuss the French perception of the ring's wider meaning. I talked about my recent book, *Liberty! The American Revolution*, which stressed how much France had helped the infant United States win its independence. I praised the Marquis de Lafayette, the fervent young idealist who had spent his personal fortune to support the Americans in their fight for freedom.

My father's ring recalled how the Americans had repaid that debt by coming to France to fight the Germans in 1917. On July 4 of that war-torn year, General John J. Pershing, the commander of the American Expeditionary Force, had led an honor guard to the grave of the Marquis de Lafayette in Paris. A staff colonel who was fluent in French declared, "Lafayette! We are here!"

While the TV cameras whirred, Gil placed the ring on my finger. For a moment I was almost undone. I remembered the shock of losing it. For a week I had roamed the Argonne Forest and the twenty-mile-wide valley beside it, where over a million Americans had fought the Germans for almost two months, taking appalling casualties from massed machine guns and artillery. Never had I felt so close to my father, so full of admiration for him. Then came the desolating moment when I realized that the ring was gone.

I remembered wondering if Teddy Fleming was wryly informing me that I was not as close to him as I had imagined. Was he suggesting I would never really understand him? Our pasts were too different. What did I know about the humiliations of poverty, the embittering sense of being treated as a member of an inferior race? Had I ever talked back to a sneering WASP or gotten out a ninety percent straight ticket vote?

Forty years of reading and writing American history steadied me. I now knew a great deal more about the complicated reality in that much-misunderstood term *Irish-American*. That enabled me to understand a lot more about the tough, angry man who had worn the Argonne ring. I managed to conceal these old but by no means quiescent feelings from the camera's staring eye.

That night at seven o'clock, Gil and I saw ourselves on French national television at our Verdun hotel. The story opened with my father's picture in his World War I lieutenant's uniform, with his broad Sam Browne belt across his burly chest. A French commentator translated my remarks. Gil added a moving statement about his belief that finding such mementos as the ring on a battlefield was a way of defying death's seeming omnipotence.

Back in Paris, Senator Paul Loridant, who represented Gil Malmasson's district, invited us to the Luxembourg Palace. At a reception in the Victor Hugo room, Senator Loridant presented me with the medal of the French Senate. "Your coming here to retrieve your father's ring reminds us of what fathers mean to sons and what sons mean to fathers," the senator said. "It also reminds France and America of the sacrifices brave men have made for their democratic freedoms."

The splendid rugs and gilded ceilings of the Luxembourg Palace were a long way from the mud and blood of the Argonne in 1918. They were equally far from the shabby industrial city of my Depression-era boyhood. They were light-years from the waterless, unheated downtown tenement in which my father had been born. The ring indubitably linked us with the poilus and doughboys of their distant decade. The connection to these vanished Jersey City worlds was equally strong—and growing more intense by the hour. Deeply as I appreciated Gil Malmasson's generosity, I began to think the loss and rediscovery in the Argonne were only the surface meaning of the ring's return.

Back in the United States, the ring's reappearance attracted newspaper, magazine, and television attention. The *New York Times* devoted almost a full page of its Metro section to its discovery and my trip to France. *People* magazine ran an article on it. The Pax TV network devoted a half hour to the story. All these reports remained on the surface of the event. Hardly surprising—there was plenty of surface to write about.

Then came a telephone call from Jersey City. Mayor Brett Schundler wanted to give me a reception in City Hall. This was good for a private laugh. Until recently, my status in Jersey City was somewhat anomalous. In 1969, a decade after my father's death, I had written "I Am the Law," a long profile of Mayor Frank Hague in *American Heritage* magazine, coolly analyzing his ruthlessness, his corruption, and the near perfection of his version of machine politics. Hague loyalists found it lacking in sympathy for the mayor. I came close to being called a turncoat—an experience I have recently replicated by writing equally dispassionate books about Franklin D. Roosevelt and Woodrow Wilson.

In another magazine article, "City in the Shadow," I chastised Frank Hague's successors for continuing a tradition of corruption that had already landed several of them in the penitentiary. The followers of these discredited pols liked this commentary even less. Once, when I ventured across the Hudson to speak in my hometown, people knocked knives on coffee cups and interrupted my observations with catcalls and insults.

As a writer, I had moved beyond my birthplace as a subject. I had written a dozen history books and novels about the American Revolution. Next came a history of West Point, followed by novels set in World War II and Vietnam, as well as in pre–Civil War Washington, D.C., and post–Civil War New York. On the surface at least, neither my father nor Jersey City were topics that had occupied my imagination for decades. But by this time I knew I was not dealing with surfaces. I was aware that on a deeper level Teddy Fleming and his wife, Katherine Dolan Fleming, and the Irish-American political and religious world of Jersey City had been with me every year of my literary life.

I accepted Mayor Schundler's invitation. My wife, Alice, and I journeyed from our New York City apartment via the subway and then a PATH train that whizzed beneath the Hudson River to Jersey City. In my youth, PATH had been an independent railroad called the

Hudson and Manhattan Tubes. The cars had been dirty, groaning relics from the era of World War I. My uncle Al Gallagher had been the night superintendent and often regaled us with predictions of catastrophe when (not if) the wheels fell off or the brakes failed. Now the trains were run by the Port Authority of New York and New Jersey and were clean and relatively noiseless.

In a half hour we were sauntering down Grove Street toward City Hall. For a moment I recalled meeting my father here after staying late at my nearby high school, St. Peter's Prep, rehearsing a play. In the twilight, the massive granite and marble "Hall" loomed like some huge mythological creature with a hundred staring eyes. At the curb, a row of gleaming seven-passenger Cadillacs waited for the ward leaders to finish their conference with Mayor Frank Hague and his fellow commissioners. Power, I thought. Irish-American power. The cars, the building, had emanated it. Gone now, gone beyond recall.

Looking up at City Hall, I realized something else had vanished: the bravura brass cupolas on the corners and the soaring central tower that had given the building a touch of grandeur. As my old friend Gene Scanlon soon explained to me, the chemicals in the city's once omnipresent smog had not been kind to metals. A recent mayor had chosen the less expensive part of valor and amputated these architectural grace notes. But the imposing gray façade, with its array of windows flanking the porticoed entrance, still managed a semblance of dignity.

In the mix of private and public memory through which I was moving, another group of buildings were at least as important as City Hall. A mix of brick and wooden two- and three-story structures, many with businesses on the first and second floors, they were on the opposite side of Grove Street and lacked even a hint of grandeur. In 1906 or 1907, when my father was in his late teens, one of the second floors had been a dentist's office. One winter day, Teddy Fleming sat down in the dentist's chair, pointed to his teeth, and said, "Pull'm out."

"All of them?" the startled dentist said.

"All of'm," my father said.

It took the dentist two hours and cost my father almost every cent he possessed. I don't know whether the dentist used novocaine or gas to stifle the pain. Probably the latter, since novocaine had only begun its career as an anesthetic in 1905. Teddy Fleming went home to his family's flat on Communipaw Avenue in the Sixth Ward and dulled the ache with whiskey until he went to sleep.

A few days later Teddy returned to the dentist's office and the dentist inserted a set of upper and lower false teeth that transformed his appearance. His natural teeth had been a protruding, twisted mess, which would have forever condemned him to inferiority with women and even with most men. In 1908, everyone admired the strong-jawed Anglo-Saxon Protestant types that dominated the stages of Broadway and the advertisements in newspapers and magazines.

Whenever I walked past City Hall during my adolescent years, I looked across the street at the site of the dentist's office, which was long gone. My mouth hurt. I felt my father's pain. I admired his guts. I wondered if I could do something so amazing. Teddy Fleming had done nothing less than change himself from an ugly lower-class Irish-American—a mick—to a man with the good looks of the WASP elite. The price he paid in pain and money was unquestionably worth it.

There was something profoundly American about this transaction. An aura of wonder, even myth, surrounded this vision of my father. Its many meanings still throbbed in my chest in 1998, almost a hundred years after it happened. It was an ineluctable part of my private memories of Teddy Fleming.

Inside City Hall, Mayor Schundler's reception was held in the council chamber where Frank Hague once presided over meetings of the city's commissioners. Maybe it was my recent exposure to the Luxembourg Palace, but the room looked unutterably dingy. It had not seen a paintbrush in several decades. In Hague's day the place had gleamed.

In the audience was a delegation of smiling teachers and students from St. Peter's Prep and a scattering of old-time Jersey Cityans who remembered Teddy Fleming and pumped my hand. Reporters from the *Newark Star-Ledger* and the city's local paper, the *Jersey Journal*, interviewed me and Mayor Schundler.

The atmosphere was incredibly good-natured. No one had a negative word to say about Mayor Frank Hague or the bare-knuckled political organization he had created and Sheriff Teddy Fleming had helped him run. On the contrary, everyone, including Mayor Schundler, the first Republican mayor in almost a century, seemed ready to hail the Democratic chieftain and my father as men who had given Jersey City an aura of national power. At times they seemed to be using my modest literary celebrity to say the bad old days were not so awful as a lot of people once claimed.

This was so contrary to the experience of my youth, when "Hagueism" was an epithet in newspapers, magazines, and books, that I felt almost disoriented. But I managed to play my part in the cere-mony, expressing my genuine gratitude for this expression of affection from my hometown. I coated my remarks on the old days in a glaze of sentimental glory.

Back in New York, as my wife and I walked from the subway down East Sixty-ninth Street toward our apartment, another memory stirred. On the south side of the street was a huge modern apartment house. On the north side was a row of nineteenth-century carriage houses—now garages with apartments above them. One night early in 1920 Teddy Fleming and Katherine Dolan, known to her friends as Kitty, were visiting a couple who lived in one of these carriage houses. Teddy and Kitty were not yet married but both had marriage on their minds.

The host, Eddie Shanaphy, was my mother's cousin. He was a chauffeur for the Wall Street millionaire James Cox Brady. The gray Rolls-Royce that Eddie drove was in the garage below them. His wife, Mae, enjoyed living in the aura of the very rich. She was always talk-ing about "the Madam"—Mrs. Brady—what she wore, what she said, where she traveled. It gave her—and my mother—a vicarious thrill to imagine people with unlimited cash at their disposal.

It was a snowy night. On Third Avenue, the El loomed in the streetlights. Trains rumbled past, rattling the windows. In 1920 my father had just returned from France, where he had won a lieutenant's commission for his performance on the battlefield at St. Mihiel and in the Argonne. Friends were telling him—and my mother—that he had a future as a politician.

On the first floor of the carriage house, my father had seen several sets of skis on the wall. "Let's try those toboggan shoes out in Central Park," he said.

In spite of the newly passed Eighteenth Amendment, which theoretically banned alcohol from America, everyone had downed enough rye whiskey to put them in the mood for some fun. They were young and they wanted to pretend they were rich. In those days, skiing was mostly a rich man's sport. You had to travel to Switzerland or Colorado to try it. They bundled into their winter coats and trudged four blocks to Central Park with two sets of skis on Teddy's muscular shoulders.

It was well after midnight. The park was dreamlike, blanketed in gleaming snow, random lamps glowing with a fiery light. The skis did not require boots. There were clamps on them, like old-fashioned roller skates, and binders that wound around the ankles to give the skier control. For two hours they slithered and floundered and flopped in the snow, laughing at each other's crashes.

I suddenly saw Teddy Fleming in the middle of this snowy stillness, surrounded by the towering apartments of the rich, helping beautiful dark-haired Kitty Dolan to her feet, brushing her off, urging her to try again. He careens downhill himself, crouched low for balance. Everyone yells their admiration. He smiles. Why not pretend to be rich for a night? He had survived thousands of German bullets and shells in France. He had helped beat the kaiser. Maybe the world was his oyster.

My mother thought it was. She saw vast potential in my father. She thought she could polish him for a march to big things by cleaning up his grammar and lower-class Irish accent. She succeeded in both departments. But he never rose beyond the wards and precincts of Jersey City.

Back in our apartment, I gazed at the picture of my father in his U.S. Army lieutenant's uniform on the dresser in my bedroom. Not for the first time, I admired the toughness in those blue eyes. Beside the lieutenant was a smiling picture of Katherine Dolan Fleming on her wedding day in 1923. Her smile concealed many sorrows.

I suddenly thought of the worst day of my life.

*"I can't stand it, I can't stand it any longer," Kitty Fleming screamed. She ran out to the kitchen and pounded on the red Formica tabletop with her fists. "I'm going to kill myself!" she cried.*

*I raced out to the kitchen and found my mother on her knees in front of the open oven. "I'm going to do it," she sobbed. "I'll show everyone what a monster he is. I'll tell the whole world he doesn't love anyone or anything."*

I retreated to the study at the rear of my New York apartment, where I wrote my books, and pondered a large framed picture of my father as I remembered him when he was sheriff of Hudson County and leader of Jersey City's turbulent Sixth Ward. The face was fleshier than the lieutenant's but it had the same tough eyes. The mouth was tauter, more knowing—almost sad. There were sorrows here too. But Teddy Fleming had accepted them with the fatalism of a man without illusions. You win some and you lose some.

What was he saying to me? Something like: You've written a lot of history about a lot of guys. How come you've left out the mayor and me and the rest of our crowd? We made a little history too. We got a few things done, even if some people didn't like the way we did them.

What if I tell the whole thing? The inside and the outside? You and Mother? The day in the car when what you said changed everything? The poem I found in your dresser drawer? What you said when you lost your leg?

You're the writer. It's your call. But if you want my advice: tell it straight.

On the opposite wall was a picture of Mayor Frank Hague, glaring defiantly into the camera. He looked ready to take on the whole Republican Party single-handed. I remembered the first time I met him, when I was seven years old.

We were in the parking lot outside Roosevelt Stadium, Jersey City's baseball park. My father steered me around a big puddle and caught up to Hague as he was getting into his gleaming black Cadillac limousine. "Mayor, I'd like you to meet my son," Teddy Fleming said.

I held out my small hand. His Honor glared at me as if he had just caught me scalping box-seat tickets and crushed my fingers into a throbbing pulp. Simultaneously he growled, "Your old man is a hell of a guy."

Maybe it was time to tell the whole story. The public triumphs and the private tragedy, the gritty laughter and the bitter regrets, the courage that transformed public defeat into a private victory. Maybe, in the words of my favorite Irish poet, I should live it all once more:

> *Endure that toil of growing up,*
> *The ignominy of boyhood, the distress*
> *Of boyhood changing into man.*

Maybe I could finally explain to myself and others how fear of Teddy Fleming turned to forgiveness and dislike to admiration. Maybe I could track the way love won a subterranean battle against historic wounds and silent reproaches. Maybe I could face—and understand, and forgive—Katherine Dolan Fleming's embittered attempts to make me a fellow antagonist of the man she publicly admired and privately disdained.

Maybe I could unite the tragic history of a people and the tragic history of a family. I had long since decided that the Irish who emigrated to the United States had become radically different from the Irish who had stayed behind and suffered under England's brutal heel. Maybe the Flemings and the Dolans summed up a lot of that history-charged term *Irish-American*.

*Yes*, I thought, *yes. I'll try it—even if it involves lying down one more time in the foul rag and bone shop of the heart.*

# 2

# The Bad Old Days

Oh Teddy Boy,
The soap, the soap is sliding
Around the tub;
Where sits your dear backside!

One of my father's earliest memories was this comic variation on Ireland's most famous song, "Danny Boy." His petite red-haired mother, Mary Green Fleming, sang her version to him as she bathed four-year-old Teddy in the kitchen sink of their tenement on Jersey City's Halladay Street.

Teddy's real name was Thomas James Fleming, after his father's two brothers, Tom and Jim. But Tom already had a son named Tom, and to avoid confusion at family gatherings the new arrival was nicknamed Teddy. It would be his name for the rest of his life. As Irish nicknames went, it was relatively mild. Many of them revealed the wicked eye of the bestowers—"Mouse" Connell, "Footo" Moran, "Pasty" O'Brien.

From an early age, Teddy's older (by one year) brother, Dave, was called "the Turkey." In an address book my father kept while he was in France during World War I, he casually listed Dave by that name, as if he did not have another one. I don't think the moniker had anything to do with an ability to "talk turkey"—to tell the blunt truth to people.

That was much more my father's style. Some family members say the nickname was derived from the gobbling sounds Dave made in his cradle.

Teddy's brawny father, David Fleming, known to his family and friends as Davey, did not approve of his wife's lighthearted distortion of "Danny Boy." "Sing the lad the real worrrds, Mary," he growled in a brogue so thick, Teddy and his brother often found it hard to understand him. "'Tis the finest truest song ever sung about Ireland. Sure it will tell him the truth about our people's sad lot—driven to foreign shores by the English thieves and murderers, when we weren't starrrved to death by the side of the road in our own country."

"Sure I see no point in fillin' the lad's head with our tales of woe," Mary Green Fleming replied, as she dried Teddy off with one of her discarded skirts as a substitute for a towel. "He's American born, with never a form to fill out or an oath to take to become a citizen in a strange country. America is his land of freedom and opportunity as much as anyone's."

"Freedom to do what?" Davey Fleming said. "Say yessir to some two-faced Protestant boss or starve as quick as the poor devils we left behind in Ireland? I want him to learn the truth while he's in his kneepants, Mary. As long as he's got an Irish name and the Prods are runnin' things over here, he's goin' to havta' fight with his fists and maybe with a gun in his hand to get a daycent livin' in this country."

"I'm not so gloomy as you about America," Mary replied. "Sure I know we're havin' hard times and you're bearin' the brunt of them. But things'll be better for the lads, I'm sure of it. For one thing, they'll know their letters, and for another they won't have the brogue that marks us as soon we open our mouths."

"I'm no more ashamed of me brogue than I am of me Irish blood!" Davey Fleming bellowed. "I'm no bookman or scrivener, I admit, but I know the old stories from me father's lips as he told them around the fire on winter nights. We come from kings who were pitched low by fate for reasons only the old gods understand. The blather of the priests is our consolation and a poor one, to be sure."

"Don't you go on with your pagan drivel in earshot of this inno-cent lad!" Mary cried.

"Dammit Mary, I want him to know the truth and not a lot of

pious malarkey," Davey roared. "If y'drive me to it, I'll give yez an *order*, so help me I will. I won't have yez fillin' me sons' heads with jokes and foolery and empty promises about America. I want them to be Irishmen! Proud fightin' Irishmen!"

"You can order me till you're red in the face, Davey Fleming," Mary said. "They're my sons too and I'll say what I please to them. I want them to be American as well as Irish. Maybe more American than Irish. I don't want them spendin' their days lamentin' Ireland's fate when there's nothin' in the world they can do about it."

"You want them to forget our dead? The two million that died starvin' in their cabins or on the roads in forty-seven and forty-eight while the English feasted on Irish beef and bread the landlords shipped them by the ton?"

"That's forty years back now, before either of us were born," Mary said. "'Twas awful no doubt. But what's the point of spendin' our days grindin' our teeth and vowin' revenge? It can't bring back the dead or persuade the English to sink their fleet and give up their ill-gotten millions."

For a long time, Teddy Fleming would remember that moment with a clutch of dread. His father was almost six feet, with a massive neck and thick shoulders and arms that rippled with muscles. There was a saying in the family that Davey Fleming could lift a horse for the fun of it. Yet there stood Mary Green Fleming, all five feet two of her, defying this angry slab of a man to his face.

She got away with it. That was all four-year-old Teddy knew for the time being. Mary Green Fleming was able to defy her husband and get away with it, though she was only a fifth his size and weight. When my father told me this story, we were sitting on the porch of our summer house in Point Pleasant, New Jersey, in 1943 or 1944. In our driveway sat a gleaming black Cadillac. The slum world of downtown Jersey City was fifty years in Teddy Fleming's past. But there was a kind of rueful wonder in his voice. For him, that tangled moment of affection and fear might have happened only yesterday.

Davey Fleming and his wife had come to America almost forty years after the devastating famine of 1846-50, which killed over a million Irish and sent another million and a half fleeing to America as desperate starving refugees. The famine Irish, as historians now call them, were a defeated, demoralized people. Davey's generation had a very different attitude. They were angry men, full of fury at Protestant England for what they saw as a colossal crime and determined to resist similar treatment from their American counterparts.

The argument about Ireland erupted repeatedly in the family, and Mary Green Fleming usually won, because she was quicker with words and she could turn Davey's anger into a joke. But one night at dinner, his mother triggered an explosion Teddy never forgot. Davey Fleming was telling them about the glories of Ireland. "Long before that dago, Columbus, discovered America, there was Irishmen comin' here to fish and trade with the Indians. And while the Englishman was still livin' in caves with nothin' on his back but deerskin, Ireland was a land of saints and scholars."

"Saints and scholars?" Mary Green Fleming said. "Swillers and spalpeens is more like it."

*Crash! Crash! Crash!* Three times Davey Fleming's big fists came down on their kitchen table. Milk danced in the glasses. Dishes rattled in the cupboard. "This time you've gone too far, woman," Davey thundered. "How dare ye fling that insult in me face? The very words that drove me from Ireland, as you well know."

"Spalpeen?" Mary said. "Sure in Ireland 'twas an insult, but not here in America, where a man's labor is paid in daycent money."

"Daycent money? You call the miserable pay I bring home daycent money?" Davey roared. "I'm still a spalpeen to the thievin' Protestant millionaires who run this country."

"Your pay keeps food on our table, with a bit of management," Mary said. "I had no intention of insultin' you with the word spalpeen. There's no husband in this city who's spoken of with more respect, I can assure you. Now calm down and eat your dinner."

"'Twould sicken me to eat at the same table with you!" Davey Fleming roared. He stomped out of their flat, slamming the door behind him with a crash that shook the building.

Six-year-old Teddy, his seven-year-old brother, Dave, and their sister, Mae, who was barely three at the time, sat staring at their mother in bewilderment. "Eat up," Mary said. "Da'll be back soon enough. 'Twasn't my words that aroused him. 'Tis an old wound from Ireland."

In Ireland, Mary told them, a spalpeen trudged the roads with a shovel on his shoulder, looking for any kind of work, no matter how dirty or filthy. Some people feared him as a possible robber, others regarded him with contempt as a man who was the lowest of the low. "Spalpeen" was often flung at him as an insult. "Be off with ye, ye spalpeen, we want none of your kind in our barns."

There was no work in their home county, Mayo, for Davey Fleming and his older brother Tom. Their family's rented farm barely fed his parents and their three younger children their daily diet of potatoes and sour milk. Tom and Davey set out to make a living as spalpeens. The times were hard. Crops were failing. No one had a farthing to spare. Out of money and food and desperate for work, they knocked on the door of a landlord's house in Donegal and got "spalpeens" hurled at them by the Protestant owner.

Davey drove his fist into the man's face. Tom added a kick in the belly. The landlord reported them to the police, who drew a warrant for their arrest. Davey and Tom fled back to Mayo, where they borrowed money from Mary's father to pay the passage to America.

"My da didn't want to part with the cash, little though it was," Mary said. "But I told him: 'Da, I'm in love with Davey Fleming. I'm goin' to marry him, even if he's in the lockup.' My ma cried until Da parted with the money—and I followed your father to America in a year's time, though Da did everything in his power to discourage me."

It was easy to see why Mary Green was a magical person in Teddy's early years. Along with her funny songs and strong opinions, she was amazingly beautiful, with white skin that contrasted marvelously with her gleaming red hair. Unlike her husband, Mary never seemed to get angry at anyone. "'Tis better to go laughin' than cryin' through this worrrld," she often said. "Sure there's enough sorrow to go 'round without lamentin' woes night and day."

When her third child was a daughter, Mary proclaimed herself the happiest woman in America "with two gossoons and a princess." She named the baby after herself but gave her an American nickname, Mae. She was a redhead like her mother with the same white skin and green eyes. Mary pronounced herself equally pleased when her fourth child was a boy, whom they named Charles after her father. "Three gossoons can't be any more trouble than two," she declared.

Mary's good cheer could not always keep tragedy at bay. Davey's older brother, Tom, and his wife caught typhoid fever, a common disease in Jersey City, where the water supply came from the polluted Passaic River. Both Tom and his wife died and his orphaned children were distributed among relatives. Mary took the oldest boy, Tom, into the family, and gave him the same affection she bestowed so bountifully on her own children.

Looking back, Teddy Fleming would find his mother's good humor all the more amazing, because they were so poor. Their four-story flat-roofed tenement had no heat and no running water and was not connected to the city's sewage system. As I began work on this book, I went over to Jersey City and visited Halladay Street. The tenements were all gone, except for one slightly tilted survivor that had long since been renovated to meet the standards of our more compassionate era. No longer was the unpaved street littered with the piles of rotting vegetables my father recalled, interspersed with heaps of ashes from the tenements' coal stoves, and stretches of muck when it rained or snowed.

In the winter, the Flemings kept warm around their coal stove in the kitchen. The other rooms were "like the North and South poles combined," Mary Green Fleming often said. To fetch water, Mary had to descend four floors with buckets and fill them from a well in the center of the nearest intersection. Teddy and his brothers were too small to be any help. Up the long flights Mary would struggle, often stopping to gasp for breath. She made more trips than most women in the building because she was a devotee of cleanliness.

Mary was always after the boys to wash their hands and faces. "We may be poor but that's no excuse to be dirty," she would say. "A smeared jib is worse than a ragged shirt. It convinces the Prods the Irish live in the muck and like it."

Even worse than the lack of heat was the cesspool toilet in the tenement's backyard. Between twenty and thirty people used it every day. When it rained hard, the thing often overflowed, creating a terrific stink—especially if it happened on a hot summer day. There was nothing they could do about it but "put a clothespin on your nose," Mary said.

Though few people knew enough about the causes of disease to make the connection, this primitive sanitation combined with the city's polluted water system to produce fearful mortality among the downtown poor. Another problem was the city's milk; almost all of it was adulterated slop that had been rejected by New York City health inspectors. The young were especially vulnerable. Seldom a day passed in the summer without the sight of a child's white coffin winding through the filthy streets on an undertaker's carriage.

No one seemed able to do much about the abominable living conditions. Between 1880 and 1910, the population of Jersey City leaped 120 percent. Worse, the city was perpetually on the brink of bankruptcy, which meant the number of public employees was kept to a miserly minimum. Twenty-five percent of the municipal property was owned by the seven trunk railroads that made the city a terminal. They paid no taxes to the city and only a pittance to the state, thanks to their warm friendship with the Republican Party.

The downtown landlords were faceless, nameless creatures in New York, who sent agents around on the first of the month to collect five dollars from each family. Davey Fleming called the agents "the squireens" and explained to his sons and daughter the Irish meaning of the word. In Ireland, squireens were the representatives of the absentee English landlords on the great estates. They collected the exorbitant rents the tenant farmers paid to enable the landlords to live in luxury in London.

Teddy often heard his mother say, "We come from Mayo, God help us." When he asked her what that meant, she explained that County Mayo was the poorest part of Ireland. More than half the people still spoke "the old tongue," a language called Gaelic. It was what the Irish spoke before the English conquered them. "Y'don't want to learn it. 'Twould make your head ache for a month," Mary added.

There were almost no schools in Mayo, and the few that existed charged fees far beyond the pocketbook of a tenant farmer. So most people grew up like her and Davey, Mary said, "not knowin' the difference between a book and a brick." That was a shame because an illiterate man could never learn a trade or get a job in an office and move up in the world. He was condemned lifelong to the same sort of "shovel and shoulder" jobs he had done in Ireland.

In Jersey City Davey Fleming dug ditches for sewer lines and foundations, he shoveled coal from railroad cars into wagons, he lugged lumber and cement for new buildings. He worked six days a week from dawn to dusk—ten or twelve hours a day in the freezing winter winds that whipped off the Hudson River and in the blazing heat of summer. Many summer days he came home covered with coal dust or mud, so exhausted he could not talk until Dave or Teddy raced to the corner saloon and returned with a bucket of beer. Davey would down it in one long swallow and gasp, "Arrrrgh!"

Recalling this scene, my father wondered if that guttural sound of satisfaction was why the dash to the saloon and back was called "rushing the growler." There are other possible explanations—among them the tendency for Irish drunks to get nasty and beat up their wives and children. That was something the Flemings never had to worry about. Davey Fleming drank but he never got drunk. Mary Green Fleming had a lot to do with that phenomenon. Along with deploring dirty faces, she decried the Irish tendency to overindulge in John Barley-corn. She mixed sarcasm and ridicule to convince her husband—and her sons—that anyone who got drunk was a fool.

No matter how hard Davey Fleming worked, he never had a steady job. When the coal was shoveled or the ditches dug, Davey and his fellow laborers were laid off. He would come home cursing the Protestant millionaires. Often Mary would remind him that it was an Irish contractor who had laid him off. Not all the Irish were poor. By 1890, a fifth of all the contractors in America were Irish. Many of the refugees from the Great Famine of 1846–50 lived in fine houses and rode around Jersey City and other cities in handsome broughams pulled by good horses. But it was the era of primitive capitalism. There was no such thing as a minimum wage. Employers paid as little as possible. Laborers were lucky to earn a dollar a day.

In 1893, when Teddy was five years old, an economic cyclone struck the country. Banks collapsed, businesses went bankrupt by the thousands. There was no work anywhere. Mary had to beg food on credit from the mostly German butchers and grocers in the Sixth Ward. The ward's leader gave them coal but it soon ran out. For a while, the specter of the almshouse loomed before the Flemings.

This government refuge was out in the mosquito-ridden Hackensack River meadowlands west of Jersey City. It was considered a humiliation and a probable death sentence in the bargain. The food was abominable and the sanitation deplorable. The insane were mixed with the penniless, creating bedlam as well as disease.

"The only thing worse than the almshouse is the city hospital," Mary told Teddy and his siblings. "Anyone who goes to either one makes a full confession and takes the last rites on the way."

A desperate Davey Fleming looked for ways to supplement his erratic and now all but vanished laborer's wages. He offered his brawn to the ward's leader, who annually backed a slate of candidates and held rallies on street corners and open lots. In those days, the ballot was several yards long. Everyone down to constable was elected each year. Opposition candidates—often also Irish—were prone to attack these rallies with clubs and rocks, unless the ward leader had some sluggers like Davey to discourage them.

Davey often made more money from a few hours of political work than he took home from a week of shoveling. He enjoyed the action. Like most of his fellow Irish, nothing pleased him more than a fist-swinging, foot-kicking brawl. It helped get some of the rage that was boiling inside him out of his system.

Angry Irishmen like Davey Fleming were even more useful on election day. In a close contest, one of the basic tactics was preventing the other side from voting. That meant the ward leader stationed sluggers like Davey in the vicinity of the polling place. They belted into insensibility any man (women did not vote) known to favor the opposition candidate. The police, usually loyal to the ward leader and the party boss, were in the game and made no attempt to stop the mayhem. On election day Davey often brought home ten dollars, the equivalent of two weeks' pay.

Davey's enthusiasm for this sort of work was bolstered by his passionate devotion to the Democratic Party, which had helped him and his brother Tom find food and shelter and work when they came to America in 1882. Davey understood the importance of sticking together behind a leader. It was the "regulars" who won his allegiance, not only because they had the money to pay him. He had imbibed from his father the sad tale of how the English had divided and conquered the Irish, enabling the Sassenachs, as Davey called the Anglo-Saxons, to commit the atrocity of the Great Famine.

Davey's inability to read or write did not exclude him from Jersey

City's political world. Far from it. In the saloons that operated on almost every downtown corner, politics was the main topic of conversation. The pertinent information was delivered with a lot more verve than any newspaper story that ever appeared in the monotonously Republican *Jersey Evening Journal*.

Davey Fleming quickly absorbed the essential message of the Democratic Party in Jersey City. It was the downtown riverside Irish Catholics against the uptown mostly Republican Protestants. The "Prods" regarded the Irish with fear and loathing. Many were members of the American Protestant Association and similar nativist groups committed to keeping Irish Catholics at the bottom of the social ladder. They put "No Irish Need Apply" signs in their store and factory windows and exchanged solemn oaths not to hire an Irish Catholic if there was a Protestant available for a job.

This violent antagonism was by no means peculiar to Jersey City. In the long-defunct *Chicago Post* I found a description of a typical Irishman in action on election day:

> Teddy O'Flaherty votes. He has not been in the country six months. He has hair on his teeth. He never knew an hour in civilized society. He is a born savage, as brutal a ruffian as an untamed Indian, the born criminal and pauper of the civilized world. The Irish fill our prisons and our poorhouses. Scratch a convict or a pauper and the chances are you tickle the skin of an Irish Catholic!

In Jersey City, the sheer numbers of Irish intensified this political-cultural war. No less than 21.5 percent of the population was Irish. Only Boston, with 22.5 percent, had a higher number of Celts. In the 1870s, Jersey City's Protestants had persuaded the Republican-controlled state legislature to pass a law that gerrymandered the city's Irish into a single ungainly state assembly district along the Hudson River. It was shaped like a huge horseshoe, and the Irish promptly gave it this ironic nickname, knowing it was unlikely to bring them good luck.

Meanwhile, a Jersey City Republican convention called for a new city charter that placed the public works, police and fire departments in charge of state- (aka Republican) appointed commissions. The mayor and the board of aldermen became figureheads with little more than the responsibility for licensing street-corner salesmen. The new commissioners fired almost every Irish Catholic on the city payroll. "Irishmen," they proclaimed, "were nowhere."

Listening to this story, Davey Fleming had no difficulty comparing such pseudo-legal persecution to the British manipulation of state power in Ireland to keep the Irish landless and oppressed. He was delighted to learn that eventually the Democrats had elected a governor who helped overturn the gerrymander in court. By the time Davey Fleming and Mary Green arrived in 1882–83, the Irish had regained their influence in Jersey City's politics and one of their own had emerged as the leader of the Democratic Party.

Robert "Little Bob" Davis was a short, cherubic, good-humored man whose parents had been famine refugees. He had grown up in Jersey City, gone into politics, and married the daughter of a chieftain in New York's famed political machine, Tammany Hall. "Little Bob" planted Robert Davis Association clubhouses throughout Jersey City and the rest of Hudson County. They staged picnics and boat rides for their Democratic followers, and dispensed food and coal to the poor in their tenements, when their pleas for help got loud enough to attract attention. Davis was known as "the Easy Boss" because he seldom issued orders. He let individual ward leaders operate semi-independently and in some cases get almost as rich as he was. Little Bob had a plumbing business that received more than its share of government contracts.

Along with a reliance on sluggers, another much-valued tactic in Little Bob's political repertoire was the use of "floaters." Equipped with fake identities, Davis's men took ferries to Manhattan and voted there for the candidates of Tammany's choice. Tammany returned the favor by shipping hundreds of Gotham floaters across the river to Jersey City to give Davis's candidates a boost in a tight race. A floater had to be ready and able to use his fists if he was challenged by the guardians of a foreign polling place. Davey Fleming was a natural candidate for this sort of job, once he learned to laboriously sign his fake name to the bottom of a ballot. Often he would return home with twenty dollars in his pocket from a Tammany leader who was feeling flush.

With the depression of 1893 continuing to paralyze the economy, these election benefactions were thrice welcome, but the Flemings remained desperately poor. That meant the younger Flemings had to go to work when they were barely out of kneepants. The Turkey (eleven-year-old Dave Fleming) got up at 5 A.M. to mop the floor of a nearby saloon. In 1898 ten-year-old Teddy Fleming rose at the same dismal hour to catch a ferry from Jersey City to New York, where he sold the *New York World* on West Street, not far from the foot of Houston Street. Davey Fleming had used his pull with the Sixth Ward's leader, who asked "Little Bob" Davis to put in a word with Tammany to land Teddy the job.

Teddy soon learned that getting hired was only the first step in a newsboy's career. To hang on to a corner, a boy had to fight for it. Teddy asked his father to show him how to throw a punch for maximum impact. Davey Fleming cheerfully obliged, remarking that now and then a kick could also come in handy, along with a thumb in the other fellow's eye. Soon no one challenged Teddy for his corner on West Street.

Teddy learned something else from this first job. An amazing number of newsboys had no fathers or mothers. They were orphans who lived on the street, sleeping in police stations and saloons on winter nights. It made him realize that the Flemings, poor as they were, could still claim they were lucky. They had parents who cared about them.

By 7 A.M. wide, cobblestoned West Street would be jammed with horse-drawn cabs and wagons and scurrying commuters off the ferries. Teddy soon found that 1898 was a good year to sell newspapers. In February someone blew up the battleship USS *Maine* in the harbor of Havana. Soon the United States was at war with Spain to liberate Cuba—a conflict largely engineered by Teddy's putative boss, Joseph Pulitzer, publisher of the *New York World*, with some help from William Randolph Hearst, publisher of the rival *New York Journal*.

To an Irish-American kid the most exciting event of 1898 was the municipal election in New York that fall. It was the first contest for control of Greater New York, a new political entity that merged Manhattan, Queens, Brooklyn, the Bronx, and Staten Island into one consolidated city. This was an idea Protestant reformers had concocted as a way to demolish Tammany Hall, which had controlled Manhattan for most of the previous century. Rising to the challenge, Tammany ran on the slogan "To Hell With Reform!" and won in a landslide. A stream of Jersey City floaters, which no doubt included Davey Fleming, added to the margin of victory.

On a good day Teddy would make twenty-five cents from selling several dozen copies of the *World*. At eight o'clock the commuters would dwindle. Teddy would spend a cent for a cup of coffee and head back to Jersey City, where he had to be at his desk in the fourth grade at All Saints Parochial School by nine o'clock. At the end of the school day, he would head home to Halladay Street and proudly hand twenty-four cents to his mother.

I always see Teddy in gray dawnlight on West Street, a skinny kid with a peaked cap over his reddish blond hair, wearing a ragged jacket or a sweater or both plus an old scarf around his throat. Blowing snow whips across the street's cobblestones. Teddy's teeth are crooked and protruding. He is an ugly little kid. He glares at me. *Could you do this?* he seems to ask. He whirls and slugs a newsboy who is trying to take his corner. "Hey, getcha *Woild!*" he shouts.

# 3

# An Uptown World

I don't want to play in your yard,
I don't like you anymore!
You'll be sorry when you see me
Sliding down our cellar door!

Pert six-year-old Kitty Dolan was the hit of family parties, singing this song while her handsome black-mustached father, Tom, accompanied her on his fiddle. Her four-year-old brother, George, also won applause for the lively way he danced to "There'll Be a Hot Time in the Old Town Tonight."

Kitty Dolan was born in 1891, only three years after Teddy Fleming. But her childhood world was so different, it is sometimes hard to believe they grew up in the same city. She lived uptown on the long ridge that ran from north to south through Hudson County, more or less parallel to the Hudson River. The paved streets were wide and clean and lined with the gracious homes of the city's mostly Protestant businessmen and professional men. Widest of all, running almost the length of the ridge, from Bergen Point on the south, opposite Staten Island, to Fort Lee on the north, was the Hudson County Boulevard.

Not long after the boulevard was opened in 1895, a schoolgirl named Ida Rickerich wrote an essay about it for a composition lesson in Public School No. 3. She described how pleasant it was to ride on such a smooth surface. Since it was on the very top of the hill, "you can see everywhere." Ida was sure it cost "a great deal" because it was cut through numerous farms and orchards. Ida was also sure that the boulevard would improve all the cities and towns through which it passed—especially Jersey City, by far the biggest town in populous Hudson County.

Ida was right. To live on or near the boulevard became the fashionable thing to do in Jersey City and in the satellite towns of Bayonne, Union City, and North Bergen. Several years after Katherine Dolan was born, her parents moved from Montgomery Street, one of the main arteries that ascended the hill to the crest of the uptown ridge, to the second floor of 4 Garrison Avenue, a comfortable street of two-family houses that ran parallel to the boulevard. The rent was twenty dollars a month, a sum that would have reduced the Flemings to starvation. But Tom Dolan was a skilled carpenter who made as much money in a single day as laborer Davey Fleming made in a week.

Tom Dolan had been born in America, not long after his parents arrived in South Amboy, a town on Raritan Bay, forty miles south of Jersey City, in the 1850s. There was not even the hint of a brogue in his speech. Further bolstering his self-assurance was the presence in Jersey City of a large extended family, including two cousins who had mastered the intricacies of building construction, and often hired him to work with them. Tom's younger brother, Bart, was a successful gentleman's tailor in New York City. The Dolans were a cheerful family, with dozens of outlying cousins and a fondness for big boisterous parties. When my mother reminisced about her girlhood, a party was frequently mentioned as a nostalgic synonym for happiness.

Kitty's mother (and Tom's wife), Mary Fitzmaurice Dolan, was as different from Mary Green Fleming as Tom Dolan was unlike Davey Fleming. Mary was tall, about five feet nine, and she carried herself in a proud, straight-backed way. Her hair was thick and dark, like her husband's. She spoke with only the hint of a brogue, like most people from County Wicklow, which for centuries had been part of the Dublin "pale," territory controlled by the English.

Mary was the daughter of a schoolteacher, who had taught her to read and write. She had emigrated with her sister, Margaret, and for several years worked as a servant in a mansion on New York's Fifth

Avenue. For many young Irish women, such a job was a kind of graduate school in American manners and taste. By the time she married Tom Dolan in 1881, Mary knew how to decorate a home with skill and elegance, and she was a superb cook.

In the 1880s, the Dolans had three daughters, on whom they lavished affection. I remember seeing a photograph of them (alas lost) sitting in pretty white ruffled dresses, their long dark hair beautifully combed and curled. They could have been daughters of a wealthy man. Within reason, Tom and Mary believed in living well. Their apartment was comfortably furnished in warm colors. A baby grand piano was the centerpiece of the parlor, and the oldest daughter, Mary, began taking lessons on it. The wall of the master bedroom was decorated with two large framed photographs of Tom and Mary that resembled paintings. They were an attractive couple, happy members of the Irish-American middle class.

I don't know whether Mary Fitzmaurice Dolan had lace curtains on her parlor windows. They were a favorite decor of the well-to-do Irish, a kind of public announcement of their affluent status. At the very least, the Dolans were aspirants to the lace curtain class. Mary Fitzmaurice Dolan certainly saw no reason to criticize such genteel touches. Only lower-class "micks" said "lace curtain" with a sarcastic edge in their brogues.

Seldom if ever was Ireland mentioned in the Dolan household as a source of anger and sorrow. To Tom Dolan, the mother country was not even a memory. Mary Fitzmaurice had never experienced the horrendous poverty and near starvation that was commonplace in County Mayo. Instead, the Dolans felt a subtle discomfort about their Irish Catholic name in mostly Protestant uptown Jersey City.

The *Jersey Evening Journal* never ceased deploring the scandalous political tactics of "Little Bob" Davis and his downtown followers. In 1889, sixty-five Irish Americans were convicted for stuffing more than ten thousand illegal Democratic ballots into various voting boxes. Little Bob persuaded New Jersey's Democratic governor, Leon Abbett, who was from Jersey City, to pardon all of them. Even more dismaying to seekers of middle-class respectability like the Dolans were downtown's filthy, saloon-dotted streets, full of strolling prostitutes and swaggering gamblers and brawlers. Worst of all were the numerous dance halls, where ladies of the evening pranced the floor with hard-drinking "sports."

Unfortunately, uptown Jersey City was no more immune to the dangers of a polluted water system and adulterated milk than downtown. One June day in 1889, the word that filled the hearts of every parent with terror wound down placid Garrison Avenue: *typhoid*. A young girl at the head of the block had contracted the disease. She was in the same class at Public School 23 as Mary, the oldest Dolan daughter. They sometimes walked home from school together.

The next day, Mary began running a fever. Two days later, her sister Margaret became ill. The day after, her sister Kathleen awoke in the middle of the night, vomiting. All three had the telltale rose spots on their chests and abdomens, the grim sign of typhoid's presence. Frantically, Tom and Mary Dolan summoned a doctor. But physicians of the 1880s could do little or nothing for victims of typhoid except quarantine the house and prescribe cold towels and a liquid diet to reduce the destructive fever.

A week later, Mary died after a day and night of delirium. The next day, her sister Margaret died in similar incoherence. Kathleen lingered another two days, but the doctor had already told the Dolans there was no hope. She sank into a stupor and died so quietly, at first her dazed parents did not realize she was gone.

In one horrendous week, death had swept away the Dolans' daughters, leaving the couple overwhelmed with grief. Tom's numerous relatives and Mary's sister, Margaret, who lived in New Rochelle, north of New York City, rushed to offer them sympathy. The pastor of their parish church, St. Aloysius, visited their house and urged them to accept God's will.

"God's will?" Tom Dolan cried. "God's will? I say the hell with God's will."

He left the shocked priest with Mary and bolted down Garrison Avenue to Montgomery Street, where there were several saloons. That night Tom came home so drunk, he could do nothing but sob like a brokenhearted child. Mary held him in her arms until dawn, weeping herself, but sensing that for some reason, she was the one who had the strength to respond to their tragedy with courage and hope.

"We've still got each other," she whispered to him. "We'll have other children."

This was the house of sorrow into which Katherine Lillian Dolan was born on Friday, November 13, 1891. Fortunately, her mother was not superstitious about the number thirteen. In her part of Ireland, it was considered lucky. Mary Fitzmaurice made a joke of it, calling it "Kitty's number"—and noticing when good things happened to her on the thirteenth of the month. It made Kitty feel special.

Two years later, brother George arrived. Both children exuded high spirits, with George an especially handsome, playful charmer. Kitty was soon proclaimed a future beauty. To an outside observer, or even a member of the extended Dolan-Fitzmaurice clan, Tom and Mary seemed to be recovering from their terrible loss.

Only within the family was another reality becoming painfully apparent. Tom Dolan could not reconcile himself to the deaths of those three innocent children. On Saturday nights, when he received his week's pay, anxiety would seep through the second floor of the Garrison Avenue house. Mary Fitzmaurice Dolan would peer out the front windows as dusk thickened on the street. When darkness fell, Kitty and George would start asking why Papa had not come home. Mary would make some excuse—he had to go to a union meeting; his brother Bart had invited him to a party in New York. They would eat a mostly silent dinner and Mary would put the children to bed early.

Hour after hour, sometimes until 3 A.M., Mary would mount a vigil in the parlor. She would try to read the newspaper. She would pace the burgundy rug. More than once, she fell to her knees and prayed. But seeking God's help only seemed to underscore her own helplessness, and she soon abandoned that recourse. Finally would come Tom's slow, stumbling steps on the stairs. Sometimes another man, often two men, would be with him to lend a helping hand or arm. Tom was frequently too drunk to stand.

"He's a bit too much taken," one escort would say.

"He'll be good as new in the morning," the other would chortle.

Mary would steer Tom to a chair in the parlor and say, "Did you drink it all again? Is there anything left?"

"Aw Mary," Tom would mutter. "Aw Mary. May have a few dollars somewheres."

Half weeping in shame and anger, Mary would go through his pockets. Rarely did she find anything but loose change. "Y'don' understan', Mary," Tom would mumble, his tongue so thick he sounded as if he had a brogue. "In bar when fellows buy y'drink y'gotta buy'em one. Iz called blowback. Iz the way men drink. Makes money go fass—"

"I don't care how men drink!" Mary would cry in a stifled voice. She wanted to rage at him but it would awaken the children—and she knew it would not do any good. It was pointless to remind him they had bills to pay at the butcher shop and the grocery stores on Montgomery Street. She knew why he drank—but she could not excuse it, because it was threatening their existence as a family.

Mary was all too aware that she was confronting the curse of the Irish race. The *Jersey Evening Journal* regularly reported the appalling number of Irish-Americans arrested for drunk and disorderly behavior. In New York during her servant days, Mary had often overheard her employers making derogatory remarks about the drunken Irish in the slums of Gotham's downtown wards.

In the morning, Tom would be all repentance and apology. He would borrow money from Bart or one of his cousins to pay the meat and grocery bills. For a month or more, he would come home on Saturday with a smile and a pocket full of candy for the children and hand Mary his pay envelope without a dollar missing. But Mary knew it would not last. She sensed that behind his temporary good cheer, bitterness still gnawed at his soul.

Tom Dolan was having a quarrel with God. He revealed it in small ways—casually refusing to go to Mass on Sundays, making derogatory remarks about the Catholic Church. At times his bitterness stirred a response in Mary's soul. She too had moments when she could barely endure the memory of those three lost little girls romping around the house. But motherhood rescued her from bitterness. Kitty's and George's innocence was a kind of balm, reminding her that she still had a capacity—and a responsibility—to create happiness.

At times Tom's drinking bouts seemed like a bad dream that had never happened. On Saturday nights when he came home sober, he would tune his fiddle and play lively songs, both Irish and American. On other evenings they would join Tom's cousins and his brother

Bart for a family dinner that always ended in a round of songs, climaxed by the four Dolans singing "Down Went McGinty" barber-shop quartet style.

> Down went McGinty to the bottom of the sea;
> He must be very wet,
> For they haven't found him yet . . .
> Dressed in his best suit of clothes.

One day Tom got into an argument with one of his cousins about the wood they should use in paneling a room in a new building going up near Jersey City's Bergen Square. The cousin made a nasty comment about how much money Tom still owed him. It was not a great deal—about thirty dollars. Mary had managed to save enough to pay back most of the loans. That Saturday night, Tom Dolan did not come home until dawn—and his paycheck had vanished. There was not even any loose change. He ranted about being insulted, about everyone treating him with condescension, including Mary.

On Sunday, Mary asked Tom to go to St. Aloysius Church and take a pledge of total abstinence. Tom refused. On Monday, he went back to work, borrowed money from a fellow carpenter, and came home drunk again. He skipped work the next day, claiming to be sick. That was true to some extent. He had a hangover of awful proportions. Soon this new pattern of drinking in midweek as well as on Saturday night and missing work—and a day's pay—became established.

By this time, Kitty was in the third grade at Public School 23. One day she asked her mother, "Was Papa drunk again last night?"

"No," Mary said indignantly. Tom had gone to a union meeting and come home sober. "Where did you hear such a thing?"

"Alice Kennedy heard her father telling her mother that Papa is always drunk. He saw him falling down in the street one night last week."

"Your father is not always drunk!" Mary said. "Don't listen to such things!"

That night, after Kitty and George had gone to bed, Mary told Tom what his daughter had said. "The next time I see Pat Kennedy I'll knock his teeth down his throat," Tom stormed.

This was bravado. Tom Dolan was no bruiser like Davey Fleming.

He was slightly built and mild-mannered by nature. "I'm not telling you about it to push you at Kennedy," Mary said. "He's a loudmouthed fool. Doesn't it trouble you to think your daughter knows such a thing?"

"It troubles me, it troubles me," Tom said. "But I'll be damned if I'll take the pledge, Mary. Only henpecked yes men take that thing."

"Don't take it if it pleases you—but stop drinking! If you don't, you won't be welcome in my bed, Tom Dolan. I can't and won't love a husband who mortifies me before the neighbors and our relatives and friends—and now embarrasses our own daughter!"

"You mean that, Mary? Do you really mean that?"

"I mean every word of it. I won't have another child by a man who can't support the two we've got."

"I can't believe you'd say that, Mary. Say it and mean it."

"I mean it, Tom."

Tom Dolan seemed genuinely amazed. With a clutch of fear, Mary realized that in some strange indefinable way, her husband was an innocent. He did not or could not understand or accept the consequences of his acts. He did not seem to know how hard and demanding life could be. His carpenter's skills, the relatively good money he made from them, the sheltering shadow of his older cousins who were too ready to forgive and forget his lapses, had dangerously distorted his view of life. There was something almost childish about this charming man. He confirmed it by weeping and promising to do everything in his power to stop drinking.

Listening at the door of her bedroom, ten-year-old Kitty Dolan felt her body swell with an awful mixture of fear and sorrow. She slid under her blanket and clutched her pillow, wondering why her father drank too much and why her mother threatened to exile him from her bed. She did not know exactly what those words meant, but they were enormously threatening. They had reduced her father to pathetic submission.

Tears stained her pillow as Kitty asked God to help Tom Dolan. He was so good, so kind, so gentle, so full of fun and songs most of the time. She loved him more than she loved her mother, who was often stern with George and insistent on Kitty doing her homework. *Please, please, please help Papa*, Kitty prayed.

# 4

# Three Beauties

Who made the world?

God made the world.

Who is God?

God is the creator of heaven and earth.

Why did God make you?

God made me to know Him, to love Him and to serve Him in this world and be happy with Him forever in the next.

How shall we know the things in which we are to believe?

We shall know the things in which we are to believe from the Catholic Church, through which God speaks to us.

By the time Teddy Fleming got to the fifth grade in All Saints Parochial School, he knew these and many other questions and answers in the Baltimore Catechism by heart. The small softcovered book, which had won the imprimatur of the American bishops at a meeting in Baltimore in 1891, was the Catholic Church's primary teaching tool in its massive effort to instill the faith in the children of immigrants and persuade them to accept the church's guidance for the rest of their lives. Everyone in All Saints Parochial School was required to memorize the answers and recite them in daily lessons before the stern eyes of the black-robed Sisters of Charity who staffed the school.

I memorized the same questions and answers thirty-five years later, at St. Patrick's Parochial School. In fact, in the second grade, I had a teacher who had taught Dave, Teddy, Mae, and Charlie Fleming. She was very old by the time I got to her and her temper had grown extremely short. Her convent name was Sister Lamburder. We called her "Sister Lambaster." She frequently belted boys and girls in the face when they failed to recite the day's catechism lesson satisfactorily.

In All Saints School in the Flemings' era, that kind of physical punishment was taken for granted. They were dealing with kids who learned their morals on the harsh downtown streets. The younger generation thought nothing of invading the city's ubiquitous railyards on summer evenings and stealing from boxcars loaded with merchandise, while one of the gang watched for the railroad cops. Each winter, a lot of the coal burned in tenement stoves traveled from the trains the same way.

Every child in All Saints School was required to go to Mass and receive Holy Communion each Sunday. In the hope that an additional injection of religion might inspire better conduct, those in grades five through eight were also assigned a weekday on which groups from each class were ordered to attend Mass and receive communion. Still selling newspapers in New York in the dawn, Teddy Fleming decided to skip this weekday appearance at the altar rail. To keep his job and protect his corner on West Street, he had to show up every day.

Teddy noticed that the priest who said the midweek eight o'clock Mass and distributed communion merely counted the number of communicants in each class. He did not know them by name. In school later that morning, the fifth-grade teacher asked those who had gone to Mass on the assigned day to stand up. If the count tallied with the priest's count, all was well.

Teddy decided to acquire a substitute at the communion rail. He selected a red-haired, pink-cheeked classmate named Timothy Mullaney. Timmy was a momma's boy. For the first three years, his mother had walked to school and stayed with him in the schoolyard to make sure no one picked on him.

One day on the way home from fifth grade, Teddy dragged Timmy into an alley. "I want yez t'go t'choich t'morra in me place," he said, in the unlovely argot of the downtown Irish.

"Why should I?" Timmy said.

Teddy seized him by the front of his shirt and held his fist in front of Timmy's terrified eyes. "If y'don't want dis down y'troat, you'll go. T'morra and every Wednesday 'til summer. Get me?"

By now Teddy was acknowledged as the toughest kid in his class. He had graduated from slugging it out with newsboys on his West Street corner to boxing in the many rings that people set up in the Sixth Ward's backyards. The Irish-Americans were crazy about prize-fighting. They had been fielding winners in every class, from heavy-weight to flyweight, for decades. For a while, many people said every immigrant ship carried a champion in its hold. Teddy Fleming's ambition was to be one of those champions. Meanwhile, he was inclined to use his fists to get his way on less momentous matters.

Teddy's cavalier attitude toward going to church was something he had probably picked up from his father. Like many Mayo men, Davey Fleming had never been a regular mass-goer. In his youth, church attendance in Mayo was seldom more than twenty-five percent of the population on any given Sunday. In his arguments with Mary over Ireland's hard fate, Davey's attitude toward the Catholic Church was frequently hostile, because the priests opposed any and all forms of violent resistance against the British.

Teddy warned Timmy Mullaney under pain of several punches in the mouth not to tell his mother anything about their arrangement. If she asked why Timmy was going to Mass on two weekdays, he was to tell her it was his way of letting God know how much Timmy loved Him. Already coping with two younger children, Mrs. Mullaney was unlikely to press the matter. She probably thought Timmy's outburst of devoutness was a blessing from on high.

The terrified Timmy performed beautifully for three months, showing up each Wednesday to be counted as Teddy Fleming at the altar rail. In class, when Sister asked those who had gone to Mass that Wednesday to stand up, Teddy rose and was counted. More than a few members of the class knew what was happening, but no one snitched. They feared Teddy would exact revenge in a convenient alley a day or two later.

Then came disaster. One Wednesday in January, when Sister asked the massgoers to stand up and be counted, Timmy rose to his feet. "Timothy Mullaney," Sister said. "Why are you going to Mass on Wednesday? Tuesday is your day."

Timmy turned bright red, a tendency that many of his male classmates found amusing, and began to blubber. "I went 'cause Teddy Fleming said he'd kill me if I didn't," he sobbed.

Sister escorted the two boys into the hall, where the full dimension of Teddy Fleming's wrongdoing was soon revealed. "Never have I seen such brazen defiance of God and His holy church!" Sister stormed. "This is something only Monsignor Meehan can deal with."

A half hour later, Teddy Fleming was in All Saints rectory, face-to-face with the pastor of the parish, large, formidable Monsignor Joseph Meehan. The Monsignor read Sister's agitated note outlining Teddy's crime.

"What have you got to say for yourself?" Monsignor asked.

"I guess I'm sorry," Teddy said.

"Sorry for what? That you got caught?" Monsignor said.

"No doubt about dat," Teddy said.

"'That.' Don't say 'dat,'" Monsignor said. The son of a wealthy contractor, he deplored the street argot Teddy and other poor Irish-American kids spoke. He knew it would stamp them as forever lower-class. Meehan urged the nuns to teach them good English, but it was a virtually hopeless task.

It never occurred to Teddy to plead for mercy, to explain that the Flemings needed the twenty-five or thirty cents he brought home from selling the *New York World* each day. That was none of Monsignor Meehan's business. Already Teddy was struggling against feeling ashamed of his father because Davey could not read or write, which left them perpetually desperate for money.

"Why do you think we want you to go to Mass and communion an extra day each week?" Monsignor Meehan asked.

"You got me," Teddy said.

"Because we think mugs like you need some extra sanctifying grace, that's why," Meehan said. "Do you know what sanctifying grace is?"

"I guess so," Teddy said.

"Recite the answer from the Catechism. What is sanctifying grace?"

"Sanctifyin' grace is d'grace dat makes d'soul holy and pleasin' t'God."

It was clear that Teddy did not understand a word of it, nor did he have any interest in trying. At the age of eleven, he had some things figured out. One was that school was pretty much a waste of time. The guys who made big money in this world, the boxing champions and the major-league baseball players and the politicians, didn't get to the top by knowing all about sanctifying grace.

"Do you think you need that kind of help from God?"

"Who doesn't?" Teddy said.

"Now I'm going to give you another kind of help. Something you'll remember for a while. Bend over and put your hands on the desk."

Monsignor took a large paddle out of a drawer and circled the desk. Teddy knew what was coming. Before he left All Saints School, he had ducked into the boys' toilet and inserted a half dozen sheets from his writing tablet inside his underpants.

*Whack!* The paddle sent pain surging through his buttocks. *Whack! Whack! Whack!* The pain brought tears to his eyes. But Teddy never made a sound. He was showing Monsignor Meehan—and himself—that he could take it. A champ had to know how to take a punch as well as throw one. This was good training.

*Whack! Whack! Whack!* Twenty-five times the paddle stung him. The last few felt like liquid fire. The sheets of paper helped a little. But it still hurt. Meehan was a big man, at least six feet tall, with meaty shoulders. Teddy tried to take his mind off the pain by picturing what he was going to do to Timmy Mullaney on the way home from school. It almost worked. His eyes were perfectly dry by the time the Mons delivered the final whack.

"Go and sin no more," Monsignor Meehan said. "Do you know who said that?"

"You got me," Teddy said.

"Jesus. If you get sent here for another caper, you'll get fifty strokes. Remember that."

At noon recess, all the boys in the fifth grade swarmed around Teddy, wanting to know how many whacks he had gotten from Monsignor Meehan. "A hunnert," Teddy said.

Everyone was amazed that he was so casual. "Didn't it hoit?" somebody asked.

"Nah," Teddy said. "I stuck some paper inside me pants. I hardly felt it."

Awe swept the circle of faces, making Teddy almost glad he had gotten sent to Monsignor Meehan. He liked to impress his fellow eleven-year-olds. You did it two ways—by being tough, and by being smart. Outsmarting Monsignor Meehan was a new high. He would ride on it for a month.

That afternoon, Teddy waited for Timmy Mullaney on the corner of Halladay Street. "Hey, birdbrain," he said. "I'm out twenty-five cents a week because of you. Got any idea how t'make't up f'me?"

Timmy shook his head.

"You betta figger it out," Teddy said. "Any Wednesday you don't come tru' wid d'dough, you'll be black and blue all over."

"Whattya want me to do, steal it?" Timmy wailed.

"Sure. If you got d'nerve," Teddy said.

At home, twelve-year-old Dave Fleming and six-year-old Charlie greeted Teddy with sympathy and vows of revenge on the whole Mullaney family. Both boys denounced Timmy and urged Teddy to demolish him. Even eight-year-old Mae got into the act. "I'm gonna punch Milly Mullaney in d'nose!" she proclaimed, to everyone's amusement. Milly was Timmy's younger sister.

Mary Green Fleming overheard the chatter and soon got the whole story. She escorted Teddy into her bedroom and examined his inflamed buttocks. "I've got half a mind to tell Cardinal Meehan what I think of him," she said. "But 'twould do no good. He's too much in love with himself to change his opinion on my say-so."

Mary had taken the lead in nicknaming All Saints' pastor "the Cardinal." Meehan had an imperious, almost regal style. He had inherited a large personal fortune, which he spent freely to furnish the rectory and hire a cook as well as a housekeeper. In his spare time he raced trotting horses.

"Don't waste yer breath, Ma. I'll get d'money outta Timmy Mullaney," Teddy said.

"You'll do no such thing. You'll only make more trouble for

yourself. His mother will be weepin' and wailin' into the Cardinal's skirts. We'll do without it."

"We need d'dough, don't we? Da ain't woiked in a week. We ain't had nothin' to eat but p'dadas—"

"We've got some hopes that Da'll get steady work. I've been sayin' rosaries by the dozen for it. We may find out at dinner tonight."

A few hours later, Davey Fleming came home and told Mary her prayers had been answered. Through the intercession of one of the Horseshoe's politicos, Davey had landed a job as a laborer at the Eagle Oil Works. On the border between Jersey City and Bayonne, Eagle was a subsidiary of Standard Oil Company, which had a huge refinery in Bayonne. An Irish-American named Patrick Donnelly ran the Eagle shipping department and hired as many Celts as possible.

Eagle's parent corporation had made John D. Rockefeller America's first billionaire. Standard Oil was a colossus that dominated the fuel business throughout the nation. In 1900, its profits totaled $20 million—the equivalent of $200 million today. David Fleming's pay did not reflect this stupendous cash flow. It was fifty cents a day—three dollars for a six-day, sixty-hour week.

The job was still a great leap forward because it was steady money. No longer would Davey have to worry about layoffs. The Flemings celebrated by moving to a cold-water flat on Communipaw Avenue. Running water, even if it was not hot, meant no more pails for Mary to lug up steep stairs. Best of all, the building was connected to the city's sewage system, and there was a bathroom in each flat.

They had scarcely moved to their new address when another worry began shadowing their lives. Mary Green Fleming had little or no energy to cook or clean or shop for food. Often she had "spells" during which she had trouble catching her breath. She complained frequently about the cold in their unheated tenement. In the winter, her fingers, often her whole hand, would turn blue in the course of a bitter night.

Eventually friends and relatives persuaded her to go to St. Francis Hospital's clinic for an examination. After the doctor heard her symptoms and listened to her heart with a stethoscope, he looked grave. He told her husband that carrying all those pails of water up the stairs of their Halladay Street tenement had damaged Mary's heart. She would have to avoid any and all heavy work if she hoped to prolong her life. She should never have another child.

That was when Davey Fleming revealed to his sons and daughter the love he felt for this beautiful woman who had chosen him in their youth. He got his temper under control; there were no more shouts or pounded fists at the dinner table. He even started going to church, where he prayed for Mary to a god in whom he only half believed.

Mary continued to be an important figure in Teddy's life. But as he moved into his teenage years, the combination of her illness and his growing maturity diminished her influence. Tired of selling newspapers for a few pennies a day, he looked for other work. They always needed money to supplement Davey's tiny salary.

In the summer between the seventh and eighth grades, Teddy's older brother Dave heard there were jobs at a nearby watch factory, pasting faces on watches as they moved down an assembly line. The pay was fifty cents a day—the same pay his father got when he started at Eagle Oil. Davey's pay had inched up to a dollar a day as the depression of 1893 relaxed its grip on the nation's jugular.

Teddy and cousin Tom Fleming joined the Turkey in the employment line. If they all got hired, it would add ten dollars to the family's weekly income. Little Charlie trailed along, hoping to get some sort of errand-boy job.

In the factory's front office, they encountered a balding clerk with a sour bony face. As each job seeker came to his desk, he asked, "Protestant or Catholic?"

If the job seeker said "Catholic," the clerk's face twisted with annoyance. "No work today."

Anyone who said "Protestant" was sent into the factory to go to work. Teddy got the idea instantly. "He's rubbin' our faces in it," he growled.

"What can we do about it?" the Turkey said, as the line moved forward. "We need d'dough."

"Yeah," Charlie said. "Who cares what this birdbrain tinks?"

When Dave got to the desk, he answered the question with, "Protestant. Can't you tell by lookin' at me? I'm always protestin' somethin'."

"Very funny," the clerk said. He waved Dave toward the door of the factory. It was obvious that he did not really care what religion anyone was, as long as they answered his question the right way.

The owner of the factory probably belonged to the American Protestant Association or some other nativist group. He had sworn an oath to exclude Catholics from the factory. But the workforce was all Catholic, so he ordered his clerk to make each boy deny his religion so the owner could tell his Protestant friends he was keeping his promise.

Teddy was next in line. "Protestant or Catholic?" the clerk asked.

"Go to hell, you son of a bitch," Teddy said. He pulled a pair of dice out of his back pocket. "I can make more dough wit' dese than you'll ever see."

"Get out! Get out of here before I call the police!" the clerk shrilled.

Teddy pointed to Dave. "He's me brudder. As Cat'lic as I am! So's dese guys." He pointed to Charlie and Tom.

"All of you get out!"

On the street, the others looked at Teddy with bewilderment. "What the hell's the point in pickin' a fight with the guy? Now we got no jobs, no dough," the Turkey said.

"We'll get dough. Plenty of it. Wit' dese." Teddy held up the dice. "I been studyin' how dey roll. Every fort' time they come up seven. Every sixt' time they come up snake eyes. They must be loaded some way."

"Where'd you get'm?" Charlie asked.

"I lifted'm from Repetey O'Brien's back pocket while he was sleepin' one off on his porch. I seen him win a bundle wit'm at a big game in Maloney's basement."

Joe Maloney ran one of the ward's dice games. Repetey O'Brien was one of the neighborhood's hardest drinkers. He was called Repetey because he kept promising to get off the booze and never did. O'Brien lived on the third floor of their tenement. When he came home drunk, his wife banished him to their back porch, even in the middle of winter.

"Jesus," the Turkey said. "He'da t'rown you off d'porch if he caught you." O'Brien was a six-foot-two bruiser.

"Yeah, but he didn't," Teddy said. "D'bum was out cold. Come on. Let's show dose Protestant bastards a t'ing or two."

They cruised over to Pacific Avenue and headed for the Lafayette section. In 1900, the name designated a residential neighborhood where mostly Protestants lived. They were the families of lawyers and doctors and managers in the numerous factories. The Irish on Halladay Street often clashed with them in gang fights on summer evenings. Their leader was a big kid named Bobby Blaine, who even Teddy Fleming admitted could throw a pretty good punch.

They found Blaine and a half dozen friends sitting on his porch steps. "Hey you guys," Teddy said, shaking the dice in his hand. "In d'mood for a little craps? I got ten bucks that says you ain't got the nerve to play d'game."

Dave and Charlie were terrified. They were sure the Prods would catch on to the loaded dice and beat their heads in. That was close to Bobby Blaine's first thought. "Those dice must be loaded," he said. "You micks don't play with anything else."

"The hell you say," Teddy replied.

Teddy amazed Dave and Charlie by pulling ten one-dollar bills out of his pocket and throwing them on the ground. He must have extracted the bills from Repetey O'Brien's pocket along with the bones. Bobby Blaine examined the dice and rolled them a half dozen times. They did not display any of the standard symptoms of loaded dice, such as coming up nothing but sevens.

"We'll go for a buck a roll," Bobby said.

Teddy shrewdly lost the first roll, convincing Bobby he had a sucker on his plate. They upped the ante to three and then five dollars a roll and Teddy started timing his bets to the dice's peculiar rhythm. In two hours a cursing Bobby Blaine and his friends had lost fifty dollars. To the Flemings, it made perfect sense. The Prods had tried to make them crawl to get a job at the watch factory. Their fellow Prods deserved to get taken by O'Brien's dice.

"You guys tell Ma d'watch factory story," Teddy said as they headed home. "Make it good. Give her a laugh."

Mary Green Fleming was sitting by the window, looking wan. Ten-year-old Mae was reading the newspaper to her. "Ma, wait'll you hear the screwy thing this guy just did," the Turkey said, pointing to Teddy.

"Glory to be God, what now?" Mary said.

Dave told the story of Teddy's dice-waving defiance of the Protestant clerk at the watch factory, adding details that had the clerk with a build like the current heavyweight champion, Jack Jeffries, and threatening to tear them apart. Charlie confirmed everything, making the clerk sound even bigger.

"Dere's Teddy, he barely comes up to d'guy's waist, ready to box'm, for God's sake," the Turkey said, going through the motions of a prizefight with Charlie. "Whoa!—the Prod takes a swing and Teddy ducks just in time. The guy spins like a top and falls on his puss."

Dave swung, Charlie ducked, and Dave nosedived to the floor. "Dat's when I dragged him outta dere before d'cops come," the Turkey said, sitting up.

Mae Fleming listened wide-eyed. Mary was shaking her head. "Your Da could get away with such antics," she said to Teddy. "You're not his size."

"Yeah, but Ma, wait'll you hear d'resta d'story," the Turkey said. "We ankled over to Lafayette and found ourselves a crap game. Them dice a'Teddy's is magic. Lookit what we won."

With a big grin, Teddy handed his mother the fifty dollars. "I bet dat's more dough than dat Protestant watch guy makes in a month," the Turkey said.

"In a year," Charlie said. "And the best thing is, we won it all from Bobby Blaine and his Prod pals!"

"Me three beauties," Mary said, beaming at them. "Glory to be to God. Me three beauties. Sure I don't know what I've done to deserve you."

Thirty-five years later, when Mae told me the story of Repetey O'Brien's dice, she summed it up, her eyes shining with nostalgic admiration, "That Teddy—he had nerve and then some."

# 5

# My Rosary

**W**hile Teddy Fleming was coping with All Saints Parochial School and the rough streets of the Sixth Ward, Kitty Dolan was growing up in a mostly Protestant world. In her public school, P.S. 23, no one asked her to recite the Baltimore Catechism each morning. No one got paddled by Monsignor Meehan or belted by Sister Lamburder. But Kitty did not feel comfortable in P.S. 23. No one showed any overt hostility or prejudice because she was Irish-American and Catholic. Kitty was an excellent student, who got close to the highest marks in her class. She was clearly not one of the lower-class Irish who inhabited downtown Jersey City.

There was a gulf between Kitty and her female classmates for a different reason. Most of them had hardworking fathers who bought them pretty dresses and bonnets. Kitty had to make do with hand-me-downs from cousins. Tom Dolan's drinking continued to haunt the family. It had grown so bad, he was having difficulty finding work with anyone except his tolerant cousins. When they had nothing to offer him, the family bank balance sank toward zero.

In desperation, with money borrowed from her in-laws, Mary Fitzmaurice Dolan opened a small grocery store on Montgomery Street, not far from their Garrison Avenue home. She sold candy, bread, milk, and canned vegetables and fruit that a busy housewife might need in a hurry to complete a dinner menu. The store did not make much money, but it was better than no money—and it served as a stark reproach to Tom Dolan, a sort of visible witness of his drinking.

By now Kitty and George knew what was happening. Tom Dolan and Mary Fitzmaurice Dolan began having bitter arguments in front of the children. Mary seemed to think or hope that embarrassment would force Tom to take a total abstinence pledge. She told him that was the only way he would regain her love and his children's respect.

By this time, like many alcoholics, Tom was a master of evasion. "Ah Mary, Mary," he would say, gazing mournfully out the window. "Would you deprive a man of the pleasure of a night with his fellow men? Do you want a manly man or a creature fit for skirts? It's no crime to clink a glass now and then. I haven't had too much to drink for six months now."

Mary would furiously contradict this lie, and sometimes call on the children to support her. Kitty would shake her head and run crying to her room. George, still in kneepants, would be almost as tearful but would sadly tell his father, "Momma's right, Poppa. You were drunk last Saturday night. I saw you."

"Jesus God, what sort of a son are you, to sell me into slavery this way?" Tom would say, half angrily, half humorously. "That's what the woman wants, Georgie. Your momma wants me to be her slave. Her obedient slave."

"I don't want anything of the sort!" Mary would cry. George too would flee the room in confusion and dismay.

Both children retreated from the pain of the wounded marriage and the failed father. George became a passionate baseball fan, keeping scrapbooks of his heroes and talking about them constantly. Kitty escaped into books. By the time she graduated from eighth grade, she was reading popular novelists such as Mary J. Holmes, who wrote uplifting stories about small-town American life.

Kitty also learned to play the piano and found music another escape. She especially loved the melodies of Ethelbert Nevin, author of the most famous song of the era, "My Rosary," and other hits such as "Mighty Like a Rose." They had a vein of melancholy that fit her prevailing mood.

Kitty never dreamt that the words of "My Rosary" would stir a profound response in her father's troubled soul. It was not a new song, having been introduced to the public in 1898, when Kitty was in the second grade. It was regularly sung in concert halls and from vaudeville stages. But the words could still have special meaning—especially to a lapsed Catholic like Tom Dolan. The rosary was one of the most powerful devotions of the Catholic faith.

The fifty beads were divided into five "decades," with a prayer to the Virgin Mary recited on each bead. At the bottom of the loop of beads was attached a crucifix, symbol of Jesus's sacrificial suffering and death to save the world from sin.

On a spring afternoon in 1905, Kitty sat down at the piano and began playing the song and singing the words.

> The hours I spent with thee, dear heart
>> Are as a string of pearls to me;
> I count them over, every one apart,
>> My rosary, my rosary.
>
> Each hour a pearl, each pearl a prayer
>> To still a heart in absence wrung;
> I tell each bead unto the end,
>> And there a cross is hung.
>
> O memories that bless and burn,
>> O barren gain and bitter loss!
> I kiss each bead, and strive at last to learn
>> To kiss the cross;
>> Sweetheart! To kiss the cross.

Suddenly Tom Dolan was standing beside her. "Play that again," he said. "Sing it the same sweet way."

Kitty played and sang it again. Tom sank down on the bench beside his daughter and began to weep. "To kiss the cross," he whispered. "To kiss the cross. That's what I've never been able to do."

He was thinking of his three lost daughters, his inability to accept their deaths. "Oh Kitty, dear sweet Kitty, do you hate me?" he said.

"No Papa!" Kitty said, flinging her arms around him. "I could never hate you. But I wish—oh I so wish—that you and Momma were happier."

"I promise you—and I'll promise Momma—that I'll try to be a better father—a better husband. I'll try. I swear it!"

He kissed her and asked her to play "My Rosary" again. They sang it together. Tom got out his fiddle and they played it as a duet, with him singing the words. He had a pleasant tenor voice. At the close he sat down on the bench beside her and said, "Don't ever forget this, Kitty. It was your love that brought me to this understanding."

"No, Poppa, it was God," Kitty said. "I've prayed so hard for you."

"That's part of your love," he said.

Our postmodern era may find Tom Dolan's transformation hard to believe. But it happened at a time when both Catholics and Protestants considered religion the chief, if not the only, hope in the struggle against alcoholism. Women's Crusades knelt in prayer outside saloons. Children, organized into a Cold Water Army, chanted their hatred of "whiskey or gin, brandy or rum, or anything that will make drunk come."

On the stage, plays dramatized the damage alcohol inflicted on families. *Ten Nights in a Barroom and What I Saw There* featured a little girl singing, "Father, dear Father, come home with me now, the clock in the belfry strikes one . . ." She returns every hour, begging him to help her sick baby brother, until the child dies.

When Mary Fitzmaurice Dolan came home from the grocery store, Kitty expected her father to tell the story of his change of heart and bring her mother into their circle of new hope and happiness. But Tom said nothing to his wife. Weary from spending twelve hours on her feet behind a counter, Mary cooked them the usual perfunctory dinner, and conversation at the table consisted mostly of George talking about the chances of the New York Giants winning the pennant that year.

After dinner, as Kitty helped her mother clear the table and wash the dishes, she told her about "My Rosary" and Tom Dolan's promise. She was shocked to find her mother unresponsive. "He's made a dozen promises like that," Mary said. "He doesn't dare make them to me anymore. I'd laugh in his face."

"Momma, I think he meant it!" Kitty said.

"He wants you to think he meant it. So you'll go on feeling sorry for him and loving him when he breaks the promise."

Mary saw what Tom was doing—setting up Kitty as a rival for his affections—and she did not like it. But Kitty was oblivious to such emotional crosscurrents. Like most young girls, she loved her father extravagantly.

"This wasn't just a promise to me, Momma. It was to God."

"Let's see if he keeps it," Mary said.

To Kitty's secret delight, Tom Dolan kept his promise. He went to the rectory of St. Aloysius Church on Westside Avenue and took a pledge of total abstinence, which the pastor signed along with him. Tom used the document to persuade employers to hire him as a carpenter again.

Mary Fitzmaurice Dolan remained skeptical, almost aloof, still half convinced the reformation would not last. As weeks passed and Tom Dolan stayed sober, Kitty was more and more thrilled. It made her believe that love was not just some silly word that singers warbled on vaudeville stages and phonograph records. It was a power that women possessed. They could use it to change men's lives—and their own.

For the rest of her life Kitty would remember her father's words: *It was your love that brought me to this understanding.* Forty years later she would tell me the story as if it had happened only yesterday. She did not seem to realize that beneath these words lurked a profound alienation between her mother and father. In his troubled soul, Tom Dolan was telling Mary Fitzmaurice that he no longer needed or wanted her love.

In a sad twisted way, Tom had transferred his quarrel with God to his wife. I can see this now, almost seventy years later. As a boy I was awed by "My Rosary." The story seemed to endow Kitty Dolan with magical powers.

# 6

# The Sporting Life

As Teddy Fleming grew up in the downtown Sixth Ward, Jersey City and the world beyond it were changing in dramatic ways. Automobiles of every shape and variety began appearing on the Hudson County Boulevard and other uptown streets. An equally magical invention, the telephone, became common in uptown homes. Even more exciting to kids were theaters that showed flickering films about cowboys and Indians and comic cops and clashing husbands and wives.

Things were changing in politics too. In 1902, the incredible happened. An Irish Catholic Republican ran for mayor of Jersey City. His name was Mark Fagan, and he campaigned on the slogan "A New Idea." An undertaker's assistant, Fagan was familiar to many families in his own Fifth Ward and he tirelessly toured the other downtown wards, talking to thousands of voters. He called Little Bob Davis a crook and promised all sorts of reforms in Jersey City.

In the Fleming household, after Mark Fagan paid a call on Mary Green while the rest of the family was at school and at work, she wondered if they should vote for him. Davey Fleming ferociously vetoed the idea. "An Irishman who's a Republican? He's either crazy or a liar or both. We'll stick with our friends. Bob Davis has put many a dollar in my pocket and many a piece of meat on our table."

"Sure what's Little Bob done for us lately?" Mary said. "He's dri-vin' around in his big motorcar while you're ridin' the trolleys. This fellow Fagan says he'll chase the harlots back to New York, arrest the bookmakers, and close the saloons on time. That'd do more for the Irish character than anything Little Bob's ever done."

Davey still voted the straight Democratic ticket. The Fleming boys agreed with their father. Loyalty, gratitude, was what counted in politics. Fagan was a reformer—another word for Protestant. Who cared if he went to daily Mass and read some book called *The Imitation of Christ?* He wanted to turn everyone into goo-goo (short for "good government") sissies. The best answer to him was Tammany's motto: "To Hell With Reform!"

To the younger Flemings' amazement and Davey Fleming's dismay, Mark Fagan won. The undertaker's triumph was a by-product of another large change in American life. With reform-minded President Theodore Roosevelt in the White House giving speeches about "malefactors of great wealth," newspapers and magazines and politicians were criticizing the way big businessmen and corrupt politicians ran the country.

One of the biggest scandals erupted in New York. Reformers began investigating the major insurance companies—New York Life, Mutual Life, Equitable Life—finding all sorts of nefarious practices, from bribes to legislators to exorbitant salaries to family members.

One revelation infuriated Davey Fleming. Equitable had been collecting fifty cents a week from thousands of small policyholders long after their policies had been paid up. Davey was one of these defrauded customers. He told Mary and his offspring that he would never pay another nickel to an insurance company and he ordered them to do likewise. "Sure it won't amount to more than a mosquito bite on an elephant, but it's better than doin' nothin'," he said.

"Don't worry, Da," Charlie said. "I ain't got a nickel."

"I'll do exactly what you say, Da," said twelve-year-old Mae. "I'll never pay them nothin'!"

"Ah the world is full of thieves," Mary Fleming said. "Let the lawyers and the prosecutors worry about them. They'll get what they deserve in the long run."

Mary was a full-time invalid now. She no longer went to Mass or anywhere else. She could not negotiate the steep stairs of their cold-water flat. Several times she was rushed to the hospital after suffering a "spell"—almost certainly a heart attack. Medicine could do little for heart disease in the early decades of the twentieth century.

None of the startling changes in politics and business altered the younger Flemings' minds about what was important in life: boxing and baseball. In Jersey City the baseball season started in March, when the major-league teams went south for spring training. On more than one morning, Teddy and his friends trudged to the Happy Nines, their local ballfield, and shoveled the snow off the infield before they started a game.

They used the cheapest equipment on the market: gloves with almost no padding, bats made of green lumber. To improve their fielding, they cut the middle out of the gloves. When they winged the ball around the infield and it hit bare flesh with the temperature only forty or fifty degrees Fahrenheit, the pain was exquisite. But no one complained. It was another way of proving you could take it like a man. Only momma's boys like Timmy Mullaney whimpered and retreated to the sidelines clutching a throbbing hand.

Teddy Fleming played third base, which meant even more pain on a cold day. Third basemen had to handle the hot smashes that came down the foul line, then make the long throw to first. Teddy soon proved he was the best fielder in the ward, with the strongest throwing arm. Not many batters got to first base on a ball hit in Teddy's territory. Teddy had only one flaw: he was not a big hitter. With his fiercely competitive temperament, he swung for the fences—and often struck out.

During these sessions, a lone spectator in clerical black often stood ten or twenty feet behind the outfielders: Monsignor Meehan. His presence made everyone play harder. When it came to baseball, Meehan was an awesome figure to every boy in All Saints School. He knew John "Muggsy" McGraw, the famous manager of the New York Giants.

In fact, the Mons knew Muggsy so well, he had performed the ceremony at his wedding. The thought of shaking the hand that shook the hand of Muggsy McGraw was enough to make almost every boy—and not a few adult males—in All Saints parish weak in the knees.

Teddy Fleming was especially impressed, because McGraw had played third base for the Baltimore Orioles before he became the

Giants' manager. Teddy saw himself pursuing the same path to fame and fortune; he would have no difficulty being as tough as Muggsy, who was famous for slugging opposing players, newspapermen, and even an occasional umpire. Throughout the spring of his eighth-grade year at All Saints, Teddy played with verve and passion, especially when Monsignor Meehan was watching them.

A week before graduation from All Saints Parochial School, Teddy was summoned to the rectory. The housekeeper led him into Monsignor Meehan's comfortable study, the scene of his fifth-grade paddling three years earlier. The big priest sat behind his desk, looking solemn.

"You're getting out of All Saints in another week, Fleming," Meehan said. "What's your ambition in life?"

Teddy stiffened his shoulders and looked Meehan in the eye. "I'm gonna play t'oid base in d'majuh leagues," he said.

"*The* major leagues. Don't say 'duh,'" Meehan said. "And it's *third* base."

The Mons sat back in his chair and Teddy saw something unusual on his wide, ruddy face: sympathy. Meehan was not big on sympathy. He was more into giving orders and issuing pronouncements. "You're not going to make the major leagues, Fleming. You can't hit a curve," he said.

"I can loin!" Teddy said. "I'll figure it out, just watch me."

Meehan's face regained its usual sternness. "You can't loin it," he said. "Or learn it, for that matter. It's something you're born with—or without. For you, baseball would be a waste of time. You'd wind up another tramp Irish athlete. We've got too many of them already. You're going to business school."

"Business school?" Teddy said, frankly astonished. "I ain't never gonna be no businessman, Monsignor." He was thinking of the factory owners he saw and heard about in the Sixth Ward. A lot of them pulled the Catholic or Protestant act with would-be employees.

"You can learn to be one," Meehan said. "You write a good hand. You're a good speller. In business school they'll teach you how to keep books, type, write letters. You can get a job in an office at twice the salary your father's getting."

The reference to his father ignited the mix of anger and shame that troubled Teddy. "My old man woiks as hard as anyone in dis crummy ward!" he said. "He brings his pay home wit'out drinkin' a nickel of it, which is more than y'can say for a lotta udda micks. It ain't his fault if them Prod swindlers in d'oil business don't pay him nothin'."

"I didn't say it was his fault," Meehan said. "I'm just telling you how the world works. You've got to start low and work hard to prove yourself."

"Nuts," Teddy said. "If I can't make it as a ballplayer, I'll do it in d'ring. I got d'best right hook in d'ward."

"You'll never be big enough to be a heavyweight," Meehan said. "They're the ones who make the real money. The rest of them get peanuts—and it's a crooked game in the bargain. You'll find yourself throwing fights—it's a quick way to lose your self-respect."

*Self-respect.* The words hit Teddy hard. He had never heard them before, but he instantly grasped their meaning. "I'll get where I wanna get and keep me self-respect, you watch!" he said.

"Teddy," Meehan said. "I'm trying to be your friend. Go to business school. The parish will pay the tuition. It's only a year."

Teddy Fleming was deeply moved—and amazed—to hear Meehan claim to be his friend. But a fierce voice inside his head still resisted the Monsignor's realism. Even though Meehan used his nickname, the priest wasn't talking to *him*, to the kid with dreams of being a famous third baseman or a champ in the boxing ring. He was trying to improve the whole Irish tribe—or at least the slice of it that was within his reach. Teddy couldn't, he wouldn't, give up his dreams for that reason.

"Monsignor, don't get sore—but I gotta do it my way. I promise you I ain't never gonna be a tramp athlete. If I don't make it I'll get an office job somehow. But first I gotta give d'udda stuff a real try."

Meehan held out his hand. "Good luck."

When Teddy Fleming told me this story in 1940, we were riding past All Saints Parochial School in his limousine, on the way to a Sixth Ward political rally. He made it sound as if "you can't hit a curve" was amusing. But I don't think the Monsignor's advice struck him as funny when he heard it in 1902.

I bet that Teddy Fleming, the fourteen-year-old with the twisted, jutting teeth, went back to All Saints School and sat there in a daze, barely listening to the nun at the front of the class. I wouldn't be surprised if he almost told Sister to shut up. He was tired of reciting the Catechism and writing down memorized answers to questions about geography and history. She could not tell him the answer to the one question that mattered. How could an Irish guy get his hands on real money when the Protestants had most of it?

Teddy decided to pursue both baseball and boxing fame simultaneously. He started hanging out at John McConville's gymnasium in the riverside Second Ward. Fighters from New York and Brooklyn trained there. It was a great place to watch professionals box. Teddy had stopped growing at five feet eight and a half. But he refused to let his size discourage him. He worked out with weights and did exercises to develop his shoulder and arm muscles. He had his father's solid torso, and he developed a formidable physique. At one hundred and forty-five pounds, Teddy soon had the makings of a good welterweight.

One of the McConville gym's trainers, a graying ex-welterweight named Eddie O'Toole, persuaded the owner to hire Teddy to keep track of the equipment and clean up before closing. In his spare time O'Toole taught Teddy the art and science of boxing.

Teddy soon learned it was hard work. Every session began with stretching. That was how a fighter avoided injuries. Teddy sat on the floor and lengthened his hamstrings, his flexors. Then came ten minutes of loosening his arms and back. Teddy ducked, twisted, bent, rotated on the axis of his hips, while Eddie barked, "Come on come on, *work* at it."

Next came a half hour of skipping rope, which not only built stamina but added dexterity to amateur feet. Basically, a boxer had to learn to dance. Then Teddy climbed into a ring with a pair of dumbbells. He circled the ring, punching the air with the bells, performing intricate steps that would enable him to escape an oncoming opponent or pivot and shatter him with a left hook or a right cross. Around and around he danced with the weights until sweat was streaming down his body.

On to twenty minutes of shadowboxing, with Eddie criticizing almost every other move, showing him how to perform a combination, throw a left hook, an uppercut, a right jab. Then twenty minutes punching a heavy bag, and ten minutes of rat-tat-tat on a light bag. Next Eddie put big padded gloves on his hands and let Teddy throw punches at him, again criticizing his stance, velocity, rapidity.

Finally came the climax of most evenings, a sparring match. Not everyone was willing to spar on a given night. Fighters often pleaded dates with girls or soreness from their last match. Teddy was always willing. He pulled on the fourteen-ounce sparring gloves and went three rounds with anyone and everyone, lightweights, middleweights, light heavyweights. Eddie drew the line at heavyweights. "Those guys can kill you with one punch," he said in his laconic way.

At the end of a three-round match, O'Toole often took Teddy out for a cup of coffee and told him what he did wrong—and occasionally what he did right. "Stick with it, kid, you got a future," he sometimes said.

In summer, McConville's gym virtually shut down. That was all right with Teddy. Summer was the baseball season and he was still playing the game. Hudson County was crowded with semiprofessional teams that attracted first-class talent. Many of the big companies with factories in Jersey City financed teams, paying players twenty or thirty dollars a game. In the *Jersey Journal* of those days (the paper had dropped the word *Evening* from the masthead) it was not uncommon to see stories headed: "Jersey City Printing Company Team Looking for Games."

Teddy continued to play third base, and he remained one of the best fielders on the local scene. But he still could not hit a curve. One summer he hired a neighborhood kid who threw a good curveball to pitch to him on the Happy Nines for hours at a time, but it was not the same thing as swinging at curves when you didn't know they were coming.

During these teenage years, women did not play a part in Teddy's life. The main reason was his passion for baseball and boxing, which most teenage girls did not share. In the first decade of the new century, few women had any interest in sports. Another reason was his ugly protruding teeth, which made him less than attractive to the opposite sex.

Eddie O'Toole played a role in prodding him into solving the dental problem. He told Teddy to get the teeth pulled or expect to lose them in bits and pieces when he got into the ring with a real fighter. The rubber mouthpieces boxers wore would not protect teeth that jutted and twisted in such an unnatural way.

Eddie liked the results of Teddy's trip to the dentist so much, he decided his protégé was ready to be introduced to the sporting world. The term included much more than athletics. "Sports" were bachelors who followed baseball, boxing, and horseracing and liked the kind of women they met in dance halls and concert saloons (an early version of the cocktail lounge). Good-time girls, O'Toole called them. They didn't expect a wedding ring on the first date—or the twenty-first. New York was full of such women and they suddenly liked Teddy Fleming's looks. But he carefully avoided playing any amorous games with women in Jersey City, where Monsignor Meehan might hear about them. The big priest was not above hauling playboys into the rectory and giving them a tongue-lashing they never forgot.

One day, Charlie, who was in the eighth grade at All Saints School, told Teddy that Monsignor Meehan wanted to see him. Teddy arrived in a defensive mood, wondering if his sporting life in Manhattan had somehow reached Meehan's large ears. But Meehan did not have the sixth commandment on his mind. "I'm waiting for you to keep your promise," he said.

"What promise?" Teddy said.

"The one you made when you got out of the eighth grade—that you'd go to business school if you didn't make it as a ballplayer or a fighter. I've been following you on the semiipro circuit. Your hitting still isn't good enough to attract any attention from a major league scout."

"You been down to McConville's gym to check me out as a fighter?"

"No."

"Eddie O'Toole says I'm ready to go. I got my first match next month, over in Brooklyn."

"Good luck," the Monsignor said.

Teddy's first fight was a big deal in the Sixth Ward. A delegation of his friends, led by Dave and Charlie and cousin Tom, traveled to Brooklyn to cheer him on—and bet money on his punches. They were ecstatic when Teddy knocked his opponent cold in the first round. They partied all night at one of the dance halls in the Second Ward and reeled home to Communipaw Avenue singing wacky vaudeville tunes.

Teddy's next fight was on a card in a Manhattan arena. Once more he put his opponent out of business in the first round. The sportswriters picked up a remark by Eddie O'Toole, "This kid's a slugger," and started calling him "Kid Slugger" Fleming. Teddy made twenty-five dollars from each fight. "I thought I was on my way to big money!" he told me with a wry smile thirty years later.

Eddie O'Toole now booked his fighter into one of the best boxing arenas in Manhattan. "You're gonna see a lot of guys with diamond studs and solid gold rings tonight, kid," Eddie said as they got off the ferry from Jersey City. With them were at least two hundred fans from the Sixth Ward, once more led by Dave and Charlie and Cousin Tom, all talking about how much money they were going to make on Teddy before the night was over.

In the dressing room, Charlie reported that Teddy was a long shot. Some bookmakers upstairs were giving odds of five to one against him. The other guy had won six in a row with knockouts. That had not stopped the Sixth Warders from betting their wads on Teddy.

"Okay, okay, beat it and let Teddy get his act together," Eddie O'Toole said, shooing Dave and Charlie and Tom out the door.

Teddy stretched out on a rubbing table and Eddie started kneading his muscles. "I got some bad news, kid," he said. "You're gonna haveta take a dive tonight."

"What the hell are you talkin' about? I seen this guy fight. I can flatten him in two rounds, tops," Teddy said.

"That ain't the way things work, kid," Eddie said. "You wanna keep boxin', you gotta do what the big shots tell you. They figure to make a lot of money on you tonight—while you're flat on ya back."

"Tell'm to go to hell," Teddy said.

"Kid—if you don't play along, you'll never box again. And I won't handle you. You'll be a tar baby. Anyone who touches you is outta d'business."

Suddenly Teddy was hearing Monsignor Meehan telling him in the eighth grade, *The heavyweights make all the real money. And you'll have to throw fights. It's a quick way to lose your self-respect.* "What's the most money you ever made from a fight?" he asked.

"Five hundred bucks," Eddie said. "When I was a contender. You gotta go along to get along, kid."

O'Toole thought his protégé would be impressed by five hundred dollars. But Teddy decided it was peanuts. The heavyweights got fifty and a hundred thousand dollars for a championship fight. Maybe welterweight boxing wasn't the royal road to riches after all. Maybe there was no royal road.

Down the aisle Teddy strode to the ring, with Eddie beside him. "Let'm hit you in the second round. Drop your right hand. He'll be lookin' for it. He ain't gonna hurt you. He ain't got much of a punch."

"How'd he win six in a row?"

"He's got some really big bettors behind him."

Teddy touched gloves and circled his opponent, an angular blond German-American who had a longer reach. He was about two inches taller than Teddy, but much leaner in the torso. Teddy decided a right to the solar plexus was the way to go. They mixed it up for most of the first round without doing much damage, until Teddy scored a left to the nose that drew blood. The guy clinched and growled, "What the hell do you think you're doin'? This is my fight."

"No kiddin'?" Teddy said. "Somebody musta forgot t'tell me."

He broke the clinch and pivoted away for a split second, then whirled and planted a terrific right in the German's stomach. It was a devastator. The German's eyes bulged; he tried to backpedal. But nothing was working. Now Teddy's weight was on his other foot, ready for the left hook. It caught the German on the point of the chin and he went down like a collapsed building.

Back in Jersey City, the Sixth Ward's bettors counted their winnings and celebrated into another dawn. But Teddy did not share their whoopee mood. In the dressing room after the fight, Eddie O'Toole had cursed him out. He had lost a hundred bucks on the German. Back in the apartment, Teddy told Dave and Charlie and Tom what had happened behind the scenes. His boxing career was over.

Charlie couldn't believe it. "You shoulda belted O'Toole in d'kisser too," he said.

"Nah. He thought he was doin' me a favor. Doin' himself one too, naturally."

The next morning, Teddy strolled down Communipaw Avenue to All Saints rectory. Soon he was in Monsignor Meehan's study. "Remember what you tole me about trowin' fights?" he said.

Meehan nodded.

"You was right. I wouldn't trow one last night and I'm outta d'game. I'm too damn old to go t'business school. Whattya think I should do?"

"You're a good-looking guy. Become a salesman. I've got some old friends in the watch business. I'll give them a call."

A salesman. Teddy went home to the family flat and lay in bed for most of the night, wondering if it was a good idea. What the hell, give it a try, he finally decided. It was better than sticking up banks or saloons. Maybe there was big money up the line somewhere. But he had begun to doubt it.

That's when it hit Teddy. Hit him really hard. He was never going to be a millionaire or a famous baseball player or a boxing champion. He would have to live with those facts, somehow. At that moment he found strength in Davey Fleming—the way his father had accepted his crummy luck and gone to work for peanuts every day and brought home his lousy pay to keep them eating.

Maybe the real fight wasn't on the ballfield or in the boxing ring. Maybe it was with life and the dirty tricks it played on you. Maybe the best you could do was come out of it with self-respect.

# 7

# The Escape Artist

In 1909, the year that Teddy Fleming surrendered his boyhood dreams of sporting fame and fortune, Katherine Dolan was in her senior year at Jersey City High School. Her life had changed and was still changing in dramatic ways. She had become a strikingly attractive young woman, with thick dark hair and a superb figure. Men swarmed around her at dances. More important to her, she had extended her horizon beyond Jersey City, where an Irish name was synonymous with inferiority to many of her uptown neighbors. On almost every holiday weekend, she took a train to South Plainfield, New Jersey, where a different world awaited her.

Her father's cousin Kate Dooling (the original family name—changed by some to Dolan) had married an Englishman named Charles Thornton, who operated a hotel in South Plainfield. They always had a room for Cousin Kitty, and a party or a dance constantly seemed to be on the calendar. Almost as popular as a destination was South Amboy, where another bevy of Dolan cousins lived.

Kitty's 1909 diary is crowded with names of young men who pursued her. One of the most ardent was her handsome dark-haired South Amboy cousin Hugh Gallagher. But Kitty had her own agenda and marrying an Irish-American cousin was not on it. She gravitated to Protestant young men in both towns, with a special fondness for those who made her laugh.

Kitty was not thinking it out step by step. But she was obviously trying to escape Jersey City and her unhappy home on Garrison Avenue—and the stigma of being Irish. Her girlish pride in rescuing her father from alcoholism had suffered some grievous wounds in the following several years.

At first the miraculous cure had seemed real and lasting. With Tom Dolan's weekly pay restored, he persuaded his wife to abandon the grocery store. That decision had removed a cloud on Kitty's horizon. Her mother had talked of making her a clerk in the store after she graduated from the eighth grade. Kitty desperately wanted to go to Jersey City High School, which had recently opened on a bluff overlooking downtown Jersey City. Her eighth-grade teacher wrote a letter to the principal, strongly recommending her as one of P.S. 23's best pupils.

Kitty loved Jersey City (now Dickinson) High School. It was big and roomy, compared to her cramped grammar school. The building featured an auditorium that seated two thousand people. Important lecturers spoke there, and the students staged plays and chorales. Mingling with the mostly Protestant young women and men who had been selected as students gave her a feeling that she had passed more than a scholastic test. She was ascending to a new level of society in Jersey City—and in the nation. Only about six percent of American grammar school graduates went to high school in 1905.

Kitty also continued to be a star pupil, with a special aptitude for math, a subject most young women disliked. By senior year she had mastered algebra, geometry, and solid geometry and had taken a course in calculus, which she found daunting. But her teacher assured her she had the ability to master it in college.

*College.* The term induced longing—and wistful melancholy in Kitty's imagination. How wonderful it would be to go to Vassar or Mount Holyoke or Wellesley or one of the other schools for women that were thriving around the nation. But she mournfully informed her teacher that it was out of the question for her. Her mother had told her she would have to go to work as soon as she graduated. They needed the money.

Tom Dolan had begun drinking again. It was not as destructive as his former sprees. He never went on a bender and disappeared for days, as he had sometimes done when he was out of control during Kitty's grammar school years. But on Saturday night he sometimes came home staggering, with half his pay missing from his envelope.

Mary Fitzmaurice Dolan would become grimly angry and summon Kitty to speak to him. "He won't listen to me," she often said. "Remind him of his promise to you."

The sarcasm in her voice was unmistakable. She was saying to her daughter, *Maybe you still love him. I don't.*

Kitty would slip into the parlor, where Tom was slumped on the couch, and play "The Rosary" on the piano. Then she would sink down beside him and talk to him in a tender, mournful voice. She would tell him how much he was hurting Mamma. She would add that he was also hurting her, because he was breaking the promise he had made to her. He had to stop drinking! Would he go to St. Aloysius's rectory and sign another total abstinence pledge? Or at least promise her he would not drink for the rest of the year?

Most of the time, Tom promised, and he kept his word for five or six months. But the fear of a slide into his old ruinous drinking pattern always loomed over them. That had been the prime reason why Kitty's trips to South Plainfield and South Amboy had begun to mean so much to her. In those prosperous country towns, there was no fear of neighbors whispering about her father's weakness. She was her own person, separate and seemingly independent from her family.

Kitty's 1909 diary began with a description of a New Year's Eve ball in South Amboy. "Danced until 5 A.M.," she wrote on New Year's Day. "Had eleven dances with Lester. I really believe I love him. Took me home. Hugh [Gallagher] was awfully angry. Only had a few dances with him."

Lester's last name was Stratton. He had a good sense of humor, which put him far ahead in the running for Kitty's affections. She saw him repeatedly throughout the year, but for some reason Kitty could not grasp, their friendship never made much romantic progress. Lester enjoyed teasing and joking with her but he never seemed to consider her a "sweetheart"—Kitty's favorite term for a boyfriend.

At times Kitty wondered if Lester had decided she was too "silly" to take seriously. One of her cousins had spread a story around South Amboy about her acting giddy when she had a glass of wine with some visitors. At one point Kitty admitted she had "an awful crush" on Lester. But Lester still declined to reciprocate.

Back in Jersey City, Lester was more or less forgotten. There Kitty's attention focused on the president of her high school class, Tom Connolly. They took long walks together and exchanged an occasional goodnight kiss. As their high school days wound down, Kitty grew more and more attracted to him. She did not seem to realize that he remained as elusive as Lester Stratton.

There is an explanation that Kitty either ignored or never put in her diary. Both these young men were Protestants. In 1909, most Protestants in New Jersey took a very dim view of one of their children marrying a Catholic—especially an Irish Catholic. Kitty's escape from Jersey City was mostly in her own imagination. Her religion and her Irish name pursued her.

Kitty saw a great deal of Tom when they both won parts in the senior class play, *In the Absence of Susan*. Kitty's 1909 diary has "REHEARSAL" in large letters above numerous pages that spring. The plot concerned the rebellion of pretty, flirtatious Maida when her prim, domineering older sister Susan goes away for an extended visit to a relative. Kitty played Maida, who engineers a romance and a proposal from Geoffrey, her brother Dick's best friend, before Susan returns. Maida works similar magic for her friend Harriet, who gets a proposal from Dick.

Tom Connolly played Geoffrey, which made for not a few onstage clinches with Kitty during the weeks of rehearsals. This imaginary love affair had a lot to do with igniting Kitty's hopes that it would lead to the real thing offstage.

Meanwhile, Kitty was wrestling with another problem: what she would do after graduation. A large number of her female classmates were planning to become teachers. Kitty resisted the idea. The image of the old-maid schoolteacher troubled her. She did not think a teacher would have much chance of meeting the kind of ambitious, get-ahead man she wanted to marry.

Her mother urged teaching as a career. "The salary isn't large, but it's steady work," Mary Fitzmaurice Dolan said in her practical way. "Schools never go bankrupt or fire people who do their jobs well."

With considerable reluctance, Kitty accepted this advice. But it redoubled her desire to persuade Tom Connolly to fall in love with her. In her imagination, he became a kind of white knight who would rescue her from a teaching career.

On May 7, 1909, *In the Absence of Susan* went off well. It drew one of the largest crowds yet recorded in Jersey City High School's splendid auditorium. Kitty noted that she was not in the least nervous onstage. Afterward, there was a dance—and a painful disappointment. Kitty "expected Tom to be nice. He was not. He never kissed me or fooled or anything and was not a bit interesting."

To her dismay, Tom seemed more attracted to another girl, Gwendolyn Hager, who had played Harriet in *In the Absence of Susan*. Kitty glumly remarked to her diary that Gwen "always spoils everything for me," suggesting she knew Tom had been smitten by her. Kitty finished this page in the diary with a heartbroken, "I know everything is over now. I'll have to go to school after this. He's gone forever."

This bitter disappointment cast a shadow over Kitty's graduation from Jersey City High School a month later. It did not seem to matter that she graduated as the salutatorian of her class, with the second highest grade average. She gave a talk, "The Relation of Literature to Life," and won the prize for the best marks in mathematics and science. It was the bleak manless future, not the achievement-rich present, that loomed largest in her mind.

In later years, Kitty would tell me a great deal about her life and loves. But she never mentioned her high school accomplishments to me—not a word about graduating as salutatorian, starring in the class play, winning the mathematics prize. Over the years, I slowly realized it was a sad indication of the intensity of her disappointment in the failure of her romantic hopes. I had to read her diary and plow through musty files of the board of education at Jersey City's public library to discover the crucial importance of this year in her young life.

When Kitty wrote, "I'll have to go to school," she meant Jersey City's training school, the two-year course that was required to win a teaching certificate. As she feared, Kitty found it boring stuff. Her ability in mathematics and science made no impression on her teachers. She seemed to relapse into the kind of passivity that occasionally turned up in her diary, when she wrote, "Sat around all day feeling tired of myself." Without giving much thought to the matter, she chose kindergarten and first grade as her field. Was she looking for some sort of lift from the innocent faces of children at this age? I think so.

No one saw much evidence of Kitty's inner melancholy. To her cousins and her family and friends she was still the lighthearted play-girl, always ready to tell or listen to a joke. She began spending almost every weekend in South Amboy or at the Thornton Hotel in South Plainfield. There, cousin Hugh Gallagher still pursued her in vain. She danced with almost everyone except poor Hugh.

Another young man began paying very persistent attention to Kitty. Handsome, self-confident Lloyd Harris was the son of a South Plainfield businessman. His mother had been a schoolteacher, and that made for a sort of bond when Kitty visited the Harrises' handsome house on South Plainfield's main street. For a while, it seemed like a repetition of Lester Stratton. There were lots of laughs and an occasional goodnight kiss—but Lloyd avoided serious conversation about love and marriage. One reason may have been his age; he was several years younger than Kitty.

Kitty's best friend in South Plainfield was Loretta Thornton, daughter of Aunt Kate and Uncle Charlie, operators of Thornton's Hotel. A short, pert brunette, Loretta soon became as close as a sister; she and Kitty had similar temperaments. They were always laughing and ready to flirt with any good-looking man who came along. Loretta was particularly gifted in this department; Kitty called her "spicy." When Loretta was around, there was "always something doing and then some." But they both remained very firmly in the good girls department.

One of the pleasures of Thornton's Hotel was a nearby lake, where couples could retreat after dark in rowboats and do a little "spooning." Aunt Kate had her doubts about this pastime, and made them evident by embarking in her own rowboat to patrol the lake and rebuke those who were in danger of going too far. As Lloyd Harris's lips met Kitty's, Aunt Kate would emerge from the darkness to say, "Kitty, haven't you been out here long enough? You'll catch cold!"

Loretta got the same treatment, as did the half dozen other young women in their crowd. This good-conduct patrol inspired one of the men, perhaps Lloyd Harris, to improvise a parody of the popular song, "The Moon Has Its Eyes on You." The Thornton's Hotel version was "Aunt Kate Has Her Eyes on You." They often ended an evening of dancing and off-key singing (Kitty called their vocalizing "screeching") with this number for a closing serenade.

Aunt Kate would give them a frosty smile and snap, "You bet I've got my eyes on you. Especially you, Loretta!"

By 1912, twenty-one-year-old Kitty was teaching as a substitute in the Jersey City schools and making a modest $600 a year. But she still yearned for a sweetheart, a marriage that would lift her to a world beyond the anxious unhappy house on Garrison Avenue. She never dreamt that her status as South Plainfield's favorite party girl would win her an opportunity to make that dream come true.

Like many things in life, the process was circuitous. Early in 1912, the *Plainfield Courier-News* launched a contest to raise its circulation. The five people who produced the most subscriptions would win a six-week grand tour of Europe. One of Kitty's cousins, perhaps yearning Hugh Gallagher, came up with a novel idea. Why don't the weekend denizens of Thornton's Hotel beat the local bushes for subscribers, and credit them all to Kitty Dolan? As Hugh put it, "We ought to send the prettiest girl in town on this trip!"

Kitty was more than willing to accept the offer. The Thornton's Hotel team went to work. Soon dozens, then hundreds of subscriptions were being credited to Katherine L. Dolan. Lloyd Harris proved to be among the hardest workers, and was rewarded by more than a few kisses on the darkened lake, in spite of Aunt Kate's ubiquitous eyes. Early in April, the newspaper announced that Kitty and four other women were winners and sent a photographer to take her picture. At Thornton's Hotel, Kitty's backers celebrated until Aunt Kate turned out the lights on them around 3 A.M. Lloyd Harris insisted on seven dances in a row with Kitty, and ended the evening warbling a slightly altered version of another popular song.

> K-K-K-Kitty, beautiful K-K-K-Kitty,
> You're the only g-g-girl that I adore!

Suddenly Kitty Dolan believed in happiness. In some wonderful incomprehensible way her dreams were coming true. She was escaping Jersey City and its legacy of shame and angry exchanges between her father and mother. She had found a handsome young Protestant swain who obviously loved her. She had won a prize that would vault her into the ranks of the sophisticated few who had toured Europe and absorbed its culture. What more could a woman ask?

# 8

# Salesman's Blues

"Otto, how the hell are ya? How're those new Elgins doin'?" Teddy Fleming asked.

"Lousy. Vy I let you zell me dem lemons?" Otto Kunhaldt growled. "Ingraham's new line iz ten times better."

"Elgin's goin' great in Rochester. My best customer there just doubled his order."

"Iz sellink zero in Glens Falls. I don't know why I listen to you. I should learn by now a mick will say anything to make a sale."

It was the spring of 1913. Teddy Fleming was in upstate New York, several hundred miles from Jersey City, selling a line of watches for the biggest distributor in the business. By now he had learned the first principle of a salesman's life: you had to eat a lot of horse manure.

When a watch didn't sell, the jeweler who ordered thirty or forty of them took it as a personal insult and gave you hell the next time you showed up. Otto Kunhaldt was especially prone to throw "mick" into the conversation. In 1913, it was the equivalent of calling a Jew a "hebe." Both terms were in frequent use. Political correctness was far in the future.

Teddy had never been fond of Germans. In Jersey City most of them were Republicans. They owned the butcher shops and the grocery stores, which meant they could let a family starve when the father was laid off or got sick. Most of them weren't that coldhearted—they were usually Catholics—but it gave them a chance to talk down to, and look down on, the Irish. A lot of the people in the jewelry business were Germans. A fair number of them were like Otto Kunhaldt; they talked down to Teddy the minute they found out he was Irish.

Teddy soon learned to expunge all references to his ethnic background from his conversation. Fleming was not an especially Irish name. But it irritated him to have to pretend to be an Anglo-Saxon. He could almost hear Davey Fleming in full cry: *Surrre I never thought a son of mine would be ashamed of his Irish blood.*

Monsignor Meehan had made good on his promise. He had gotten Teddy this job with the help of Horace Stoneham, the owner of the New York Giants. Teddy worked hard to learn the watch business. You had to know a lot about watches to sell them. You had to remember what your competition was selling, plus arguments that proved your brands were better. Even if some of your stuff was junk, you couldn't say so. A salesman was part joker, part liar, and part magician. He was supposed to make lost money come back by laughing a lot and swearing a ton of cash was just over the rainbow.

Teddy went to work on Otto Kunhaldt. He told him Elgin was launching a huge new advertising campaign to back their watches. They were offering twenty percent discounts to anyone who ordered more than fifty copies. Otto's ugly German puss continued to resemble an umpire's ten seconds after Muggsy McGraw questioned his sanity. Teddy went to his last option. "Lemmy buy you lunch, Otto. We'll talk this thing over and maybe come up with an angle that will get your stuff movin'."

Lunch meant an hour of listening to Otto complain about his bunions and the deadbeats who bought wedding rings and got divorced six months later and declined to pay the balance. Up here in Protestant land, it was amazing how often people were getting divorced these days. It almost made a guy think marriage wasn't such a bad idea, if you could bail out of it whenever you felt like it.

All Teddy got out of lunch was a promise to think about a reorder if business picked up. He made three more calls in the afternoon and wrote one decent reorder. He ate dinner in a restaurant next door to the hotel. The food was okay but he found himself back in his room by eight o'clock.

Teddy started thinking about what he would be doing in Jersey City. Heading for New York with a few friends, maybe. Or standing at the bar in a Sixth Ward saloon talking about the New York Giants or the black heavyweight champion, Jack Johnson. Maybe listening to Charlie or the Turkey telling jokes or kidding the socks off Timmy Mullaney, who was still trying to be one of the boys.

If he went to a saloon in Glens Falls, he'd either drink alone or get picked up by a worn-out floozy who didn't interest him. Or maybe encounter some drunk who thought Syracuse's or Buffalo's International League baseball team was better than Jersey City's Jerseys. That could lead to a brawl and jail time. For what? To show some jerk from the boondocks who's boss?

That was the night Teddy realized he hated this job. He hated listening to jerks like Otto Kunhaldt. He hated spending three out of every four weeks on the road. Losing touch with his family, his friends, the rhythm of life in the Sixth Ward. Maybe he wasn't a baseball star or a boxing champ, but he was somebody in the Sixth Ward. He was the guy with nerve, the Kid Slugger who refused to throw a fight and screw his friends, the guy who knew where sporty girls hung out in New York and Newark. Who was he in Glens Falls or Rochester or Buffalo? A salesman. Another way of saying a zero.

Back in Jersey City, Teddy was still living at home with the rest of the Fleming family. With some help from Teddy and Charlie and modest raises that Davey had won at the Eagle Oil Company, they had moved to 122 Randolph Avenue, on the outer edge of the Sixth Ward, to a flat with hot and cold water. The neighborhood was a lot better than Communipaw Avenue, a main artery down which trucks lumbered day and night.

The comforts of their new apartment were small consolation for the sadness that pervaded the Fleming household. In 1910, Mary Green Fleming's damaged heart had stopped beating. A weeping Davey Fleming had cradled her in his big arms and kissed her farewell as her breathing grew slower and slower. A tearful Mae and Charlie had been at the bedside.

Teddy had been on his salesman's circuit in upstate New York. He had ridden trains day and night to get back for the wake and funeral. It was a mournful three days, remembering Mary's jokes and laughter—

above all the day she had called him and Dave and Charlie "my three beauties" for coming home with those fifty larcenous bucks from Repetey O'Brien's loaded dice. Teddy still carried the dice in his pocket as a good luck charm.

Also missing from Mary's deathbed was Dave Fleming. The Turkey was a married man. He had succumbed to the charms of Elizabeth Whelan, who had lived next door to them on Communipaw Avenue. Lizzie, as she was known in the family, seemed a good match for Dave—she was full of jokes and fun. They were also having fun in bed; Lizzie gave birth to a son within nine months of their wedding, and they named him Thomas, a sign of Dave's high opinion of his younger brother. At the christening, everyone agreed the kid was going to be a heavyweight champion.

Privately, Teddy thought Dave had made a big mistake. Now he had no room to maneuver. He would soon be like his father, forced to take almost any steady job to keep his wife and kids eating. Davey Fleming was talking to various politicians about getting the Turkey a job on the fire department. The money was okay, but that's all it was and all it ever would be—okay. Teddy nourished hopes of making a lot more than a fireman's salary.

There was another reason why Teddy was unhappy with his salesman's job. It could be summed up in two words: Frank Hague. The big fellow, as people were already calling the Second Ward leader, was shaking up Jersey City's politics in a new way. He was telling people it was time for the Irish to take charge of City Hall and tell the Protestants and the German Republicans to go to hell. Davey Fleming, no slouch at local politics, was saying Hague was "the boyo to watch."

In 1911, Boss Robert "Little Bob" Davis had died and Jersey City's politics had gone berserk. Things had been bad enough with the Irish Catholic Republican, Mark Fagan, as mayor for three terms. Mark self-destructed by getting too liberal for the GOP bosses and infuriating the Catholic Church by building too many new public schools. A German-American reformer named Otto Wittpenn got elected mayor on an anti-Davis Democratic ticket with support from Germans and the uptown Irish, who bought his goo-goo approach to politics. After Davis died other big shots got into the picture, trying to inherit Little Bob's power. The Easy Boss left an estate worth

$800,000 (the equivalent of $15 million today), which was nice ammunition for the reformers.

Then Hague started calling Otto Wittpenn a front for the railroads and other big businesses that owned most of Jersey City. The message resonated with Davey Fleming and his friends, who were still ready to denounce any and all Protestant millionaires. It also rang bells uptown. Overnight Hague took Wittpenn's reformer image away from him.

To everyone's surprise, Monsignor Meehan started backing Hague. The Mons had been impressed by an endorsement Hague got from his pastor, Monsignor John Shepherd, who assured his fellow priests that the Second Ward leader was committed to closing the brothels and prostitute-filled dance halls. This was something Mark Fagan and Otto Wittpenn had failed to do.

That idea also rang bells in the Fleming family. Mae Fleming had become a very attractive young woman, with red hair that all but glowed in the dark and her mother's delicate white skin. The Fleming males had already put out the word that anyone in the Sixth Ward who got close to Mae without a wedding ring in his pocket was in danger of serious harm. The fewer temptations for her to go the route of a sporting girl, the better.

Teddy Fleming liked Hague's belligerent style. He liked him even more when he threw Otto Wittpenn another political curveball. Hague got behind a proposal for a new kind of government for Jersey City. The *Jersey Journal* was pushing it in every issue. The idea was to run the city like a business, with five commissioners in charge of everything. That eliminated the board of aldermen, which the *Journal* called a debating club that specialized in giving a mayor hot-air headaches.

A lot of other cities in the country had adopted commission government and were enthusiastic. Mayor Wittpenn sat on the fence, which was a gutless way of saying he was against it. That amounted to a strikeout in the Fleming household.

When Davey Fleming dropped by to remind Sixth Ward leader Doc Holland that the Turkey was still waiting for his appointment to the fire department, Doc said, "What about your other boy, Teddy? He's got a lot of friends in this ward. I could use some help in gettin' them to vote the right way in this commission government fight."

"Teddy's on the road a lot, sellin' watches," Davey said.

"Tell him if we win this thing, I can arrange for him to make a lot more dough than he'll ever make sellin' watches," Doc said. "And the Turkey will have that fire department job so fast, it'll make his head spin."

Davey ordered Mae to send Teddy a telegram reporting Doc Holland's offer. It reached him in Glens Falls, where he had just had another dismal go-round with Otto Kunhaldt. Teddy's first reaction was no thanks. He had a sure thing with this job. People would always buy watches. Why throw away three years' experience on a political gamble? Still, it was nice to know Doc Holland had his eye on him. Even nicer to know there were still a lot of young guys in the Sixth Ward who admired him.

Teddy decided to have a drink and think it over. The saloon was crowded with locals talking sports and politics. He nursed a rye and ginger ale and wondered what Doc meant by giving him more money than he could make in the watch business. Maybe he'd let him run a card game. You could take a nice cut from a good game, if you had the cops' okay and no worries about being raided. If Hague won, maybe that would be a possibility. But was Hague going to win? Teddy hadn't spent enough time in Jersey City lately to be sure.

"Hey Flem, how's the watch business?"

The chalky face, the gray hair, the tired eyes were familiar. Teddy had seen the guy on several trains. He quickly attached a name to the details: Miller. Pete Miller. He sold a line of men's hats. He liked to hold forth on the virtues of his hometown of Buffalo.

Pete had already bought himself several drinks. He insisted on buying another one for Teddy, who told him the watch business was doing fine.

Teddy asked Pete how long he had been on the road. "Twenty-five years this November," Pete said.

"You still enjoy it?" Teddy said. "Is that why you ain't moved up to a home office job?"

Teddy got an earful of the one home office job that Pete had tried—and hated. He denounced what he called "office politics." The bosses and assistant bosses were all skunks who were out to get him because he talked back to them. He knew what hats sold and what ones didn't and they were ignoramuses. Pete had decided he preferred the road, where he was his own boss.

"Don't you get tired of bein' away from home so much?" Teddy said.

Pete smiled mournfully. "My first two wives did. Pair of selfish bitches. Now I take my nooky where I can find it. That's another nice part of the road. One-night stands. You don't promise them anything more than a good dinner. Maybe a present so you can visit the next time around."

Teddy bought Pete a blowback and wondered if this was what he had to look forward to after twenty-five years. Still on the road getting laid where and when something turned up. Taking guff from jerks like Otto Kunhaldt. Still afraid to admit to anyone that he was Irish. Was a jail sentence much worse than this for a future?

The next morning, Teddy caught the nine o'clock train to New York, where he told his employers he had decided to quit the watch business. The first person he visited in Jersey City was Monsignor Meehan. Teddy told the Mons he had bagged a sales career. He had come home to play some politics and help his brother Dave get into the fire department.

Meehan nodded. "I gave Doc the idea of asking for you. I think you can do some good around here. This commission thing needs help in the ward. Frank Hague's the only politician in sight with the drive to take charge of this city and get the Irish a square deal. We've had enough of New Idea Republicans and pompous German reformers."

By noon that day, Teddy was at Doc Holland's clubhouse on Pacific Avenue in Jersey City's Sixth Ward. "My father says you wanta see me," he said.

"Have you still got that road job?" Doc said.

Teddy shook his head. "I'm home to stay."

Doc pushed his derby back on his bald head and gave Teddy a big grin. "We've got work to do," he said.

Doc was nine or ten years older than Teddy. He had been born in the Sixth Ward and had grown up with Little Bob Davis's approach to politics—let's everybody have a good time. But he was smart enough to see that reform was a bandwagon a politician had better get aboard or else.

With Teddy Fleming pushing day and night to get out the

younger Democrats, the Sixth Ward voted big for the commission form of government. The referendum won going away and candidates lined up by the dozen to run for the five commission seats. Doc Holland declined to back Frank Hague in the election. He was playing his cards very carefully. But Doc was soon admitting privately to Teddy that Hague was getting too popular to resist.

Frank Hague ran against "Boss Wittpenn." He asked the voters whether they wanted commission government or machine government. He blasted Wittpenn for doing nothing about the outrageous tax deals enjoyed by the railroads. Convinced that Hague was a genuine reformer, the uptown Irish and even some Germans voted for him. He finished among the top five and became commissioner of public safety, which gave him control of the police and fire departments.

The police department was a mess. A lot of cops were drunks. Almost all were on the take from saloonkeepers who wanted to stay open until dawn and the madams of brothels who did not want anyone hassling their visitors. The real boss of the department was the Patrolman's Benevolent Association, which had faced down previous police commissioners who tried to change the system. For instance, if a cop had a ticket to a political dinner or dance, he didn't have to show up for work that night. Often that meant instead of thirty men on duty in a precinct, there were five or six.

Hague began holding departmental hearings, which led to the dismissal of as many as thirty policemen in a single day. When the PBA resisted, he fired the bosses. When they retaliated by trying to form a union, Hague summoned every cop in the city to a meeting in a downtown theater and told them that anyone who did not resign from the union immediately was fired. He said the idea of public employees forming a union was ridiculous. Who were they going to strike against—the people? Everyone resigned on the spot and Hague fired the organizers of the union.

For those who resisted Hague's authority, the "Zeppelins" were the last resort. These were large, tough off-duty cops who waited in dark alleys for a holdout as he walked his beat. A voice or a beckoning hand would lure him into the alley, where he got a battering that convinced him an anti-Hague policeman's lot was not a happy one. In a year, every cop on the force was a Hague man.

In the Sixth Ward, Doc Holland maintained his political independence, but he began sending signals that he recognized Frank Hague as the coming leader. Meanwhile, Doc gave Teddy Fleming the right to run a traveling poker game in the back rooms of the ward's several saloons. Teddy's cut was ten percent, five of which went to Doc. It was nice money—about three thousand a year. Teddy bought himself several new suits and decided maybe he could afford to sample New York's nightlife.

It had been a gamble, coming back to Jersey City and teaming up with a stubborn Irishman like Doc Holland. But Teddy Fleming was encouraged by how many young people in the Sixth Ward saw him as Doc's right-hand man.

Teddy had long since decided that life was a gamble from beginning to end, with some guys having runs of luck and others never getting a break. So the possibility of this roll of the dice coming up snake eyes did not bother him. When he looked in the mirror, he saw a good-looking guy who could talk himself into a deal somewhere.

In the meantime, it was great to be home, listening to Old Davey blast the millionaire Prods and the British empire, talking baseball and boxing with the Turkey or Charlie over a couple of beers—and making sure Mae Fleming headed for the altar with a decent guy.

Teddy Fleming was already thinking like a leader who cared about his people, starting with his own family. Mary Green Fleming had done her job well. Along with her jokes and laughter, she had given her sons and her daughter a sense of the central importance of love in every life.

# 9

# To Europe with Love

On July 6, 1912, Kitty Dolan took a bus from South Plainfield to the Plainfield railroad station. With her were her parents, Uncle Charlie Thornton, Lloyd Harris, Loretta Thornton, and several other girl-friends. Kitty and Lloyd had spent the previous night having a heart-to-heart on the lake; he had begged her not to fall in love with anyone else on her trip. If she returned with an engagement ring on her finger he would be miserable for the rest of his life.

This plea was very close to the proposal for which Kitty yearned. She was so sure she would soon be moving to Lloyd's hometown that in the front of the diary of the trip she planned to keep she wrote, "Katherine L. Dolan of Jersey City and South Plainfield."

At the dock in Hoboken a half dozen friends from Jersey City joined the party and came aboard the Hamburg-American Line's steamship SS *Pennsylvania* with flowers and gifts. The four other winners and the group's chaperon, Elizabeth Kiernan, also had numerous friends wishing them bon voyage. As the ship sailed, Kitty stood on the stern until America was just a blur on the horizon. Descending to her stateroom, she unpacked and confided to her diary, "Am simply crazy or enthusiastic about everything."

The next day Kitty met two Pennsylvanians, Christine McGinley and her younger sister, Irene. They were also winners of a subscription contest. Kitty and Irene were the same age—twenty-one—and became instant friends. They decided to sleep on deck rather than in their stuffy staterooms. Many other passengers did likewise. At the end of the first day at sea Kitty told her diary, "I never felt so positively grand in all my life."

Within another twenty-four hours, she and Christine began flirting with the ship's doctor, a blond, handsome twenty-five-year-old German. They soon declared he was a joint "crush"—not only because of his good looks but his age. None of the "young fellows" their age on the ship looked interesting.

They were soon visiting the doctor in his small hospital, and finding him more and more fascinating. He was just learning English, which added a touch of humor to their conversation. Occasionally he threw in shocking "cuss words," which they told him no respectable American male used. He invariably blushed and apologized. Kitty found him "so polite and gentlemanly."

The flirtation with the doctor continued for the twelve-day voyage. She and Christine had tea in his cabin one night from ten to eleven o'clock; another night the doctor tried to persuade them to share some wine. They said no. Kitty had the first dance with him at the opening party in the ship's lounge. She noted how many people commented on what a striking couple they made, he blond, she dark, he in white, she in pink.

Christine was soon telling Kitty that the doctor was insanely in love with her. Kitty, having had more than her share of romantic disappointments, cautioned her diary, "You can never be sure of a man."

When they went ashore at Cuxhaven, Germany, the doctor waited for Kitty on the dock and asked her for a farewell kiss. She said too many people were watching, so he settled for a hug and the promise of a letter to his home. She liked being told by the other passengers that she had "captivated" the doctor. One woman said the mesmerized young German had told her he thought Kitty was "the sweetest loveliest girl he had ever met."

Kitty did not waste much emotion on the doctor after they parted. "It's a shame such friendships have to end so quickly," she wrote, and never mentioned him again in the rest of her trip diary. She was not in the market for a casual affair. What she wanted was a sweetheart, an engagement, a wedding ring.

Kitty liked Germany and the Germans. They were friendly and invariably polite. She was pleased that she had seat number 13 on the train to Hamburg. She noted that they had thirteen pieces of luggage in their party and aboard ship their dining table had seated thirteen "My number follows me," she wrote.

Further observations made her less pleased with German men, who were "altogether too dapper looking to suit me, with their high pointed collars, long tailed coats and wide straw hats." Kitty seems to have thought the style made them look like "sports" or "swells"—on the prowl for willing women. She was more impressed with the way German women her age felt free to visit beer gardens and drink in public, something no respectable woman would consider doing in America.

Christine and her tour had taken another route, and Kitty soon decided she was less than thrilled with her group. They did not know how to have a good time. One night, after they left a Berlin beer garden at 10 P.M., Kitty glumly told her diary, "If I had a fellow I never would leave that early."

The itinerary took them from Hamburg to Berlin to Dresden to Frankfurt, with Kitty admiring the art and historical buildings but grousing, "There is no fun with this bunch. You have to be just so." On the other hand, she was not about to go off on her own in search of adventure. In Dresden she met three young women from their steamer, "out flirting." Kitty added, "They ought to be more careful, I think."

The closest Kitty came to misbehaving was in a Dresden beer garden, where their English guide persuaded her to try German Rhine wine. "We had two bottles and I had three glasses. *Shocking*," she wrote. She took her wineglass with her as a souvenir of her daring.

In Frankfurt Kitty had her fortune told by one of her traveling companions. She was informed that "a light [complexioned] fellow I like very much was an unfaithful friend." She wondered if the fellow were Lloyd Harris but decided against it. Those endearing words Lloyd had spoken on their last night on the lake in South Plainfield were still alive in her memory.

At Wiesbaden they got their first mail. There was "a dandy long letter from Mama," an equally good one from Loretta, and several others from male and female friends. But there was nothing from Lloyd Harris.

Kitty was upset. "I'm afraid after all his extreme youth shows," she wrote. "Out of sight, out of mind, and I hardly think he meant all he said, altho' I find it rather hard to believe that." She decided to hope for a letter in Paris.

The City of Light lived up to most of the expectations Kitty had acquired from reading about it as a girl. She loved the food, the Louvre museum, the Champs-Elysées, Notre Dame, the Arch de Triomphe, the palace of Versailles. But when she drove through the green-glowing Bois de Boulogne, she found herself wishing she could stroll the woods and fields with "a fellow."

Alas, the one fellow she wanted to hear from remained absent from mail call. "I do not know what to make of it," Kitty told her diary. "It is not at all like him. But then I don't think you can depend on a fellow altogether. He may mean what he says for the time being but after a while he forgets he even said it." Memories of Tom Connolly and Lester Stratton were painfully visible in those lines.

Four days later, with still no letter from Lloyd, Kitty could barely control her disappointment. "I never thought he of all fellows could be so mean. I'm afraid I have considered him too perfect so far and he is like most other fellows after all. It really hurts an awful lot."

She resolved that Lloyd would never find out how she felt. She retaliated by leaving him off her extensive mailing list. Before she left Paris, Kitty sent an awesome fifty-two postcards to correspondents in Jersey City, South Plainfield, and South Amboy. It was a glimpse of how eagerly she sought and tried to keep friends.

Kitty also sent an excerpt from her diary to the *Courier-News*. The editors were so pleased with it, they ran it on the front page. They also published letters from the group's chaperon, Elizabeth Kiernan, and some of the other winners. All personal references were, of course, excluded from Kitty's diary. She made it sound as if the tour was a wonderful culturefest.

For the rest of the trip, Kitty could not get Lloyd off her mind. As she toured the Luxembourg Museum, she reminded herself to be sure to tell Loretta about all the "shocking" nude statuary she had seen.

"I'm glad I did not go through any of these museums with a fellow I was intimate with, Lloyd or Lester, for instance. Oh heavens!"

From Paris Kitty and her companions traveled to Brussels and then to Amsterdam, where they stayed at a very good hotel overlooking one of the canals. Kitty's room had a "dear little balcony" that enabled her to step out and gaze down at the shining water. She suddenly imagined herself in Venice on her honeymoon, but there was something missing: a bridegroom. "The dream fell flat," she ruefully concluded. Traveling would be ideal, she added, "with a little romance attached. I always miss that."

Kitty made several more trips out on the balcony in the next few days, wishing Loretta or Lloyd were with her, or both. "It would not be conventional, but what's the difference?" she wrote forlornly. Neither was likely to appear. Some of her traveling companions started teasing her about her tendency to daydream. One suggested she was enjoying "visions of unalloyed bliss," which was not far from the yearning truth.

In London there was still no letter from Lloyd. By now Kitty's diary entries were growing short. The sheer duration of the trip, the number of museums, cathedrals, restaurants visited, began to make further annotation seem a waste of effort. She was starting to think of home. "A dear letter" from Lester Stratton cheered her up. She called it "a sweet one, nicer than he ever wrote before." The last country Kitty visited was Ireland. After a swift tour of Dublin, they took a train to Killarney and its famous lakes. Kitty was enchanted by the scenery, calling it "a heavenly place." She and a friend visited the fifteenth-century ruins of Muckross Abbey, one of the many monasteries destroyed in Ireland's wars with England. Kitty's almost total lack of interest in Irish history was evident in her reaction. Wandering through the ruins alone, she stopped and "just listened to the stillness." It was "really inspiring." Not a word about British brutality or Ireland's sad fate.

Later that day they walked to the shore of the largest Killarney lake. Kitty found the view breathtaking. "Beautiful shadowy mountains rising and the sheen of the water below. To say I was awed is not at all strong enough. To the right and left tall thick trees added to the lovely effect." Then came a last burst of the wish that was haunting her: "Oh *how* I longed for a sweetheart!"

After dinner Kitty went for a walk with Elizabeth Kiernan, the tour's chaperon. They talked about life and love as the intense darkness of a moonless Irish night descended. The diary ended with a line that the coming years would make more than a little prophetic: "No lights on the road."

On the voyage home Kitty had a flirtation with an officer aboard the Hamburg-American Line steamer SS *Dominion*. This time he was the ship's purser, another blond, handsome German. They spent several nights spooning on a secluded part of the deck. On their last night at sea, he asked her to join him in his cabin. For a moment Kitty almost said yes. So many things seemed wrong with her life, in spite of her glorious tour of Europe.

Was this man telling her to become a woman of pleasure, a good-time girl, as the sports called the women they met in saloons and dance halls? Without Lloyd, her life seemed so empty, so uncertain. But something deeper than desire and disappointment stopped Kitty. How could she ever face her mother after doing such a thing? She often felt that Mary Fitzmaurice Dolan's penetrating eyes could read her inner thoughts. Kitty said no, leaving her panting purser the most frustrated sailor in the Hamburg-American Line's fleet.

As the *Dominion* docked in Philadelphia, Kitty's parents waved a cheerful greeting. Tom Dolan gave her a warm kiss and so did her mother. Several friends from South Plainfield were with them. There was no sign of Lloyd Harris. The other winners also had family and friends to greet them. On the train to New Jersey, the travelers raved about the trip. Several people asked Kitty if she was going to publish her diary. Everyone had read the excerpts in the *Courier-News*.

Back at 4 Garrison Avenue in Jersey City, Kitty could not restrain the question: "Mama—have you heard anything from Lloyd Harris? He never wrote me a single letter."

Mary Fitzmaurice Dolan put her arm around Kitty. "I'm afraid there's some very bad news there. Your Aunt Kate tells me poor Lloyd has come down with a terrible disease. It's called scleroderma. There's no cure for it. Gradually, his body will turn to something very like stone."

For a moment Kitty thought her heart, her brain, had turned to stone. "Oh my God," she said. "I was so angry with him—I *hated* him. I want to see him—as soon as possible!"

"First you better think very carefully about what you're going to say and do," Mary Fitzmaurice Dolan said in her deliberate way. "A man in his condition is likely to cling to you—to try to turn you into a combination wife and nurse. You don't want a life like that."

"Momma, I love him! I love him more than ever now!"

"That's the way you feel for the moment. But you haven't promised him anything. You're not even engaged. Offer him sympathy, of course. But don't let him put a ring on your finger."

"I'll make up my own mind about that, Mother!"

Kitty did not sleep well that night. She tossed and turned in her bed, wondering why she had a job she did not really like and a sweetheart who was doomed to a lingering death. What had she done to deserve such disappointment? Wisps of Tom Dolan's rage against God drifted through her soul. She struggled to believe that somewhere, somehow, her love could rescue Lloyd, or at least offer him some consolation for his hard fate. In the morning, ignoring her mother's reproachful looks, Kitty took a train to South Plainfield.

# 10

# You're in the Army Now

For a while, Teddy Fleming enjoyed life back in the Sixth Ward. With his cut from the card game, he had money to take himself and Charlie and the Turkey to baseball games and boxing matches. Or to vaudeville shows at Keith's Orpheum in Jersey City. Sometimes they hit the Broadway musicals, where their favorite star was blonde, curvaceous Marilyn Miller. How that babe could put over a song!

Charlie Fleming fell in love with a local girl named Mae Leahy. They tied the knot and had a baby—a girl—so fast, it was almost magical. Pretty soon the two sisters-in-law teamed up to keep their husbands home nights. That prompted sister Mae to start telling Teddy it was time he got married, but he just said, "Yeah yeah," and she usually dropped the subject.

Old Davey spent most of his time in his favorite saloon, talking politics. Teddy did more of the same with Sixth Ward leader Doc Holland. There was plenty to talk about. Frank Hague was coming on strong but there were still quite a few people who had other ideas about who should be running things.

On the side Teddy picked up extra money as an umpire on Jersey City's semipro baseball circuit. He liked keeping in touch with baseball. He also organized some of the young guys in the ward into a gang that was for hire when a striking union wanted to rough up some scabs (aka strikebreakers) or Tammany needed a little outside muscle to solve a problem with wiseguys who tried to disrupt an election. They were also available as floaters. It added up to plenty of dollars in Teddy's pocket. All in all it was a pretty nice life.

In the summer of 1914, everything started going kerflewy. A war exploded in Europe. England and France and Russia against Germany and Austria-Hungary and Turkey. The newspapers were full of it. Everybody talked about it. President Woodrow Wilson said the United States was neutral. But the New York papers all favored the English. Ditto the *Jersey Journal* and the city's uptown Protestants. In the downtown wards a very different attitude prevailed.

Most downtowners rooted for the Germans, with Davey Fleming one of the most outspoken. Davey could not read the papers but he had Mae and Teddy report the war news to him every night. When the reporters made it sound like the French and the British and the Russians were thrashing the huns, Davey fell back on hoping Ireland would start a revolution in England's backyard. "England's difficulty is Ireland's opportunity," he said. That was a slogan among the English-haters.

Charlie Fleming was just as hungry for a German victory. He started reading the *Gaelic American*, a newspaper that damned President Woodrow Wilson as a liar and a fake because he was letting the British buy millions of dollars' worth of ammunition and guns in the United States and protesting when German submarines sank ships carrying the stuff to England. He never said a word about the British fleet's blockade of Germany. Charlie and Davey went to rallies in New York and in Jersey City calling for a law banning arms sales to both sides. But the big banks were all pro-English and the big-business fat cats could not resist the profits they were making in the weapons and ammo game, so the protests went nowhere.

Woodrow Wilson was a Democrat and a former New Jersey governor but he was not popular with the Irish-Americans in Jersey City. The inside word went that he was honest but not "level" (as in "on the level"). That meant he wouldn't take a bribe but he was more than willing to make a promise and then break it—the lowest thing a politician could do in an Irish-American's opinion.

Wilson had accepted the 1910 gubernatorial nomination from Boss James Smith of Newark and Boss Little Bob Davis of Jersey City with the understanding that the pols would hand out the jobs and

Wilson would back Smith for U.S. senator. Wilson welched on both promises and turned into a Mark Fagan–style progressive reformer before the bosses' appalled eyes.

Wilson's reform act got the New York newspapers behind him and he won the Democratic nomination for president in 1912. That did not excite anyone in Jersey City, even though a guy named Joe Tumulty, born in the Fifth Ward, was giving the candidate shrewd political advice. The Democrats had lost four presidential elections in a row, three by nominating a Nebraska loser named William Jennings Bryan who liked to rant about how unfair life was for poor people. As if that was news.

To everyone's surprise, Wilson won the election, mostly because Teddy Roosevelt split the Republican vote by running as the candidate of a new party, the Progressives. Before Woodrow could do much, the war in Europe distracted everyone, including him. In 1915 the Germans sank the British liner *Lusitania*, drowning more than a thousand people, including a hundred-plus Americans. A lot of people, especially ex-president Teddy Roosevelt, called for war. Wilson said Americans were "too proud to fight," whatever that meant.

Next the president began talking about negotiating a "peace without victory," which prompted Teddy Roosevelt to call him "a Byzantine logothete." Charlie looked it up in a dictionary and reported it meant windbag.

Wilson also started using nasty names—on fellow Democrats. When the Irish-Americans started screaming for a ban on arms sales to both sides, Wilson called them "hyphenates" and accused them of "pouring poison into the veins of our national life." That did not digest well at the Fleming dinner table—and a lot of other dinner tables in downtown Jersey City.

Irish-American dislike of Wilson became even more intense when the Dublin Irish tried to stage an uprising on Easter Sunday 1916. The British brought in heavy artillery and smashed them in a couple of days. Davey Fleming was so mad he could not stop cursing, even when his daughter Mae was in the room. Charlie, the *Gaelic American* reader, was equally upset. He said the British were murderers, barbarians, the scum of the earth. He was even harder on Wilson, who had not said a word on behalf of the Easter rebels, even when the British ruthlessly executed the leaders.

Teddy, who had little or no interest in Ireland, was cooler. "Does this mean you guys won't vote for Wilson when he runs in the fall?" he asked.

"I'll have t'think about it," Charlie said.

"No you don't," Teddy said. "You're gonna vote the straight ticket, like always. That goes for you too, Da."

Davey and Charlie knew what he meant. They owed Doc Holland for Teddy's card game and they were still pushing for the Turkey's appointment to the fire department. They were also thinking of trying to get Charlie on the police department. Doc would not be impressed by their splitting the ticket on behalf of dear old Ireland. Holding their noses, they did as Teddy told them and voted for Windy Woodrow, as Charlie called him.

In other cities in the 1916 presidential election most of the Irish-Americans stuck with Wilson for similar reasons. They did not dislike him enough to vote Republican. Besides, the Republicans, egged on by Teddy Roosevelt, sounded like they could not wait to get into the war on the English side. Wilson's campaign slogan was "He Kept Us Out of War." It went over big with the goo-goos and pacifist Protestants and he won by a whisker, thanks to somebody switching 4,000 votes in California after the polls closed.

By that time, no one in Jersey City had much good to say for the Germans. In the middle of the night of July 29–30, 1916, Jersey City was jolted by a tremendous explosion that blew out windows all over town. The sky turned reddish purple and the ground shook. At 122 Randolph Avenue, the building swayed like a heavyweight who had just taken a knockout punch. As more explosions added to the chaos, people rushed into the streets screaming with terror.

Davey Fleming reeled into the kitchen, where Mae had already set the table for breakfast. She had recently invested in new dishes and they were on Davey's mind. "Saaave the dishes!" he shouted, clinging to the dancing table. Teddy rushed to the kitchen window, which looked out on the Hudson River. "It's Black Tom!" he shouted. "It's blowin' up!"

Black Tom was originally the name of a marshy island at the tip of Caven Point, a peninsula that jutted into the Hudson. By 1916 it was known as the Black Tom Terminus. Three-quarters of all the ammunition the Americans were shipping to England passed through its warehouses. Boxcars carrying every imaginable variety of high explosive rumbled down Caven Point each week. A thousand tons of this murderous matériel were detonating with fantastic fury, less than a half mile from the Flemings' apartment.

The Flemings decided to stay indoors. All sorts of flying metal might be in the air. Not until morning did they venture out into the streets, which were covered with shattered glass. Over in Manhattan was another million dollars' worth of broken windows. By the end of the day, everyone was convinced that the explosion was sabotage and the saboteurs were Germans. In later years, Teddy Fleming often said Black Tom convinced him America was on its way to war.

Meanwhile, life—and local politics—continued. Dave and Charlie were both fathers of growing families. Mae was dating a quiet young guy from South Amboy named Al Gallagher. He was a whiz mechanic who had a good job at the Hudson and Manhattan Tubes, the subway that had recently started running under the Hudson River between Jersey City and New York.

Mae started working on Teddy day and night to get married. He was almost thirty years old. Teddy told her to find him a good-looking girl. He claimed all the lookers were in New York, which made Mae tear her red hair and give him hell for talking down Jersey City girls.

With Teddy nudging hard, Doc Holland went down to City Hall and reminded Frank Hague that Dave Fleming was still waiting to get into the fire department. Doc talked about what a great job Teddy Fleming had done turning out the younger vote in the ward. Hague was coming up for reelection in the spring of 1917, and by this time he had the police department under control. He liked the idea of getting Hague Democrats into the fire department too. So, presto! the Turkey was a fireman as of January 15, 1917. The Flemings quietly celebrated that one in their Randolph Avenue apartment.

The Turkey's appointment was not the only reason the Flemings liked Frank Hague. They also appreciated his tough style when it came to confronting other city problems, such as the big-business habit of importing armed goons when unions went out on strike. Not long after Hague became commissioner of public safety, three major express companies with headquarters in Jersey City faced a strike. Hague phoned their chief executives and told them no strikebreakers would be tolerated. The Jersey City police would protect the companies' property and make sure no violence occurred on the union side.

This was a startling contrast to a previous express strike, when armed thugs aboard the horse-drawn express trucks shot down strikers in Jersey City's streets. The new strike lasted only thirty hours and was settled by arbitration. Hague used similar tactics to block strikebreakers in a trolley car walkout. A few months later, Eagle Oil Company, where Davey Fleming now worked as a watchman, faced serious violence. More than 3,000 Eagle workers voted to strike in sympathy with the workers in the Standard Oil refinery in Bayonne, where terrific violence had been raging for weeks. Strikebreakers had killed workers and policemen had been assaulted by the outraged union men.

Standard Oil imported five hundred rifle-wielding scabs to give the Eagle workers the same brutal treatment they had administered in Bayonne. But Eagle was in Jersey City and Commissioner Hague was determined not to let gunfire erupt in his bailiwick. The big fellow rushed to the Eagle plant with a detachment of policemen and told the superintendent to send the strikebreakers back to New York. When the superintendent refused, Hague ordered his policemen to take the rifles away from the goons. For a while, it looked as if a shootout might ensue. But the cops' determination—and their hands on their guns—decided matters. The strikebreakers surrendered their weapons and marched meekly to the ferry that had brought them from New York. Hague sat down with the workers and arbitrated their grievances in hours of tough negotiating, and everyone was back at work the next morning.

Watchman Davey Fleming, who would have been in the middle of any crossfire between the strikers and the riflemen, became a Hague devotee after that performance. "The fellow has the nerrrve of a burglar goin' up the side of the Woolworth buildin'," he said.

Down in Washington, Woodrow Wilson went from keeping the United States out of war to denunciations of the Germans because they were intensifying submarine attacks on American ships carrying food and ammunition and weapons to England. Charlie still insisted Windy Woodrow had it all wrong: the Germans were just trying to even the score for the British blockade. But Wilson seemed to think it was some sort of crime. He got even madder when the British slipped him a copy of a telegram the kaiser had sent to the Mexicans, urging them to form an alliance if the United States declared war on Germany.

On April 2, 1917, the president went before Congress and asked them to declare war. He said Americans would fight to "make the world safe for democracy." Charlie Fleming, still reading the *Gaelic American*, laughed out loud. The slogan, which originated with the British, was a sick joke—the British ran an empire that ruled 444 million people, and about five percent of them had a vote.

Nobody listened to Charlie and his handful of fellow *Gaelic American* subscribers. Once Congress declared war, patriotism became the only thing that counted. Were you a good American? Everybody had to get on the team. Just in case, Congress passed laws making it a crime to criticize the government.

In the midst of this international hugger-mugger, Jersey City had another election. This time Doc Holland handed the Sixth Ward over to Frank Hague with no reservations. Teddy Fleming worked harder than ever to turn out the youth vote. All five Hague candidates, including the big fellow, won, and they promptly named Hague the mayor.

For most people, the war dominated the news. On June 5, 1917, by order of Congress, all American males aged twenty-one to thirty were required to register for "selective service." That was a goo-goo way of saying "draft." Dave, Charlie, and Teddy Fleming registered, but Teddy was the only one who had any chance of getting Uncle Sam's invitation. Married men were going to be exempt until the draft boards got through with the bachelors.

Nobody was very excited about the draft because everyone thought the war was as good as won. The New York papers said the United States only needed an army to make the Mexicans behave. The British, French, and Russians were taking care of the Germans nicely. All they wanted from America were more guns, ammo, and U.S. Navy ships to help them deal with the kaiser's submarines. If your number was picked, you were more likely to get a vacation on the Rio Grande than a visit to Europe.

That was why Teddy Fleming was not particularly worried when his number was one of the first plucked from the government goldfish bowl by the secretary of war. He talked it over with Doc Holland and they both agreed he shouldn't—and probably couldn't—duck the call. Frank Hague was telling everybody the Irish were going to prove they were the most patriotic Americans in the country. The new mayor ran huge ads in the newspapers, announcing a citywide send-off when the first draftees left for the training camps.

Davey Fleming was the only member of the family who felt badly about Teddy's call-up. "To think a boy of mine is goin' to be defendin' them miserable thieven' Sassenachs," he groaned.

"First of all, Da, he ain't a boy," the Turkey said. "He's twenty-eight years old, and I'm ready to bet he'll spend his time givin' Mexican señoritas the eye instead of shootin' at Germans."

"I'm not so sure," said Charlie, the *Gaelic American* reader. "What if the limeys are lyin' in their pearly teeth? What if them and the frogs are losin' the war?"

"Then we'll have to win it for'm," Teddy said. "A coupla regiments of micks can handle the whole damn German army if they give us the chance."

That was the Teddy Fleming they loved. The tough guy who liked a fight and knew how to win one. The Turkey and Charlie beamed at him. Davey had to admit he liked this confidence in the fighting Irish, even if they ended up shooting and slugging for the wrong side. They poured some beer and drank a toast to their favorite soldier. Teddy was off to what Teddy Roosevelt was calling "the Great Adventure."

# 11

# The Limits of Love

Is it true, Kitty? Is it true what I've heard? You're seeing Lester Stratton?" Lloyd Harris said, bitterness all but clotting his words. "Is that why I haven't seen you lately? Tell me the truth."

Kitty Dolan gazed forlornly at the pale, emaciated face on the pillow. It was hard to believe that this was the vibrant young man with whom she had danced into the dawn at more than one festive party at Thornton's Hotel. Five long years had passed since Kitty had returned from Europe to find Lloyd stricken by this mysterious disease. Ignoring her mother's advice, she had rushed to South Plainfield and tearfully embraced him. She had spent almost all her weekends in his sickroom for the next two years, reading to him from his favorite books, discussing films and plays she had seen in Jersey City and New York.

Every morning before Kitty went to work at P.S. 27, she had gone to mass at St. Aloysius Church and prayed for Lloyd's recovery. She had been one of the leaders of a fund drive in South Plainfield to raise money to send him to Germany, where a specialist had reported progress with a treatment for scleroderma. They had staged a dinner dance that netted a thousand dollars. Kitty had charged everyone who wanted a dance with her ten dollars. It had been another kind of trip—into a strange new country where pity mingled with desire. Even though Lloyd had not offered her an engagement ring, Kitty had proclaimed herself his sweetheart.

In spite of her prayers, Lloyd continued to decline. The eruption of the Great War made a trip to Germany out of the question. Kitty soon found herself in the worst imaginable situation—half engaged to a permanent invalid, who was deeply depressed by his harsh fate. No young man in South Plainfield dared to date Kitty. They were afraid people would accuse them of depriving Lloyd of his only consolation.

Behind the scenes, Kitty's best friend, Loretta Thornton, tried to help. She urged Lester Stratton and others to take Kitty out. They danced with her at Thornton's Hotel parties but went no further. Worse, the parties were dwindling; the "old crowd," as they now called themselves, began pursuing careers in Newark and New York, and others got married. Loretta started getting serious with a handsome Pennsylvanian named Lyman Barr. That did nothing for Kitty's morale.

In Jersey City, Mary Fitzmaurice Dolan began urging Kitty to cut back on her visits to Lloyd, to go to South Plainfield every other week or every third week, and stay in Jersey City. "Make up excuses," Mary said in her blunt way. "Tell him you're studying for a graduate degree. Your brother George needs tutoring. Anything."

Kitty was not a good liar. Lloyd saw through her withdrawal almost immediately, and made her next visit a torment. For a while she relapsed into coming every weekend. Meanwhile, she had made new friends at work. Two fellow teachers, short, dark-haired, direct Mary McNamara and tall, willowy, red-haired Marie Hannaway listened sympathetically to Kitty's description of her plight and gave her the same advice she was getting from her mother. It was time to say goodbye to Lloyd.

"Write him a farewell letter and just stop seeing him," Mary said. "Take South Plainfield off your social calendar."

Marie was more ready to understand Kitty's complicated feelings. "I'd try to talk to him. Tell him you've met a man in Jersey City."

"But I haven't met one," Kitty wailed. "I've lost touch with all my old beaus!"

"So what?" Mary said. "You'll meet one eventually. It's only a white lie."

Mary and Marie decided to launch a rescue operation. They invited Kitty to parties on weekends, where she met some of their male friends and had a valid excuse to avoid Lloyd. But Kitty was so half-hearted about meeting other men that the program went nowhere. The males all interpreted her reluctance as rejection and the telephone at 4 Garrison Avenue remained silent.

The only man with whom Kitty spent much time was her mother's cousin Lee Shanaphy. He was several years older and had usually ignored her at family parties. But her good looks and her sad plight with Lloyd had inspired Lee to befriend her. Skeletally thin, Lee had no illusions about being attractive to a pretty woman. But he was witty and often wise. He shared Kitty's fondness for the theater and they read many of the same books. He listened to her agonizing over Lloyd and also urged her to end the sad affair.

One night, while they were coming home from a play, Lee offered to go to South Plainfield and talk the situation over with Lloyd, man to man. "I'll tell him I'm insanely in love with you," he said. "Which is the absolute truth. I'll ask him if he intends to deprive you of the chance for a lifetime of happiness with yours truly. After he surrenders you, Loretta can claim she talked you out of such an awful mistake."

Kitty kissed him. "Oh, Lee," she said. "I wish I could love you. I really do. I do love you but—"

"There's no need to explain," Lee said. "I know exactly how to rate my chances. They're about the same size as my muscles. Nonexistent."

Kitty decided against sending Lee as her emissary to Lloyd. Somehow she wanted to say the words herself. But she could not imagine speaking them. She could not even find the words she wanted to say. So she drifted through weeks and months, her spirits lifted only by the kindergartners in her classes. Unfortunately, they also reminded her that the clock was ticking. She was twenty-seven years old, on the brink of thirty, which was synonymous in most circles with old maidhood.

Then came America's plunge into the war in Europe. Kitty's interest in politics had never been strong. Woodrow Wilson's abrupt reversal of course came as a shock—which soon led to dismay. Uncle Sam drafted every bachelor in Jersey City and South Plainfield and South Amboy. Even Lee, with his nonexistent muscles, was swept into the ranks. As a crack stenographer and typist—he had been making good money as a private secretary in a Wall Street brokerage house—he was selected for General Pershing's staff, and Kitty began receiving lively letters from Paris.

Lee in Europe, along with every other available man, only increased Kitty's melancholy. That was her state of mind when Lloyd Harris curtly asked her if she were seeing Lester Stratton. "For your information, Lloyd, Lester Stratton was drafted two weeks ago," Kitty said. "Before that, I hadn't seen him for a month. But what if I were dating him—or someone else? Do you really think I'm going to spend the rest of my life reading books to you each weekend?"

"I suppose not," Lloyd said. "You think you've done more for me than I have any right to expect. Is that it?"

"Lloyd—I'm afraid that *is* it," Kitty said.

She began to weep. "Oh, Lloyd. I really loved you. I know you loved me. I'll always remember you—always love the memory of that last night on the lake. But I can't—Lloyd, I just can't go on this way."

"Kiss me good-bye," Lloyd said.

Kitty kissed his cold forehead, his stiff hands—and fled the Harris house. She had found the words—or the words had found her. They were not very nice words. Why couldn't she have found some lines of poetry from Tennyson or Browning? Maybe it would have been better to write a letter, where words could have been chosen carefully, tenderly. Why was life always so unexpected, so accidental, so treacherous? Weeping into an already sodden handkerchief, Kitty rode a train back to manless Jersey City.

Decades later, Gladys Matteson, a Dolan cousin who lived in South Plainfield, told me a postscript to this tragic story. One day in the early 1920s, when Gladys was waiting for a bus to take her to high school in Plainfield, Lloyd Harris's mother emerged from their house and begged her to visit Lloyd. She pointed to her son, propped up in a chair by the window. "You look so much like Kitty Dolan," she said. "You know how he loved her."

Gladys visited Lloyd the next day. They talked exclusively about Kitty. Her photograph was on the dresser beside his bed. Thereafter, Lloyd sat at the window and waved to Gladys each day, until she graduated from high school. "Kitty was his dream of happiness," Gladys said.

# 12

# Over There

**S**tick it in to the hilt, pull it up—out—and stick it in again!" Sergeant Teddy Fleming snarled.

The soldier lunged toward the straw-stuffed dummy dangling from a crosstree above the sawdust pit and plunged the gleaming bayonet on the end of his Springfield rifle into the dummy's midriff, pulled it up, out, and plunged it into his chest.

"Yell!" Sergeant Fleming roared. "This ain't no kindergarten make-believe! You're killin' this guy! Call him a rotten name. Remember how them dirty sneakin' heinies blew up Black Tom!"

The soldier retreated and charged again, screaming, "Die, you German son of a bitch!" In and out and in again went the bayonet.

"That's more like it," Sergeant Fleming said. "I wanta see every man in this company do it the same way!"

For another two hours, the men of Company C of the 312th Infantry Regiment of the 78th Division charged through the cold December wind, screaming berserk curses and shredding the dangling straw pseudo–German infantryman with more and more ferocious bayonet thrusts until Sergeant Fleming pronounced himself satisfied with their prowess. Only then were they permitted to seek the relative comfort of their barracks in Camp Dix, the huge training center that army contractors had hammered together in the South Jersey pines.

Fifty years later, when I talked to one of the men who had taken bayonet lessons from Sergeant Fleming at Camp Dix, the ex-soldier recalled, "I'd grown up in a nice neighborhood in Newark. I'd never seen anything like him before in my life. He made my hair stand on end. We were all terrified of him."

Teddy Fleming and the U.S. Army of 1917 were an almost perfect fit. The officers of the 78th Division were looking for men like him—old enough to win some respect from the mostly twenty-one- and twenty-two-year-olds in the ranks, and tough enough to shape them into fighting soldiers. The brass made Teddy a corporal almost as soon as he donned a uniform, and they liked his performance well enough to make him a sergeant a few months later.

The army wanted more than screaming bayonet thrusts. They demanded marksmanship from every soldier—and Sergeant Fleming was just as tough on the rifle range as he was in the bayonet pit. He wanted every man in Company C to be a sharpshooter, and he flayed anyone who did not take this goal seriously.

The army also wanted endurance. Day after day, the 312th Regiment trudged the narrow roads of southern New Jersey with sixty-pound packs on their backs. Sergeant Fleming strode beside Company C, wearing the same pack, matching them every step of the way. He had his eye out for wiseguys who lightened their packs with bedsheets or underwear. When he caught someone pulling this act, he made him carry bricks on the next march.

The army also wanted instant obedience to battlefield orders. Sergeant Fleming made sure the men of his company were the best performers in the regiment on the drill field. They did the manual of arms so often, they recited it in their sleep. When he shouted, "By the right flank, *march!*" or "To the rear, *march!*" they wheeled and headed in the new direction as if they were a giant centipede with a single brain named Fleming.

Most of the men in Company C were Irish-Americans, many from Jersey City. Twenty thousand of the 78th's twenty-eight thousand men were from New Jersey. Sergeant Fleming's soldiers soon got used to his tough-guy style. They liked the self-confidence he emanated. Most of them realized they might need some toughness on the Western Front.

By the fall of 1917, everyone knew this was where the Yanks were going. According to the army's rumor mill, the limeys and the frogs had sent some generals to Washington, D.C., who confessed the Allies were hanging on by their fingernails. Fritz was very close to winning the war. The stuff about the Allies having the war as good as won had been British baloney manufactured for the newspapers, just as Charlie Fleming had suspected.

There were all kinds of arguments about how the Yanks were going to fight. The limeys and the frogs wanted to march them into their armies, but the American generals already in Europe said nuts to that. So it was up to the Americans to get a couple of million men over there and win the thing. That was how Teddy Fleming saw it as the 78th Division headed for the Hoboken docks and their grand tour of Europe.

On their shoulder patches was a lightning bolt, symbol of their recently coined nickname, the Lightning Division. The brass said it signified what they were going to do to the Germans. The wiseguys in the ranks said it was a tribute to "Jersey Lightning," the mind-numbing hooch that the South Jersey natives brewed in illegal stills in the pine forest around Fort Dix.

The trip to France was hell for Sergeant Fleming. Every time he looked at the water, it stirred one of the worst memories of his life. In the summer between the fifth and sixth grades, he and his two brothers and a half dozen friends had taken a streetcar out to Bayonne, where people swam in the Kill Van Kull, a swift creek that separated New Jersey and Staten Island.

Jimmy O'Brien, a son of the dice player, had dared Teddy to jump in. He could not ignore such a challenge to his nerve. He stripped to his underwear and jumped. Teddy went down like a corpse in a lead-lined casket, while the water got darker and his chest started to explode. The Turkey yelled for help and a stranger who could swim dived in and pulled Teddy to shore, where he puked water for an hour.

After twenty years, Teddy couldn't understand why butterflies still flew in his belly every time he looked at the water. He told himself it was ridiculous. He had a life preserver. If the krauts hit them with a torpedo, he stood a fair chance of surviving. But the butterflies kept fluttering.

The insects folded their wings as the troopship reached the mouth of the river Thames. They had made it across "periscope pond" with only a single brush with a German submarine, which their escorting destroyers swiftly sank. For the next twenty-four hours, they steamed slowly up the famous river, with thousands of English men and women cheering along the banks. They were the first American troops to land in England instead of going directly to France. Private Harry Ross, Company C's joker, thumbed his nose at the limeys and said, "I wonder if they'd be cheerin' if they knew how many micks there were in this regiment."

"They'd cheer anyway," Sergeant Fleming said. "We're here to save their necks."

Debarking in London, the Lightning Division marched to troop trains that took them to barracks on the white cliffs of Dover. After a brief stay in the shadow of Dover Castle, one of the most ancient buildings in England, they boarded coastal steamers that ferried them to Calais. There they marched five kilometers into the country to a rest camp, which the men promptly dubbed "Camp Restless." For one thing, the tents were too small and too few, forcing fifteen men to jam into each one. It also started to rain and did not stop for the rest of their stay. The chief reason for their restlessness was the universal awareness of the Garden of Allah, a gigantic brothel not far from the Calais docks. The British sailors on the channel steamers had told them the Allah had the best nooky in France.

In ports such as Saint-Nazaire, where the Americans were in control, General John J. Pershing, the commander of the American Expeditionary Force, had closed all such establishments, to the amazement of the French. President Woodrow Wilson had decreed that Americans were going to fight a "clean" war. The army had reinforced the president's decision by requiring draftees to sit through training films showing the awful effects of syphilis and gonorrhea. Everyone had to stare at bodies with holes where eyes, noses, ears had been. "Would you borrow another fellow's toothbrush?" the government asked. "Don't borrow his whore."

Sergeant Fleming soon discovered that neither these films nor presidential exhortations prevented a hefty proportion of C Company from seeking a visit to the Garden of Allah or one of the numerous other brothels that were going strong on Calais's side streets. No moralist, either of the Monsignor Meehan or Woodrow Wilson variety, the sergeant treated them to a ferocious lecture on using condoms on such adventures. "You all saw them films at Fort Dix," he roared. "Any guy who gets the syph or clap is on my shit list!"

The sergeant did not accompany Company C to the Garden of Allah. Already he had discovered one of the key ingredients of leadership: you had to maintain a careful distance from your men. You couldn't get drunk with them and cavort with your pants down and give orders to them the next day. But it did no harm to let them cavort with your tacit blessing.

Sergeant Fleming seems to have taken a benign attitude toward an ingenious scheme by Harry Ross to increase Company C's access to the Garden of Allah. Ross borrowed one of Teddy's coats, with its sergeant's stripes, and marched a platoon out the gate of Camp Restless under the noses of the guards. Once the escapees got a safe distance, they legged it into Calais and had a memorable time.

A less pleasant Calais memory was the disappearance of their barracks bags. They were lugged off the channel steamers by French stevedores and deposited in a huge heap. When the regiment sent working parties back with wagons to transport them to Camp Restless, the bags had vanished. The French greeted furious inquiries with shrugs and chatter about perhaps mistaking them for "salvage." Extra uniforms and underclothes and all sorts of personal mementos vanished in that disappearing act, which left the 312th Regiment with less than fond feelings for their supposed allies.

Even less pleasant was a night raid on Camp Restless by German bombers. Sergeant Fleming awoke to explosions and flames filling the night, reminding him of Black Tom. He got the company out of their tents and ordered them to lie flat on their faces until the attack ended. About a dozen members of the 78th Division were killed; none were from the 312th regiment. The dead men's friends were so enraged, some of them threw hand grenades into a nearby German prisoner-of-war camp, killing several of the enemy. Sergeant Fleming condemned that attack as murder—cowardly murder at that.

A few days later the 78th discovered something that left Teddy astonished at first, and then amused. They were going to train with the

English army! Harry Ross wanted to know what was funny about that? "My father will have a conniption if he ever finds out about it," Sergeant Fleming said.

Within a week, the 312th Regiment exchanged their Springfield rifles for British Lee-Enfields (the British had no ammunition for the Springfields) and trains carried them to Blequin, in the British rear area in Picardy, about thirty kilometers behind the front lines. This was the part of France that inspired a famous song, "Roses Are Blooming in Picardy," but Company C found little that was romantic in their quarters, which were mostly barns and parts of French houses from which animals and humans were rudely exiled to make room for them. Nor were they enchanted by the Frenchmen they met in Blequin and nearby villages. They called Americans "Anglais" and overcharged them for everything.

Teddy was wary of how the limeys were going to treat him and his mostly Irish-American company. While the men were distributing themselves in their Blequin billets, he heard a pint-sized limey private chirping, "S-S-Sergeant F-F-Fleming? An-Anyone suh-seen S-S-Sergeant F-F-Fleming?"

Teddy waved him over and the private said, "C-C-Compliments of S-S-Sergeant Muh-Major Cr-Cruickshank, S-S-Sergeant Fleming. The suh-sergeant muh-major hopes you can find time to s-s-share a cup of t-t-tea with him."

Harry Ross guffawed and started prancing up and down, pretending to hold a teacup with one pinky outstretched, lisping, "Oh, I say. A cuppa tea n-n-now. Ain't that r-r-ripping?"

"Shut up, wise guy," Sergeant Fleming said. He nodded to the little limey private and said, "Sure. I'll be glad to have a cup. Where can I find the sergeant major?"

"Just f-f-follow me, S-S-Sergeant," the private said, and led him outside to a chugging automobile. They drove about a half mile while the private, whose name was Perkins, apologized for his stutter. He said he had gotten it last year when a 210-millimeter shell exploded in the middle of his platoon, killing everyone but him.

Eventually they reached a farmhouse around which numerous tents had been pitched. In the barnyard behind the house, a table had been set up and someone had put a vase with a tired-looking rose on top of it. Private Perkins disappeared into the barn and soon emerged with a short brisk man at least ten years older than Teddy.

Sergeant Major Richard Cruickshank shook hands with the greatest cordiality. "A pleasure, Sergeant Fleming," he said. "So glad you could spare time for a sip of tea."

Cruickshank snapped his fingers and two soldiers, one of them Perkins, appeared with chairs, which they placed beside the tea table. "I hope you like tea, Sergeant," Cruickshank said. "I gather most Yanks prefer coffee."

"I drank tea in the cradle," Sergeant Fleming said. "My mother served it Irish style, with plenty of milk and sugar."

"Oh-ho," Cruickshank said with a pleased smile. "We limeys like it the same way."

He snapped his fingers again and Private Perkins and his friend produced a big brown teapot, two cups, and a dish of hot buttered scones. They sat eating and drinking as if they were at the Waldorf or some other classy New York hotel. Cruickshank wanted to know what county in Ireland Teddy's mother came from. When he said Mayo, the sergeant major smiled and said, "Mayo, God help us. We've had some of them in the regiment. Fighters, every one of them."

Cruickshank said he had been stationed in Tipperary for many years and was fond of the Irish people. "I liked 'em so much I married one," he said. "She and the two brats are waitin' for me back there."

"Just like the song," Sergeant Fleming said. He was referring to one of the war's most popular songs, "It's a Long Way to Tipperary," about a soldier whose heart was still in that Irish town.

"Righto," Sergeant Major Cruickshank said. "There's a lot of truth in that tune."

This was obviously not Davey Fleming's version of Ireland—or the English. Sergeant Fleming began to relax. He liked this man. He asked how long Cruickshank had been in the army. "Fifteen years," the sergeant major said. "I joined when I was eighteen. Lied about my age. No bloody jobs in London for a bloke from the East End. That's where the riffraff hang out. No complaints. Seen a bit of the world—India, Burma, South Africa."

Sergeant Fleming made it clear that he was new to the army game. Cruickshank nodded. "You'll learn fast, I think, judgin' from the cut of your jib. The one thing to remember is, the generals are bloody fools who ask the infantry to do the impossible. Advance in mud up to your chin, that sort of thing. The junior officers aren't much better. All eager to die for king and country—glorious brainless patriotism. It's up to you to keep your men alive."

Sergeant Fleming tried to conceal his astonishment. "How do you do that?"

"Dig!" Cruickshank said. "The minute an attack stalls, start them diggin' the deepest 'oles they can manage. The entrenchin' shovel will keep you alive a lot longer than your bloody rifle. You'll be lucky to hit a single hun with the thing in a year in the lines. As for the bayonet, it's only good for stirrin' rations in the pot. It's the artillery and the machine guns that does the killin' in this bloody war. Ours and theirs."

"What do you use instead of a bayonet?"

"Trench shovels, blackjacks, brass knuckles, shivs—anything and everything that will make the bastards yell 'kamerad.'"

"Sounds like some of the fights I seen in the Sixth Ward."

"I seen'm in the East End too," Cruickshank said with a nod of approval. 'Ere's one more bit of advice. Teach your men to love the mud. To put their bloody faces in it as if it was their mothers' breasts. That's the only way to stay alive when the shrapnel starts flyin'. Anyone who stays on his feet is a dead 'ero in sixty bloody seconds."

"Another thing. Never change a machine gun! Flank the bloody things. Then grenade 'em."

Throughout this fierce lecture, they continued drinking milky tea and consuming scones. Private Perkins and his friend stood by, refilling their cups and replacing the scones, which were delicious. Recalling it thirty years later, Teddy Fleming said if we all lived several lives, as some deep thinkers claimed, the next time around he wanted to come back as a British sergeant major. No sergeant in the American army had the servants and comforts Sergeant Major Cruickshank assumed as part of his rank and privileges.

As for the sergeant major's advice, Sergeant Fleming was a little skeptical. He could not believe the tough micks in Company C would have trouble with German artillery or machine guns. On his way back to Company C's billets, he encountered the regiment's chaplain, Captain George H. Murphy. The priest grabbed him by the arm and said,

"Sergeant, I've got a new job. I'm supposed to sell you guys the government's insurance policy. It's for ten thousand dollars. They deduct the cost from your pay each month. I think you should all have it."

Ten thousand dollars was a lot of money in 1917, the equivalent of $140,000 in twenty-first-century cash. Sergeant Fleming shook his head. "A lousy idea, Father. You don't want guys thinkin' they're gonna get killed. Our casualties ain't gonna be that heavy anyway. I'll take three thousand."

"That means everyone else in the company will do the same thing!" the chaplain said.

"Three thousand is about right," Sergeant Fleming said, ending the conversation.

Maybe there was some retrospective revenge in this refusal for all those years when Equitable Life had stolen money from Davey Fleming for his paid-up policy. More likely, Sergeant Fleming meant what he said.

For the next six weeks, the 78th Division trained with the British in their sector of the Western Front. They learned to deal with poison gas by wearing their masks in buildings full of the real thing. Each company spent a few days in the front lines, which were pretty quiet. Only an occasional artillery shell was thrown by either side. The officers said the Germans were on the defensive these days. But there was a lot of talk about a big British offensive starting soon. That would heat things up very quickly. Sergeant Fleming and the rest of Company C could hardly wait. They were getting bored with the endless training routines.

Finally, the 312th was told to prepare to take over a section of the front lines near Arras, where they and the other three regiments of the 78th Division were expected to play a big part in the coming offensive. Before they could pack up and march, a Canadian division trudged past them, heading for the front. Rumors swept the regiment that the 78th was going elsewhere. Soon came orders to turn in their Enfield rifles for Springfields. Everyone knew what that meant—they weren't going to fight with the British after all. They were joining the American army again. That cheered everyone up.

Behind the scenes, this transfer was part of the bitter struggle that raged between General Pershing and the top French and British commanders about where the Americans would fight. The British had pressured Pershing into giving them five divisions, one of them the 78th. Now Pershing had recalled three of them, infuriating the king's men. If Sergeant Fleming and his micks of Company C had known about that, they would have been even more cheerful.

In a day or two came orders to pack and march to a nearby railroad siding, where hundreds of boxcars and chugging locomotives waited for them. They climbed aboard the smelly boxcars and soon they were heading south. For days they rattled through the war-torn French landscape, stopping only to resupply food and water.

They finally debarked east of Paris and headed for a sector of the front known by the name of its principal town, St. Mihiel. It was a salient, a huge bulge in the Allied lines, south of Verdun. The American First Army had been given the task of eliminating it.

For the first few days of the offensive, the men of the 78th were part of the army's reserve. The generals expected fierce resistance, and planned to relieve the frontline divisions when they suffered heavy casualties. But the Germans, already on the defensive, preferred to retreat rather than fight. Soon the St. Mihiel salient ceased to exist. The frontline divisions were pulled out and the 78th and other reserve divisions took their places. The 312th Regiment occupied a mix of woods and fields on the left of the American line. Company C was assigned largely open ground, where they began setting up machine guns and automatic rifle posts to defend themselves against a German counterattack.

As the men of Company C prepared for this first taste of frontline combat, Chaplain Murphy appeared to give the men his blessing and some words of encouragement. After his brief sermon, the priest again urged Sergeant Fleming to persuade them to take the full ten thousand dollars of government insurance. "They all followed your lead," said the exasperated priest. "Not a man has taken more than three thousand."

"We don't need it, Father. I guarantee you," Sergeant Fleming said. "I think this war's as good as over. The Germans don't have no fight left in 'em, from what I hear."

It undoubtedly looked that way, from the lack of enthusiasm the enemy had shown defending St. Mihiel. The chaplain retreated to a dugout a half mile behind the front lines. As darkness fell, German planes appeared overhead. Bombs rained down on other parts of the line. None of them fell in the 312th's sector. Their luck was holding, Sergeant Fleming thought, recalling their escape from the air raid in Calais.

The sergeant did not realize that the planes were doing more than dropping bombs. They were reporting the exact location of the American lines to their artillery. As darkness fell, a rumbling whooshing sound filled the air. Seconds later a tremendous explosion smashed down trees in all directions. It was followed by a dozen more blasts of similar size. Sergeant Fleming was encountering the kind of heavy artillery that had wiped out Private Perkins's platoon and left him with a permanent stutter.

"Dig!" Teddy shouted to the men of Company C. "Dig the deepest damn hole you ever saw."

He started digging a hole of his own as the 210-millimeter shells continued to crash around them, all but splitting his head open with every explosion. A shrill whine filled his ears. After each blast the air was thick with whizzing shrapnel and black, choking smoke. Nearby he could hear men screaming with terror. He crawled over to them and shouted, "Dig! Did you hear me? Dig!"

Back in his own hole, Sergeant Fleming ordered runners to go up and down the line to see if anyone had been hit. These messengers did not run, of course. They crawled on their bellies. The bombardment could be the prelude to a German attack. It was vital to know if Company C still had an intact defensive line. A shell that killed a half dozen men would leave a hole through which the enemy could get in their rear.

Teddy was still digging when a face appeared at the edge of his hole. It was Lieutenant Donat O'Brien, one of Company C's two platoon leaders. "Get out of that hole, Sergeant," O'Brien said. "I'm taking it over as a command post."

"Go to hell," Sergeant Fleming said. "Dig your own goddamn hole!"

Another shell exploded not more than a hundred feet away. In the glare Teddy could see terror in Lieutenant O'Brien's bulging eyes. "I'm giving you an order, Sergeant," O'Brien screamed.

Cursing, Sergeant Fleming grabbed his rifle and trench shovel and crawled out of the hole. He wormed his way through the mud toward the left flank, figuring O'Brien would take charge of the defense in his vicinity.

Another 210-millimeter shell came in, this time so close that the explosion left Sergeant Fleming in a paralyzed daze. He did not know how long he lay there, covered with mud, wondering if he were dead.

A hand shook his shoulder. "Sarge, you okay?" asked a familiar voice. It was Corporal Rodney Green.

Teddy Fleming decided he was still alive. "I think so," he said.

"That shell landed smack in your hole. There's nothin' left of O'Brien. I sent a report to the captain."

Wisps of black smoke still swirled from the hole. Teddy crawled over and stared into it. There was not a trace of Lieutenant Donat O'Brien. Instinctively, Teddy's hand went to Repetey O'Brien's dice in his pocket. Luck, he thought. Luck had kept him alive.

How much longer would he stay alive in this bedlam? The huge shells continued to slam into the muddy earth. Cries of "Medic!" filled the air. He crawled back to an aid station and ordered two terrified medics to help the wounded men.

All night the shells continued to explode around Company C's position. As dawn broke, the bombardment dwindled, no doubt to keep the German batteries hidden from Allied scout planes and artillery spotters in balloons. Thanks to Sergeant Fleming's repeated exhortations to dig, Company C's casualties were relatively few—only three killed and a dozen wounded. One man talked disconnected gibberish far worse than Private Perkins's stutter. It was Teddy's first encounter with what World War I doctors called shell shock. All they found of Lieutenant O'Brien was a piece of his raincoat.

Sergeant Fleming crawled a half mile in the mud to Chaplain Murphy's dugout. He awakened the dozing priest and said, "Father, I didn't know what the hell I was talkin' about. I'll take the full ten thousand bucks. So will every guy in the company. I'll see to it."

Thirty years later, Teddy Fleming told me about his first night under fire. "After that bombardment, I never expected to come out of the war alive," he said. "No one did. It didn't matter whether you were the toughest guy in the AEF or the worst momma's boy that ever lived. Or whether you were Irish, Italian, Jewish, or Zamboangan. No one could fight a two-hundred-and-ten-millimeter artillery shell."

He summed it up with words that showed how deeply that night affected his life: "I still feel like I'm living on borrowed time."

# 13

# Argonne

For the rest of their time in the St. Mihiel salient, the 312th Regiment and the rest of the 78th Division endured more nights and not a few days of bombardment from German heavy artillery. Someone gave the 210-millimeter shells an American nickname, "Jack Johnsons," after the black heavyweight champion with a knockout punch second to none. German planes also swooped down to strafe and bomb them. In three weeks, more than two thousand men were killed or wounded by shell- and machine-gun fire.

Some of these casualties were suffered while the 78th aggressively patrolled the forests and roads, giving the Germans the impression that the American army might renew the offensive. The idea was to pin down as many German divisions as possible, so they could not be used elsewhere.

While the 78th and other divisions created these diversions, the bulk of the American First Army marched north—toward another objective, the Argonne Forest and its neighboring valley. Plans called for an all-out attack that would shatter enemy defenses in a matter of days. Instead, the offensive floundered to a blood-soaked stop as the Germans poured in men and rained high explosives on the struggling Americans from high ground on three sides.

No one in the 312th Regiment knew anything about the situation in the Argonne when they were ordered to pull out of St. Mihiel and head for the new battlefield. The 78th's doughboys made part of the sixty-mile journey in trucks. Most of it they covered in traditional infantry fashion, "picking up one brogan and putting the other one down," as Teddy Fleming later described it to me.

Icy rain deluged them, turning the roads to gumbo that could suck off a man's shoe if he was not careful. Sergeant Fleming strode beside his men, maintaining the steady route march pace. It was hard, boring, business and a wiseguy in Company C decided to entertain the rest of the men at Sergeant Fleming's expense. He began kidding Teddy about the way he'd changed his insurance policy from three thousand to ten thousand dollars and ordered everyone else to do likewise. The wiseguy had been one of the few who stuck with three thousand.

"Does this mean the Germans are a lot tougher than you thought, Sarge? Or have you decided you're not as tough as we thought you were at Dix? Have those Jack Johnsons given you an education? Pretty hard to fight one of those with a bayonet, don't you think?"

And so forth. The wiseguy had a great line of chatter. He was known in the company as "the Mouth." Sergeant Fleming liked it less and less. A couple of times he told the guy to shut up. The Mouth obeyed, but after another two or three miles he'd go back to work. Teddy began to feel his authority as a leader slipping away from him. He saw smirks on a lot of faces.

"Sarge, is it true you wet your pants when that shell evaporated Lieutenant O'Brien? I heard you talked baby talk for twenty-four hours—"

Teddy Fleming dropped back until he was marching beside the Mouth's rank. The wise guy was in the middle of the rank, which made him think he was more or less immune from immediate punishment. Without breaking his stride, Sergeant Fleming reached into the rank and dragged him out by the collar. He spun the Mouth around and hit him on the point of the jaw with a terrific left hook. The guy flew ten feet and lay there in the rain, out cold.

"Keep marchin'!" Sergeant Fleming shouted. "Anyone else who thinks he can be a wiseguy and a fightin' soldier can expect the same thing!"

It was not quite as brutal as it looked. The division had trucks bringing up the rear of the column to collect soldiers who grew too exhausted to keep the marching pace. The Mouth would wake up in one of those vehicles and return to Company C's ranks a quieter man.

To avoid German artillery, the division marched by night along a road that ran through parts of the Argonne Forest. They had orders to be in the front lines to relieve the 77th Division by dawn on October 16, 1918. The darkness was total and the cold rain came down in torrents. No one had the slightest idea where they were going. Guides who supposedly knew the way were as lost as everyone else.

When the men of the 312th Regiment finally reached their assigned positions, it was daylight. They had orders to attack immediately. One of their first targets was a red-roofed farm appropriately identified on their maps as "La Ferme Rouge." American artillery pounded the farm and the fields around it and Company C and the other men of the 312th's first battalion charged—only to find that the fields were thick with barbed wire.

In the north, the British were using 4,000 tanks to smash through the German barbed wire. The hastily organized American First Army had only 189 tanks when they attacked in the Argonne, and most of them were knocked out on the first day. Artillery was supposed to blast passages through the wire, but it was a very erratic instrument. Again and again, men in C Company and other companies died trying to cut their way through under heavy German machine-gun fire.

Fifty years later, I knocked on the door of the same red-roofed farmhouse and was greeted by the barrel-chested owner, André Godart, who had been fifteen when the 312th Regiment stormed his father's fields. The Germans had dug tunnels running from the cellar of the farmhouse to forward trenches and blockhouses. Godart took me out in the pasture behind his house. My eye could trace the snaking line of the German trenches, while in the distance several concrete blockhouses were still visible, sunk deep in the earth, with only a slit, like a baleful mouth, for machine guns.

The 312th Regiment finally drove the Germans out of La Ferme Rouge and moved forward with the men of the 311th Regiment toward their main objective, the town of Grandpré. Built against the brow of a steep hill, Grandpré had a main street running east–west and two other streets feeding down into it from the north. The Germans controlled the north–south streets and could infiltrate men over roofs and through back doors into the east–west houses. This was bad enough. Much worse was another German-controlled piece of real estate that the doughboys dubbed the Citadel.

This was a tongue of rock that jutted into the center of Grandpré and ended in a perpendicular thirty-foot cliff. Count Bellejoyeuse, a minor figure in sixteenth-century French politics, had built a chateau on this commanding perch. The Germans had burrowed into its shattered ruins like determined moles and emplaced machine guns that could pour leaden death into the fields below it. Behind the chateau was Bellejoyeuse Farm, an ironically named piece of real estate in which the Germans had emplaced more machine guns to protect the Citadel's rear and flanks.

The 312th Regiment's commander sent a patrol into Grandpré to feel out the Germans' strength. Machine-gun and rifle fire erupted from all points of the compass. Every man in the patrol was killed, wounded, or captured. It was obvious that an assault would have to be made in force.

To get into position for the attack, the 312th Regiment crossed the Aire River, which ran through the fields not far from the base of Grandpré's steep hill. Rain had raised the normally sluggish stream and in some places the men had to wade through water up to their necks. The immersion ruined almost every gas mask.

They had barely reached the opposite bank when the Germans laid down a gas barrage. Sergeant Fleming and his men watched in horror as the noxious cloud boiled up less than fifty yards away. In another sixty seconds the entire regiment would become a strangling, coughing mob.

A breeze sprang up and the deadly vapor moved down the river valley instead of enveloping them. Luck, Teddy Fleming thought, patting Repetey O'Brien's dice in his pocket.

The 312th Regiment attacked Grandpré. It was slow, murderous work. They soon learned the Citadel could not be taken by frontal assault. Assailing it from the east was equally impossible. Bellejoyeuse Farm protected that flank, and another German strongpoint, the Bois des Loges, protected Bellejoyeuse Farm. The only hope seemed to be an assault that swung west of the town, up a narrow valley to a village called Talma. Sergeant Fleming and the men of C Company headed up this defile, which was on the extreme left flank of the American lines.

According to division headquarters, the French were in possession of Talma. But C Company soon learned this was the sort of information that the staff men in headquarters put out without bothering to find out if it was true. C Company found nothing in Talma Valley but Germans. They were in front of them and on two sides, with machine guns galore, and artillery support from a gun every American soldier grew to hate, the 77-millimeter Austrian cannon that fired a shell dubbed the "whizbang." It traveled at almost the speed of sound and exploded a second after its whiz, giving a man no time to duck.

Division headquarters rushed machine guns to support Company C against a German counterattack. They arrived just in time, but the situation grew more and more confused. "Sarge," Harry Ross screamed at one point, "I thought we were winnin' this goddamn war!" He pointed over the edge of his hole at gray-uniformed Germans dodging and twisting toward them.

"Start shootin'. That's the only way to win it," Sergeant Fleming shouted, as whizbangs gouged the earth around them.

C Company beat back the counterattack, but all thought of moving forward was put on hold for the time being. They were barely hanging on to their foothold in Talma Valley. Every time a soldier showed his head above his foxhole, machine guns flung bullets from the Bois de Bourgnone on the left or from the crest of Talma Hill on their right. It was almost impossible to get any food into the valley. For several days they lived on carrots, eaten raw or cooked and mashed into a sort of stew mixed with bread. After three days of this diet, Sergeant Fleming vowed never to eat another carrot for the rest of his life. As far as I know, he never did. They were never seen on our dinner table.

On the third day, as they waited for further orders and hoped for reinforcements, Sergeant Fleming saw an incredible sight. Up the road toward them strolled an American major. His clean, well-pressed uniform identified him as a headquarters soldier. He was apparently oblivious to the existence of the German machine guns that had the road covered from three sides.

Teddy Fleming's athlete's reflexes sent him lunging out of his hole shouting, "Get down!" He hit the major with a flying tackle below the knees and they both hurtled off the road into a shellhole filled with muddy stinking water. The major surfaced, spluttering curses and threats. "I'll have you court-martialed—"

An instant later, the German machine guns opened up, shredding the road and the ground on both sides of it. "Sergeant," said the chastened major, "would you accept an apology from a damn fool?"

Again and again the men of Company C and the other companies in the First Battalion tried to push up Talma Valley. This was where Teddy Fleming learned to apply Sergeant Major Cruickshank's dictum, that it was his job to save the lives of his men. He absolutely banned frontal assaults on machine guns, the preferred tactic, according to most generals in the American high command. Instead, he (and other sergeants and lieutenants) adopted German assault tactics. They dodged, twisted, crawled from shellhole to shellhole, firing on the guns from the flanks, trying to keep the gunner's heads down until they could get close enough to throw grenades. Only then was there a final rush to finish off survivors.

They finally captured an important German machine-gun nest at Talma Farm, about halfway to Talma village. The next morning two companies from the First Battalion tried a surprise assault on the village. Shrouded by a heavy fog, they moved forward and were within three hundred yards of their goal when the winds of chance, which had rescued them from the gas attack while crossing the Aire River, betrayed them. The fog suddenly lifted and the Germans poured in machine-gun fire from the front and both flanks. Almost every man in the advance platoons was killed or wounded; the few that survived played dead through the agonizing day and crawled back to the American lines at nightfall.

Men began to crack in the face of such carnage. One captain, after seeing a patrol shot to pieces, asked to be relieved, claiming that his "heart" could not stand the strain. Even worse was the collapse of C Company's captain as they moved out to an assault. He turned and ran in the other direction. In a fury, Sergeant Fleming raised his rifle to shoot him in the back. But whizbangs were raining down and he was afraid the bullet might go wild and hit a man in the rear echelon of the attack.

After the defeat of the two-company assault on Talma village, the Americans again dug in and waited for reinforcements or fresh orders. Each night, regimental headquarters ordered a four-man patrol to move up Talma Valley in the darkness to make sure the Germans were not gathering for a dawn assault. Sergeant Fleming was in charge of selecting the men for these patrols. After the first three did not return, he realized it was a suicide assignment. But sergeants were in no position to defy the colonel of the regiment on such matters.

On the fourth night, Teddy selected a thickset Irish-American corporal named Conroy and three of his platoon and sent them crawling into the darkness with urgent orders to be as silent as humanly possible. They too did not return. War, a cursing Sergeant Fleming thought, was a hell of a stupid business at times.

Five years later, Teddy Fleming was walking down Thirty-third Street in New York. Strolling toward him was the vanished corporal. Finally convinced he was not seeing a ghost, Teddy grabbed him and said, "I thought you were dead and buried somewhere in Talma Valley."

"Sarge," ex-Corporal Conroy said, "I'm not stupid enough to commit suicide. When you sent us out that night, we went the other way. We didn't stop runnin' until we was five miles behind the lines. Then we found some aid men and said we was gassed. We put on a good act—coughed like hell—and they shipped us back to the States."

Teddy bought him a drink. "What the hell," he told me. "The war was over. I thought about doing the same thing a couple of times up there in Talma Valley myself."

But Sergeant Fleming stayed in the fight for Talma. So did most of the other men in C Company who were not carried to the rear with wounds or hastily buried where they fell. Why? Patriotism, making the world safe for democracy, had little to do with it. For Teddy Fleming, Talma Valley was the ultimate test of his nerve, his manhood.

Another reason for staying was the men of C Company. They belonged to him far more than to the company's officers. They had slept in the same barracks and tents for almost a year. They needed his leadership now and he responded with a fierce loyalty, a ferocious concern for each of them.

Sergeant Fleming was on duty day and night, using jokes and

tough talk to steady men whose nerves were starting to shred. He reminded them to keep their feet dry to prevent trench foot. He urged them to fight the ubiquitous lice by picking the crawling creatures off each other's heads and necks. He ordered them to eat the slop that the regiment's cooks risked their necks to lug up Talma Valley in the darkness each night. He lectured them on keeping their gas masks within instant reach to survive the daily gas attacks. He tried to be compassionate as well as tough, sending to the rear men who began to babble or sob uncontrollably after too many whizbangs exploded nearby.

Through most of these hellish days and nights, cold rain drizzled from the leaden sky. Although they shivered in their wet uniforms, the infantrymen of the 312th learned to like the downpour and the mud it created. Mud meant the shells sank when they hit, and that cut down on the shrapnel. One day a whizbang struck only a few feet from a private in C Company but failed to explode. The private dug it out and discovered the number on it was identical to his army serial number.

Luck again? Sergeant Fleming thought so. So did the private.

On October 23, what was left of the 312th's First Battalion made another try at Talma. It was part of a coordinated attack the 78th Division launched, both there and in the town of Grandpré after a nightlong artillery barrage. The Germans responded with a fierce counterbarrage that caused heavy casualties among the 312th's Third Battalion, attacking Grandpré. They kept going anyway and one squad made it to the top of the Citadel.

With Company C and the rest of the First Battalion, it was the same deadly story. A vicious crossfire of machine guns and artillery pinned them down on the reverse slope of Talma Hill. They were in desperate need of artillery support, but there were no radios to get the word back to the gunners. In the AEF, the men in the front lines depended on runners to carry such messages.

Parker Dunn, a game little Irish-American from Albany, New York, volunteered to risk the lethal curtain of fire. The battalion commander told him it was suicide. Without waiting for an order, Dunn took off. He was hit once, sprang to his feet, and kept running. All around him the earth churned with shellfire and machine-gun bullets. Dunn went down a second time. Everyone was sure he was finished. But he staggered to his feet and made a few more yards. A geyser of earth exploded in front of him as a whizbang hit home. Dunn did not get up again. His medal went to his stepmother.

Perhaps inspired by Dunn's reckless courage, Sergeant Fleming and the men of C Company somehow worked their way to the top of shell-ripped Talma Hill and drove the Germans off it in ugly hand-to-hand fighting. By this time, Teddy Fleming and his men had learned that Sergeant Major Cruickshank was right—bayonets were useless in trench combat. C Company's favorite weapon was the trench shovel. Sergeant Fleming used it on a young German lieutenant who tried to surrender. "Kamerad," he screamed, raising his hands. Teddy killed him with a thrust to the chest. The memory would haunt him for the rest of his life.

Other men from C Company piled into the trenches, some swinging rifles as clubs, others wielding blackjacks and ugly knives with serrated edges, recently issued for trench fighting. The Germans fled and what was left of C Company pushed into the southern end of the Bois de Bourgogne. Their ranks too thin to go farther, they dug in while a fresh battalion of the 311th Infantry filed past them.

On the night of October 27, the 312th Regiment was withdrawn and reorganized into two (instead of three) battalions. That meant one out of every three men who had gone into the Argonne was now a casualty. That was when Sergeant Fleming became an acting lieutenant. All the officers in C Company were dead or wounded or, in the case of the company's captain, had run away.

Teddy was mainly chosen for the leadership he had displayed during the hellish days and nights in Talma Valley. Rescuing that wandering headquarters staff major from German machine guns may have also played a part in the choice.

Coming out of the Bois de Bourgogne, the new lieutenant received his only wound of the war. The trail was blocked by a large tree branch, which each man was supposed to hold for the man behind him. Maybe a private had a grudge against the ex-sergeant. More probably they were all too exhausted after nine days of almost continuous fighting to remember the simplest order. The man ahead of Teddy let the branch go and in the darkness it smashed him in the face, breaking his nose.

The battalion commander told him to consider himself wounded and go to the rear. Lieutenant Fleming refused. "I think I'm needed around here," he said. No one argued with him. The First Battalion had only four officers left. Wiping away the blood and shrugging off the pain, Acting Lieutenant Fleming stayed with his men.

That night, several miles behind the front lines, the 312th found that the rear area was as dangerous as Talma Valley. German long-range guns, probably alerted by an observation plane that had spotted a careless match or a cooking fire, poured a terrible bombardment into their camp. They dove under wagons and into ditches as the big shells screamed in like berserk express trains.

One of Lieutenant Fleming's favorite soldiers, a red-haired kid from Jersey City's Second Ward, cried out, "Sarge, I'm hit. 'I'm hit.'"

Teddy crawled over to him through the whizzing shrapnel. "My legs," the kid said. "They got my legs."

Teddy groped for his legs in the darkness to put on a tourniquet. There were no legs. Minutes later the boy was dead. The exhausted new lieutenant almost wept. The kid had reminded him of his brother Charlie.

How much longer could any of them put up with this sort of random death? The pain of his broken nose twisted through Teddy's brain and became something deeper, an angry voice that asked God why.

This was neither the time or place to debate such a question. Teddy had no answer to it anyway. There were other wounded men to bandage and get to aid stations. The lieutenant began giving orders. It was the army's answer to big questions: Do your job.

"This happened because someone got careless," Acting Lieutenant Fleming growled. "If I see anyone light a match, I'll personally shoot him between the eyes."

As an historian I learned some ironic facts about my father's ordeal in the Argonne. The American high command never expected the 312th Regiment to make any signifcant headway in Talma Valley. Their repeated attacks were part of a larger strategy aimed at making the Germans shift troops to that flank, weakening their center.

On November 1, after a tremendous bombardment by 4,000 heavy guns, the Americans launched their main attack on the weakened German center. In twelve hours they had smashed a gaping hole, forcing the Germans into headlong retreat all along the line. The 78th

Division returned to the front to participate in the pursuit of the fleeing enemy.

They were still dangerously short of officers. One battalion was
led by a captain. Acting Lieutenant Teddy Fleming was the commander of C Company. They were battle-wise veterans now. Whenever the Germans tried to make a stand, they swept them aside with
field artillery and flank attacks. They stayed in the game until November 3, when exhaustion caught up to them again.

That day, the 78th Division marched out of the Argonne for the
last time. Eight days later, the Germans signed an armistice and the
war was over. By that time, Teddy Fleming and other instant lieutenants were headed for officers' candidate camp, where they spent
three months studying the lessons of the war and the art of infantry
leadership.

For Lieutenant Fleming the Argonne was a profound personal
experience on several levels. It validated his image of himself as a lucky
man—with nerve. It enabled him to discover something that he did
exceptionally well—lead men. It certified him as an American, something no one, including the president of the United States, could take
away from him with verbiage about "hyphenates" poisoning the
nation's bloodstream.

After the graduation ceremony at officers' candidate camp, Teddy
strapped the broad, gleaming Sam Browne belt across his chest. He
felt a mix of pride and pleasure more intense, more satisfying than he
had ever known before. It did not matter that the Sam Browne belt
was a British touch that General Pershing had added to the AEF officers' uniforms. It told the world that Thomas J. Fleming had made it
into the officer corps of the U.S. Army. For a guy with an eighth-grade
education, this was an achievement worth celebrating.

In the deepest, most private level of Teddy's soul, there was less
cause for celebration. The Argonne had violated the simple Catholic
faith Teddy had been taught at All Saints School. On that murderous,
muddy battlefield, death had been so random, so haphazard, often
seemingly accidental, it became impossible for him to believe in a loving God who watched over each of His human creatures.

This unarticulated loss of faith became part of my father's life. It
did not mean he was an atheist. Like his father before him he did not

feel qualified to argue with the priests or with women like his mother, who vehemently supported the Catholic Church. He may even have retained a wary hope that somehow, somewhere, everything could be explained.

This loss could be regarded as an invisible wound. I don't think Teddy saw it that way. For him it was a confirmation of ideas and attitudes he had already acquired in the slum world of downtown Jersey City. Either way, it was an ineluctable part of the journey of his Irish-American soul to the day of his death.

# 14

# Home Is the Hero

**W**hile the war churned on in Europe and Woodrow Wilson made a dramatic speech about Fourteen Points, or principles, on which the Americans would insist at a peace conference, Kitty Dolan drifted through melancholy days and nights. She slept badly, a common symptom of depression. Her friends Mary McNamara and Marie Hannaway worked hard at trying to cheer her up. They vacationed together at the Jersey shore. They went to plays and movies.

Mary Fitzmaurice Dolan told Kitty again and again that she had finally done the right thing. Lloyd Harris had no right to expect her to spend her youth as a companion to a dying man. Her brother, George, told her in his breezy way that she was the best-looking babe in Jersey City and she ought to start enjoying herself.

Gradually, Kitty began to rediscover her old cheerful self. She decided her mother and George were right and began going to dances that the YMCA staged for soldiers and sailors who were passing through Jersey City on their way to the Western Front. She foxtrotted with men from Missouri and California and found she was as popular—and as deft on the dance floor—as she had been at Thornton's Hotel.

Kitty continued to pay minimal attention to the war, even when the Americans finally went into action in June of 1918 and the newspapers began to report hundreds of men killed and wounded every day. In

October, the newspapers reported rumors of an impending armistice—
which became a reality on November 11, 1918. Soon President Wilson
sailed to Europe with his wife to negotiate a permanent peace.

The peace conference dragged on and on, with pictures of Wilson
riding through various European cities being cheered by wild-eyed
mobs, and later pictures with mustachioed French and Italian politicians. Although Kitty recognized some of the sights she had seen on
her tour of Europe, she and her friends found the diplomacy distant
and confusing. But she began to take a little more interest in politics
when it looked as if women were going to get the vote. The woman
suffrage movement had browbeaten Congress into passing a constitutional amendment, which was rapidly ratified by the necessary two-
thirds of the states.

Another constitutional amendment passed before the woman suffrage amendment. It banned every form of alcoholic drinks from the
nation, closing saloons everywhere. Considering the woes drinking
had inflicted on her family, Kitty thought Prohibition was a good idea.
So did Mary Fitzmaurice Dolan. Tom Dolan denounced it, not
because he wanted to get drunk when he pleased—lately he had gotten his drinking under control—but because he said it was going to
make sissies of the whole country.

Meanwhile, Mayor Frank Hague was making headlines at City
Hall. He had raised the local taxes on railroad and business property
to astronomical heights, setting off howls of rage in uptown Jersey
City and the rest of Republican-controlled New Jersey.

Kitty did not think much of the new mayor. His grammar was
atrocious. He talked like a downtown Irish lug—which gave Kitty
thoughts of moving out of Jersey City as soon as possible. Several of
the men she met at the YMCA dances told her there were good teaching jobs in Chicago and San Francisco and other cities. Her brother,
George, was talking about heading for California to play baseball—he
was a very good pitcher and the Pacific Coast League often sent players to the majors. If he didn't make it to the big leagues, George saw a
movie career as a fallback. Her brother made California sound exciting. Why not go with him?

Kitty's rebellious musings were interrupted by an invitation to a
wedding on April 17, 1919. The bridegroom was her South Amboy

cousin Thomas Aloysius Gallagher, Hugh Gallagher's younger
brother. Everyone called him Al. Kitty had met him many times but
had never paid much attention to him. She instantly suspected Hughie
had put her name on the invitation list, hoping to get several dozen
dances with her and possibly persuade her to start seeing him.

Al was getting married to someone named Mae Fleming. Kitty
looked her up in the telephone book and found a David Fleming on
Randolph Avenue. Not the best address in the city but not the worst
either. Why not go? Kitty decided. She was unlikely to meet an eligi-
ble man, but Hughie was full of fun and so were the rest of the South
Amboy Gallaghers. She would have a good time.

The wedding took place in St. Patrick's parish church, a huge
Gothic structure that reminded Kitty of some of the churches she had
visited in Europe. She was struck by the bride's red-haired beauty. The
party after the ceremony was just as lively as Kitty had expected it to
be, and Hughie Gallagher was after her for every dance.

Toward the end of the evening, the bridegroom horned in on
Hughie and danced Kitty around the floor in a smooth foxtrot. "I've
been telling Mae about you," Al Gallagher said. "How you're the best-
looking woman in the family and the most fun."

After the dance, Kitty sat down next to the bride, who introduced
her brother, Dave Fleming. "Don't worry about him, he's married and
then some," Mae said. "Just had his second kid. Poor Lizzie! But he's
not bad-lookin', don't y'think?"

"Oh, definitely," Kitty said, giving Dave a flirtatious smile.

"Well, he's nothin' compared to my brother Teddy," Mae said.

"Hey, whattya mean?" Dave said with a cheerful grin. "I got that
bum beat by a mile in the looks department!"

"Teddy's got *muscles*," Mae said. "Y'know what I mean?" She
pointed across the room to her father, Davey Fleming, sitting at a distant table with several friends his age. "Like my fatha. Along with the
muscles comes brains. He got promoted to lieutenant in the army.
They commissioned him in the middle of a battle! Anyway, the point
is, Teddy ain't married. I been tryin' to get him to the altuh for a good
five years! You interested?"

"Of course she's interested," Dave said. "She wants to be in the
same family with a handsome lug like me."

"Not really," Mae said. "All you gotta do is look at a woman and she gets pregnant!"

"I'd love to meet him," Kitty said, only half meaning it. The Flemings' awful grammar and pronunciation marked them as downtown Irish, even if they were living on Randolph Avenue. But Dave was unquestionably handsome. Teddy's army commission suggested he had acquired some polish. Maybe he was a gentleman as well as an officer.

A few weeks later, a letter from Mae Fleming Gallagher appeared in Kitty's mailbox. In it was a photograph of a good-looking, strong-jawed lieutenant with a gleaming belt across his chest. The writing in the enclosed note was precise and the spelling accurate. *Teddy just sent me this. Send it back when you get a chance. That's a nice uniform, don't you think? He said he was coming home in a couple of months. Let's keep in touch. Mae*

When the newlyweds moved to 308 Arlington Avenue, Mae invited Kitty to dinner. Arlington Avenue was on the eastern, less fashionable side of Jersey City but it was a street of well-painted two- and three-family houses. Al Gallagher was working as an electrician at the Hudson Tubes. He was obviously making a nice salary to afford a mortgage on 308, which was a three-family house. The Gallaghers had taken the second floor and were renting the two other floors.

The dinner was well cooked and pleasant, except for the presence of Davey Fleming, who dominated the conversation. Mostly he talked about the war that was raging in Ireland between the British and the Irish Republican Army. Kitty had paid no attention to it. "Yes be God, one of these days Ireland shall be free, from the center to the sea!" Davey roared.

Kitty failed to recognize one of the slogans of the Irish Republican Army. She talked about the beauties of Killarney. Davey scoffed. "A bunch of tourist bootlickers, that's all them micks are down that way. They don't care whether the boots are English or German or American. The Corkonians are just as bad and the Dubliners worse. I'm inclined t'think there's not a true patriot anywhere but in Connaught, where they haven't taken the king's shillin' because there's nothin' to spend it on!"

Connaught was Ireland's western province; it included Mayo and other equally poor counties. With her minimal knowledge of Ireland, Kitty did not know what Davey was talking about. Neither did Mae. She changed the topic to Lieutenant Fleming.

"The Turkey tells me a bunch of fellas in the ward wanta run Teddy for the state assembly," Mae said.

"The Turkey?" Kitty said.

"That's Dave's nickname," Al Gallagher explained with a smile. "I think it means he's got the gift of gab."

"Do you think Teddy will run for the assembly?" Kitty asked.

"Who knows. These days, you gotta get Frank Hague's okay for everythin'," Mae said.

"I don't like him very much," Kitty said.

"You better change that tune, me darlin'," Davey Fleming said. "Hague's our man all the way. He's showin' them Protestant million-aires they can't get away with robbin' us blind any longer. I hope this don't mean you're gonna go Republican! That'll convince me women should never have gotten the vote."

"Oh no," Kitty said.

"I'll educate her, Da, now that you've educated me," Al Gallagher said, smiling at Kitty.

Back home later that night, Kitty poured out her doubts about the Flemings. "They're really *thick*, Mamma, especially the father," she said. "Thick" was a derogatory Irish term—as in "thick mick."

"If Al Gallagher can get along with them, I don't see why you can't," Mary Fitzmaurice Dolan said. The implication was clear. Kitty was getting too old to be fussy about the flaws of a man's relatives.

The weeks wound down to a November day in 1919 when Kitty got a phone call from Mae Fleming Gallagher. "Teddy's comin' home. They wanted him to stay in the army but he decided against it. He'll be here in a week."

Mae had a plan. "I want ya to be visitin' us. It's gotta look like an accident. Y'just dropped in t'see me and Al."

"How will that work? I can't spend all day in your parlor," Kitty said.

"I got the whole family involved in this. They'll phone me when he visits'm. We'll keep track of 'm and you can get over here ahead of 'm."

The next call came a week later, on Saturday. "Teddy's in town!" Mae said. "He got off the boat in Hoboken about an hour ago. He's visitin' Charlie right now. He'll go see the Turkey next. Get over here as soon as you can."

Kitty dressed with care, selecting a new burgundy dress, with the skirt just above the ankles in the latest fashion, and a wide-brimmed dark blue hat. She had just finished putting on her lipstick when the phone rang again. "Where are ya?" Mae said. "He just got to the Turkey's. He's only four blocks away! They'll do their best to slow'm down but don't waste no time!"

Kitty raced across town, arriving at 308 Arlington Avenue considerably short of breath. Hurrying up the dark narrow stairs to the Gallaghers' second-floor apartment, she missed a step and fell flat on her face. But she quickly recovered and Mae greeted her at the door with a conspiratorial smile. "He's still at the Turkey's. Relax and catch y'breath."

She led Kitty into the parlor. A half hour later, the front doorbell rang again. Up the stairs came the heavy footsteps of a male. Mae met him at the door, which opened into the dining room. There were exclamations of joy, the sound of a kiss, Old Davey roaring congratulation from the kitchen, where the hero went to shake his hand.

Footsteps approached the parlor. Kitty heard Mae say, "We got company. Al's cousin, Kitty Dolan, dropped in t'see me. She came to the weddin'. We're gettin' t'be good friends."

A moment later Teddy Fleming was at the entrance to the parlor. The Sam Browne belt across his chest gleamed in the lamplight. His black shoes had a similar shine. His uniform was as crisp and creased as a soldier's in a recruiting poster.

The lieutenant had a broad smile on his face. He was in a very good mood. "Kitty," Mae said. "This is my brothuh Teddy. I tole you about him. Our war hero."

"What the hell are you talkin'about?" Teddy said. "I ain't no hero. I'm just a lucky stiff, like everybody else that got home in one piece."

The awful grammar and the downtown lower-class accent made Kitty wince. Lloyd Harris's polished diction and gentlemanly style flashed in her head. But her smile remained intact. "I'm so glad to meet you," she said.

"Likewise," Lieutenant Fleming said.

They met, the schoolteacher and the unlettered soldier, in that small second-floor parlor on that December day in 1919. I visited the apartment a hundred times in my youth. What I remember most is the dimness and the surplus of furniture. A couch and several overstuffed chairs were crammed into a room that was not more than eight feet wide and sixteen feet long. A full dining room set of carved walnut jammed the room just behind it. Light entered only from two windows fronting on the street. In the dining room two other windows looked out on a narrow alley into which sunlight never penetrated.

In that dimness, the lieutenant saw a brunette with a great figure and a scintillating smile. She talked about the movies and the Broadway theater, which she adored. She had a brother, George, who wanted to be a baseball star. She chattered about friends from high school. That made her the closest thing to a college graduate the lieutenant had ever met. Remarks about "teacher friends" revealed she was a working woman with a salary, another novelty.

The schoolteacher saw a soldier who emanated self-confidence, command. His grammar and his lower-class accent were abominable but those were things a woman could fix, especially a woman who knew something about education. He might deny he was a war hero but he certainly looked and acted like one. That made him someone special, someone Kitty Dolan could love.

The lieutenant was attracted. He liked Kitty's flirtatious style and he liked even more the education she personified. Friends said Frank Hague was looking for guys with good war records to give his organization a patriotic shine. Maybe Mae was right, it was time he settled down. His two brothers were married and already had kids. Why not marry a good-looking woman with class? That would be a nice reward for ducking all those bullets and shells in St. Mihiel and the Argonne.

I'm writing more than history now. I'm writing *His*tory and *Her*story, about the journey of two souls, two personalities, two individuals whose profoundly different pasts were temporarily made irrelevant by a series of coincidences that can only be called fate. It is a very American story. It is also a very Irish-American story. That meant a happy ending was by no means guaranteed.

# 15

# The Man in Charge

Mae insisted Kitty and Teddy stay for dinner. The conversation swirled all over the place. Davey Fleming wanted to know what Teddy thought of the news from Ireland, where the war for independence was still boiling. Teddy replied by telling them about the day General Pershing had inspected the 78th Division with England's Prince of Wales, not long before they sailed home. The prince was a runt; he barely came up to Pershing's shoulder. As they passed C Company, Private Harry Ross yelled, "Hey General! Ask the little bastard when he's gonna free Ireland."

The prince kept walking. Either he hadn't heard the insult or he decided pretending he hadn't was the best policy. Pershing whirled, furious, and for a minute Teddy was sure they were all going to be court-martialed on the spot. Instead a big grin flashed across the general's face and he winked—then caught up to the plodding prince.

"Damn it, I wish the Democrats would run that man for president," Davey said.

"I had the same idea, Da," Teddy said. "But I checked with a couple of guys from the old regular army. He's a Republican. Teddy Roosevelt was one of his best friends." Roosevelt had died early in 1919.

"Too bad," Davey said. "Too damn bad."

Kitty asked the lieutenant if he had gotten to Paris. "A few times," he said. "Nice town."

"What did you think of the Louvre?" she said.

"The what?" Teddy said.

"The Louvre. The national museum."

"I skipped it," Teddy said. "I spent my money on the Folies Bergère." He surprised Kitty by pronouncing "Bergère" correctly. He must have met a few French people.

"What's that?" Mae wanted to know.

"A stage show. A lot of babes dancin' around wearin' as little as possible," Teddy said. "Oooh-la-la."

"That don't surprise me," Mae said. "The French have no morals, from what I hear."

"They got them. They just don't put them to much use," Teddy said. He told them about the loss of the 312th Regiment's barracks bags.

Mae was outraged. "We oughta make them pay for that," she said. "Send them a bill."

"I think they already owe us a bill or two," Teddy said. "I mean bill as in billion."

After dinner Lieutenant Fleming escorted Kitty Dolan back to 47 Boyd Avenue. The Dolans had moved to this quiet street west of the boulevard not long after Kitty had started earning a salary as a teacher. They had to walk through a black neighborhood that sprawled for a half dozen blocks in the center of the uptown part of the city. Kitty remarked that she would be much too nervous to walk through it alone. She was glad she had a soldier at her side.

The lieutenant laughed. "You afraid of meeting Jack Johnson, maybe?" he said. "I don't think I could handle him."

Kitty did not know what he was talking about. He had to explain that Jack Johnson was the former heavyweight champion, who was notorious for his affairs with white women. Miss Dolan was obviously not a sports fan or a tabloid reader.

"Mae told me you were a boxer before you went in the army," Kitty said.

"For about ten minutes," Teddy said. He told her how he had refused to throw his third fight.

Kitty said she admired his honesty. "Honesty had nothin' to do with it," Teddy said. "All my friends bet their shirts on me. I couldn't let 'em down."

"What did you do for a living before you went in the army?" Kitty asked.

"Oh, this and that," Teddy said.

He was not about to tell her he ran a card game in the Sixth Ward and had a gang who rented themselves out as sluggers when needed in Jersey City and New York. Already Teddy had Kitty figured as one of the uptown Irish who might as well be a Protestant, without any idea of how people lived downtown.

"For a while I sold watches but I decided a salesman's life was for the birds."

"You mean you were always away from home?"

"Yeah." He saw no need to tell her about Otto Kunhaldt and his fellow Germans and their putdowns of the Irish.

"I really like Mae," Kitty said. "She's so—so direct."

"What does that mean?"

"She says what she thinks."

"It's a family trait. If you listen to Old Davey for five minutes, you get the idea. Everyone says me and Mae take after him."

"Mae says you're going to run for the assembly."

"I don't know about that. It's only a rumor."

"I think you'd make a good assemblyman—maybe a congressman. But you'd have to improve your grammar, your pronunciation of some words."

"No kiddin'?"

"That's a good example. You should say *kidding.*"

Shades of Monsignor Meehan, Teddy thought. By this time they were walking down Boyd Avenue. "Here's my house," Kitty said. "We live on the second floor."

Teddy looked it over. "Nice," he said. "What's your father do for a livin'?"

"He used to be a carpenter. Lately he's been working as a mill-wright at Colgate's. Helping them set up heavy machinery."

"Sounds like good money."

"It's good enough. They let me keep my salary. I don't even have to pay rent. That's how I get to see so many shows in New York."

"Ever thought of goin' into it? Show business? You've got the looks."

"I—I thought of it. But I decided against it. Better to be safe than sorry, as the saying goes."

"Yeah—a lot of showgirls end up sorry. I've met a few."

Kitty was disconcerted by that remark. She told herself to be realistic. This man was over thirty years old and he was not Lee Shanaphy. He had undoubtedly met quite a few women.

She suddenly wanted him to kiss her boldly on the lips—or at least suggest a date. Instead, the lieutenant squeezed her hand and said: "I'll see you around, maybe. You're in the phone book?"

"Oh yes."

"I'll look you up."

Kitty had trouble getting to sleep. Had she ruined things by criticizing his grammar and pronunciation? It just came out. Maybe she could not stand the thought of listening to that lower-class accent for the rest of her life. But there was something about Teddy Fleming she liked, something *heroic*. The word was not misplaced. She liked the way he refused to brag about his battlefield exploits. He was unassuming, modest. Admirable qualities.

Teddy Fleming was having very different thoughts. He knew that Kitty had not arrived at 308 Arlington Avenue accidentally. The Turkey had tipped him off to Mae's game plan. Big brother had added a wink and said, "She's a looker. Nice dancer. Too bad you got two left feet."

"Thanks for the tip-off, wise guy," Teddy had said. Was Dave telling him not to make his mistake? Maybe.

Kitty had class, maybe too much class for him. There were a lot of things to settle before he could think about getting married. The next day Teddy headed for the Turkey's firehouse and had a long talk with him about Frank Hague. The mayor was riding high. Last month, he had elected a governor, Edward I. Edwards, a local banker. That gave Hague control of dozens of state boards and commissions, plus all the district attorneys in New Jersey. Unfortunately, you had to be a lawyer or a guy with a college education to get into those pickings.

The Turkey thought the big win meant Hague was not exactly desperate to draft war heroes for his ticket. He was doing very nicely without them. But the Turkey was pretty sure Doc Holland was still in Teddy's corner. Did he want his old card game back? Teddy shook his head. He wanted something more solid than a card game—something more respectable. He was pretty sure a classy dame like Kitty Dolan was not going to marry someone who ran a card game and could wind up in jail if the wind blew the wrong way in City Hall.

Later that day, he talked things over with Doc Holland, who whacked him on the back and made it clear Teddy was still his guy. Doc gave him a pretty good assessment of Frank Hague. He was level but very very tough when it came to bargaining about who gets what. Doc was negotiating with him about coming aboard his organization in a big way. Hague was offering to make him city clerk, one of the best slots in City Hall. But he wanted to have the final say on every job in the clerk's office—and he was insisting on a lid on the number of card games and numbers men and bookies in the Sixth Ward. Hague wanted to make Jersey City look as clean as the diocesan seminary— and he wanted most of the loose money to go to City Hall. With a governor in Trenton to give him leverage with every lawyer in town, the mayor might be even tougher to deal with next year. Doc was inclined to take his offer.

"Where does that leave me?" Teddy said.

"I'll take you to City Hall with me," Doc said. "I'll make you part of the package. It shouldn't be hard to sell you, with that great war record."

"What would the money be like?"

"Two, maybe twenty-five hundred a year."

Not great but not bad either. Old Davey's salary at Eagle Oil had been $150 a year when he started out. Now he was a watchman but he still brought home a lot less than a thousand. Teddy thought he could add another thousand to his income with some local umpiring and skimming a little here and a little there from the ward's numbers and bookie action, if he needed it. Doc was a bachelor. He wasn't hungry for money. Almost everything he made he put back into the ward, one way or another. His annual boat ride was one of the biggest parties in the city. He gave away half the tickets to people who couldn't afford them.

That night Teddy had dinner with the Turkey and his wife, Lizzie. They had two boys, Tom and Joe, and Lizzie had another kid in the oven. It was great watching Dave roughhouse with the boys. Little Joe wanted to know if Uncle Teddy really was a famous fighter, like his daddy said. "Yeah," Teddy said. "Just like he's a famous fireman."

"Didn't I tell you?" the Turkey said. "They already know I'm the most famous fireman in the state."

Lizzie wanted to know all about the "madamlaswells." Teddy told her he was too busy ducking bullets to notice any. "I bet they ain't nothin' compared to a Jersey City girl," Lizzie said.

"You could be right," Teddy said.

Tom and Joe refused to go to bed until Uncle Teddy taught them to box. He got down on his knees and showed them how to throw a left hook. Dave and Lizzie said good night with their arms around each other's waists while the boys yelled, "So long, Uncle Teddy!"

The evening left Teddy with long thoughts. Maybe there was something to getting married, having a wife who loved you, kids who looked up to you. Charlie, with a girl and a boy, seemed equally contented with life. All the way home Teddy thought about his mother's story of how she had fallen in love with his father. Could he get Kitty Dolan to fall that hard for him?

Two nights later, when Kitty answered her telephone at 47 Boyd Avenue, a man said, "Is this Miss Dolan's grammar and pronunciation school?"

"Who's speaking?" Kitty asked.

"A guy who needs a few lessons. Don't you recognize my voice?"

"When would you like to start, Lieutenant Fleming?"

"Maybe we can have our first session at a restaurant in New York. I got tickets to the Ziegfeld Follies. You can come along if you guarantee me a pass*ing* grade." He made a point of pronouncing "ing" completely.

"Oh—absolutely," Kitty said.

"I'll pick you up around five," the ex-lieutenant said.

Kitty rushed to tell her mother the news. "Don't count your chickens before they've hatched," Mary Fitzmaurice Dolan said. "You're dealing with a man who's been around. He's not going to fall into your arms like some character in a novel."

Kitty dismissed her mother's pessimism. She also ignored the wry way Teddy Fleming had launched his courtship. He wanted those grammar and pronunciation lessons—and he wanted Kitty Dolan. But he was not going to become her humble pupil, before, during, or after he got a passing grade. First, last, and always he was going to be the man in charge.

# 16

# The Big Win

$T$hose Germans wasn't the brightest guys in the world by a long shot. But they was damn well trained."

Teddy Fleming was telling a story about the Argonne to Tom Dolan. Kitty, sitting on the couch to his right, pulled at her earlobe twice. She was warning Teddy he had made two grammatical errors in that remark. Kitty had worked out a code that told Teddy when he made a mistake.

On the Boyd Avenue front porch, later in the evening, Teddy asked Kitty what he had said wrong. "It should be 'those Germans *weren't*,'" Kitty said. "And 'they *were* well trained.' If the subject is plural—Germans—they—the verb should be plural."

"I keep missing that one," Teddy said.

"At least you didn't say '*them* Germans,'" Kitty said with a smile. "You're learning fast."

Teddy was starting to like the idea of straightening out his grammar and pronunciation. He had straightened out his teeth. This was part of the same process—talking right was as important as looking right. He liked the way a woman with Kitty Dolan's class was taking the trouble to give him some polish. He did not like getting corrected, but Kitty's silent signals made it a private matter, strictly between the two of them.

Teddy was working at City Hall in the tax assessor's office. Doc

Holland had cut his deal with Frank Hague, which gave him the clout to land jobs for some of his key people. But Hague was the tough negotiator Doc said he was. He wouldn't pay Teddy more than $2,000 a year. Doc made up some of the difference from the ward's gambling take, and the umpiring business had been good for over a thousand a year, so Teddy wasn't hurting for money. But that was hardly the main point.

All the other ward leaders in Jersey City were getting into line, recognizing Hague as the Democratic Party's leader in Jersey City and Hudson County. The mayor and his four fellow commissioners had been reelected in 1921 by a solid majority. People talked about the "Hague Organization" as if it were here to stay.

At City Hall Teddy had gotten friendly with a guy named Billy Black. Billy was an uptown Catholic who had a high school education and was a reader of novels and history books. His grammar and pronunciation were perfect. Kitty liked him a lot. She said Billy was the sort of man Teddy should associate with. Teddy was not so sure about that; he thought Billy lacked political smarts. But he was useful in persuading Kitty to see Teddy as husband material.

It was a kind of game. Kitty flirted with him; those beautiful eyes seemed to be inviting him into bed; she let him kiss her good night. But she was not exactly chasing him. She took vacations with her teacher friends and went to Broadway shows without him. Sometimes she talked about her brother, George, who had moved west to play baseball, making it sound as if she'd like to follow him.

That made Teddy uncertain about the whole proposition. Maybe she was too classy for him. She had expensive tastes; she wore a new dress every time he saw her. She loved to shop for clothes. She owned a closet full of hats. Could he keep a woman like that happy?

Politics was a risky business. In 1920, the Irish-Americans had gone nuts about Ireland and wrecked the Democratic Party. Davey Fleming was one of the wildest and he took Charlie with him. They had voted Republican! It was all about Woodrow Wilson's refusal to lift a presidential finger for Ireland. Throw in total disgust in the rest of the electorate with Windy Woodrow's hot air about the League of Nations and you had the makings of a political catastrophe. The Democrats lost the White House and governorships and senate and congressional seats in one of the biggest landslides in American history.

In Jersey City, Frank Hague realized the whole Democratic ticket was going down for the count. He passed the word: *Save the Skidder*. He was talking about Thomas "Skidder" Madigan, an old Second Ward pal who was running for sheriff. This was a crucial office. The sheriff selected the grand juries that Republicans could convene to investigate all sorts of things in Hudson County. They saved Skidder with a majority that was mostly stuffed into the ballot boxes in the small hours of the morning.

Last year, the Irish-Americans had regained their sanity, thanks mostly to news from Ireland that made them swear off home-country politics forever. The independence men had cut a deal with the British to set up something called the Irish Free State in the south of Ireland. In the north the Protestants were in the majority and they became a separate state too. But a lot of the independence men did not buy the deal. They wanted a united Ireland and they did not think much of the Free State, which let the British handle foreign policy and tied the Irish pound to the Bank of England. They walked out of the Irish legislature shouting insults at the Free State guys. Among their most unpleasant cracks was, "Americans!"

Most Irish-Americans backed the Free State. They thought it was more than half way to independence. In Ireland the antis reached for their guns and a civil war broke out between the Free State and the Irish Republican Army. They were still shooting each other, with the Free State guys winning. Davey Fleming and Charlie the *Gaelic American* reader could not believe it. They were totally disgusted with the Ould Sod and everyone on it.

"If I ever send them @%# micks another dollar, may God or your mother's ghost strike me dead!" Davey roared. "If that don't happen, stick me in the nearest looney bin!"

"Ditto," Charlie said. He was so disgusted that he lost his sense of humor for a good six months. Teddy restored him to normalcy, as the new Republican president, Warren Harding, liked to call it, by talking Doc Holland into getting the kid brother on the cops. It was a nice feeling, to have the clout to take care of your own that way.

The Turkey helped by razzing Charlie day and night. "What the Ireland Irish need is one month of Frank Hague as a dictator," he maintained. "He'd straighten out the whole lousy country in a week and spend the rest of the time on vacation."

Hague was definitely a take-charge guy. He demanded top-drawer results in every ward, and if he didn't get them, he wanted to know why. That meant you had to talk all the new immigrants—Slovaks, Czechs, Polish, Italians—into voting the straight ticket. When Hague said he expected a real canvass, he meant making sure every male and female in the ward over the age of twenty-one was personally urged to vote. He had the exact numbers of how many votes were in each ward and expected to see them add up right on election night.

This was totally different from "Little Bob" Davis's approach. He had lived up to his nickname, "the Easy Boss." As long as the Democrats won the election, Bob didn't ask too many questions about who turned in the best performance. Hague piled his demand for a maximum across-the-board effort on top of the usual rallies and posters and speeches by VIP politicians. When someone told him he was turning politics into a business, the mayor growled, "You're damn right I am."

The big fellow was doing something else new—something Little Bob Davis and other bosses never tried. He was going after the corporations and the railroads as if he didn't care what they could do for him in the money column. Little Bob had made most of his personal fortune by cutting deals with the Protestants under the table and through his plumbing business. He never ran for office himself. Little Bob thought that was sticking your neck out too far.

Frank Hague liked running both City Hall and the Democratic Party, and he asked the voters to approve his performance every four years. More important, he was raising money his way. Everybody in the Organization who had a city, county, or state job thanks to City Hall had to kick in three percent of his salary every year. That created a slush fund bigger than the New Jersey Democratic Party had ever seen before. It also gave Frank Hague a private bank account no one saw. There wouldn't be any complaints about that—if he kept winning elections.

That was a large if. The big fellow had nerve—maybe too much nerve. Billy Black had told Teddy a story a couple of weeks ago. Hague called Billy into his office and handed him an old battered suitcase.

"Take this to New York and give it to the names on this list," he said, slipping an envelope into Billy's hand.

Billy got on the Hudson Tubes and found himself walking up Wall Street. He went to a brokerage house and handed the suitcase to a guy who was obviously waiting for it. Ditto to a bank, and then another brokerage house. Billy noticed that the suitcase kept getting lighter. It was unquestionably empty by the time he got it back to Hague.

"What the hell was in that thing?" Billy asked.

"Money, you idiot!" Hague growled.

Nerve—but Teddy Fleming liked it. He liked the way Hague taxed the hell out of the Republicans and beat their socks off at the polls. He also liked the way he put Jersey City on the map. On July 2, 1921, Hague had lured Jack Dempsey, the heavyweight champion of the world, to town for a fight with the French challenger, Georges Carpentier. The match attracted a crowd of eighty thousand people and grossed almost a million dollars. Newsreel films of it packed theaters around the country.

Teddy happened to be nearby when Hague arrived at the arena in Boyle's Thirty Acres. He watched as the big fellow looked over the crowd, which included huge numbers of swells and sports from New York. The mayor frowned and pointed at a tall, gangling young policeman with buck teeth and a sloppy haircut. He was from South Jersey, imported to help the Jersey City police force handle the crowd. "Put that hayseed under the stands somewhere," Hague growled.

Teddy Fleming liked Hague's determination to make Jersey City look classy whenever possible. Teddy was not quite as enthusiastic about another side of the Hague operation. The mayor was delivering a "clean" city—the sort of town the priests and the women voters wanted.

Prohibition had closed all the saloons, which gave Hague a huge head start in this department. The mayor banned girlie shows in the theaters. He ordered the cops to crack down on prostitution, either on the street or in brothels, no matter how much the pimps and madams offered to pay. Bootleg booze and gambling were the only vices tolerated—and these were limited in each ward to guys with the okay from City Hall. The bootleggers, bookies, numbers men, and card sharks were told to pay a nice split to the ward leader, who was supposed to send most of it to City Hall. Doc Holland, independent as usual, kept half of his take.

Teddy saw the value of the clean-city image from a vote-getting point of view. It wowed the goo-goos and lace curtain Irish in the uptown wards. But it made Jersey City into a pretty dull town. On the other hand, New York was only a ferry ride away, and Newark, only twenty miles away in the other direction, was still wide open.

The clean image got down to the personal level in another way. The word went out from City Hall that the Organization was not going to tolerate any wild Irishmen in its ranks. Skirt chasing was off-limits, especially if it got noticed by the cops or the newspapers. The Organization wanted married men, faithful to their wives, fronting for them everywhere. Again, it was Hague's way of lining up the priests and the women voters behind him.

This year, 1922, the Hague Organization was promising to elect another governor and put the current governor, who couldn't succeed himself under the state constitution, into the U.S. Senate. If he pulled that one off, Teddy Fleming told himself, the big fellow was here to stay and a young guy could gamble on a future in the Hague Organization.

In November 1922, Hague rammed both his candidates down the Republicans' throats. Doc Holland threw a victory party in the Sixth Ward clubhouse that lasted until 5 A.M. "The sky's the limit!" Doc shouted, three or four sheets to the wind. "We got the whole damn state in our back pocket!"

In the Sixth Ward they did not have to stuff a single ballot box. Teddy Fleming had put together an organization at the ward level that canvassed and canvassed and identified voters who were too sick or too stupid to vote and got them to the polls, sometimes with cash supplied by ex-saloonkeeper George Ormsby, now the ward's bookmaker, sometimes with promises of jobs, sometimes with a fleet of cars Teddy had lined up, sometimes with the help of Monsignor Meehan, who was with the Organization heart and soul.

It was hard work, most of it done after putting in a day at City Hall. Teddy liked both sides of the job. He enjoyed getting to know people from other wards and other departments in City Hall. People admired his war record, his boxing and baseball past. In the Sixth Ward, he liked putting together a committee that piled up the votes. It was similar to a sergeant's or a lieutenant's job, shaping up an infantry company. You picked the right people and let them do a lot of it on their own. You distributed praise and some extras the army didn't provide, like free drinks and cash on election day.

After the big win, Kitty Dolan started getting a lot more attention. Teddy had managed to see her about once a week during the election push, but now it was twice and three times a week and she was starting to complain that she was too tired to teach the kiddies in her kindergarten. In mid-December the weather turned cold and snowy but Teddy still insisted on dinners and shows. By now, listening to Billy Black and practicing in private, Teddy was close to a passing grade in his speech lessons.

As they walked down Boyd Avenue past heaps of shoveled snow, Kitty began complaining about how cold her feet were in bed last night. "How about giving me a chance to keep those little tootsies warm?" Teddy said.

There was a long silence as they kept walking. The wind moaned in a nearby alley. "Does a ring come with that suggestion?" Kitty said.

"A couple of rings," he said.

"Oh," Kitty said. "Oh."

She started to cry. "What the hell's going on?" Teddy said, giving her his handkerchief.

"I—I—love you," she said. "I was getting afraid you'd never—"

"I had to sweat out this election. We did great in the ward. I think I can talk to Hague—or get Doc to talk to him—to give me a better job. It's a gamble like everything in life. You ready to roll the dice with me?"

"Yes," Kitty said. "Yes. I don't care about the money. I—love you."

He kissed her long and hard. They were standing under a streetlight. It made Kitty feel she was on a stage. She saw herself guiding this man to fame and maybe even to fortune. She was polishing his grammar and pronunciation. Now all he needed was the inspiration to aim high. That magical elixir would come from her love.

Kitty saw Teddy Fleming standing before the state senate in Trenton or before the House of Representatives or even the U.S.

Senate in Washington, D.C., charming and occasionally intimidating his fellow politicians. While at home he held Kitty in his arms and whispered: *You're the one who deserves the credit for everything I've done.*

It was a woman's version of the American dream, the pursuit of happiness through romance. The dictionary says that romance traditionally deals with "idealized" exploits and "fictitious" tales. In most respects it is the opposite of realism. Romantic Kitty Dolan was marrying a man who was intensely realistic. It was the riskiest gamble of Teddy Fleming's life.

# 17

# Sweethearts

My Dear Baby:

Tomorrow (Tuesday's meeting) means a great deal to me and this morning I felt as though I need you. In fact I know I will always need you (not bad from a dumbbell like me, what say you, Babe?) but you know what I mean. I would like to have you here to talk about it.

I feel positively sure that something is going to happen tomorrow but I do not know what it will be. I am holding out for the three th [thousand], have given Doc a very good argument to advance to the powers that be and feel sure it will go over if he has his nerve with him. I think he should have, because if I do say so myself, I have worked hard and conscientiously for him and the big fellow.

Knowing me as you do, you know how I feel at this moment. I am wondering if you remember what I told you one time about my wishes. . . .

I surely do miss you and your pleasant greetings when I come home from business, but I miss you a great deal more when I cannot say "Good night, Baby." I am wondering if you miss me half as much as I miss my little wife. I am planning to love you to death when you come home. The best advice I can give you is to rest up for the coming onslaught of your boy friend. . . .

When I read this letter for the first time, I was amazed. Teddy Fleming, the Kid Slugger who knocked guys cold with a single punch, the snarling sergeant and lieutenant who led C Company into the shellfire of St. Mihiel and the machine guns of the Argonne, had not only married Kitty Dolan, he had fallen in love with her.

It was the summer of 1924. Kitty was taking a week's vacation in Pennsylvania's Pocono Mountains with several of her schoolteacher friends. The letter reveals just how much marriage had changed Teddy Fleming, the man who resisted the sound of wedding bells for so long.

Years later Teddy's sister, Mae Fleming Gallagher, told me with considerable amusement how nervous her brother had been on the day of the ceremony, April 2, 1923. Mae had never seen him so jittery. She remarked that it was strange that a man who had the nerve to take on the German army should be so undone by the prospect of becoming a husband.

"Kitty ain't one bit nervous," Mae had said.

"Why should she be?" Teddy growled. "She's getting what she wants."

The implication that Teddy had wanted—or at least thought about—some other arrangement seems unmistakable. But Kitty had prevailed. She had made a wedding ring an essential part of their relationship. When Kitty announced their engagement, her cousin Lee Shanaphy wrote her a witty letter of congratulations in which he remarked, "I know this has been on your mind longer than hair has been on your head." Frank Hague's insistence on sexual decorum for his leaders may have played a part in Teddy's proposal. But it was at best (or worst) a minor influence. Kitty's looks and effervescent personality were the main ingredients.

Marriage had transformed Teddy Fleming in ways that would satisfy any woman's romantic dreams. He had made Kitty his confidante as well as his wife, the recipient of his deepest hopes ("wishes") for the future.

Kitty had responded with an ardor that came naturally to her romantic nature. Her letters from Pennsylvania were addressed to "My Sweetie." She told him how much she enjoyed his latest letter. "Dear, it was adorable!" She said she liked his letters so much more now than before, "when you were only my sweetheart. Now, you are my sweetheart plus!"

In a playful riff, she said it was "worth staying away from my honey to be able to read how much you miss me." She ended the letter with an amorous directive: "If I get home after supper, I want you up in our rooms where I [can] fall on your neck. When I said my prayers [last night], looking at your picture, I just had the most terrific longing for your arms and your big wonderful body next to mine. Please don't be afraid to show me, dear, how much you love me."

Teddy's letter recorded an important development in those wishes he shared with his wife. Doc Holland was going to see the big fellow— Frank Hague—to argue for a new job and a raise for Teddy Fleming. It was hardly a leap into affluence; the salary was $3,000 a year (about $31,000 in modern dollars). But it was a big jump from the $2,000 Teddy was getting as a tax assessor. Almost as important as the salary was the job itself: he wanted to become clerk of the Second Criminal Court, a job with civil service protection.

Would Doc pull it off? It is clear that Teddy had some doubts about his mentor's nerve in a confrontation with the mayor. This was hardly surprising. By this time, Hague was well-known for his explosive temper when someone disagreed with him. Teddy was reaching for a job that many other ward leaders had probably spotted as a nice plum for a young comer in their neighborhoods.

On the other hand, there was reason to hope the big fellow might be in a benevolent mood. Elsewhere in the United States during the 1920s, the Republicans were winning victory after victory over a demoralized Democratic Party. The Democrats were reeling from the mess that Woodrow Wilson had made of World War I. They were also saddled with the responsibility for Prohibition, one of the most unpopular laws ever passed by Congress. In spite of these negative national issues, Frank Hague had elected two governors and a U.S. senator in five years.

The mayor had dealt with Prohibition by ordering his candidates to run on a platform of making New Jersey "as wet as the Atlantic Ocean." His success had made him far more than a local leader. Frank Hague was now a member of the Democratic National Committee and chairman of the Democratic Party in Hudson County and the state of New Jersey.

On a personal level, Teddy's letter underscored the distance between him and Frank Hague at this point. He was not a major player in the organization. Twelve years younger than the mayor and most of his circle, Teddy was in no position to speak for himself. Doc Holland was crucial to his prospects.

Adding to the tension were new and sobering responsibilities as a husband. Shortly after Teddy and Kitty married, Tom Dolan and Mary Fitzmaurice joined them in buying a large two-family house on Randolph Avenue. It had a pleasant second-floor sunporch overlooking the quiet tree-lined street. The Dolans occupied the first floor, the Flemings the second floor. By this time, Tom Dolan had put his drinking days behind him and seemed to be in good health, ready to bring home a satisfying salary as a millwright for the Colgate-Palmolive Company for years to come.

Within a few months of moving to Randolph Avenue, Tom began suffering pain when he urinated. The doctors diagnosed cancer of the bladder. There was little that medicine could do for this killer disease in 1923. For Kitty it was a difficult time. She still loved her father deeply. She visited him almost every day in the city hospital. Many years later, she told me that often, as she left his room, he would begin to scream. The first time this happened, Kitty begged the nurses to give him some painkillers. They told her Tom was not in any pain. "He's just mad because he's dying," one of them said in a classic bit of hospital callousness.

Tom Dolan was expressing one last time his rage at the God who had taken away his first three daughters, thirty-five years earlier. It could not have been easy for Kitty Dolan to keep this explanation at a distance while she was so rapturously in love with her husband. Was it a threat, a foreboding glimpse of similar sorrow in her own life?

Tom Dolan died on May 29, 1924. This meant Teddy Fleming was now solely responsible for meeting the mortgage payments on 123 Randolph Avenue. Kitty's brother, George, was no help. He was still pursuing a career as a baseball pitcher. He spent most of each year playing for a minor-league team in the West, whose name was never mentioned in surviving letters. When his father died, it took George twenty-eight hours on trains to return for the funeral.

By this time, Teddy seems to have acquired a somewhat negative opinion of his brother-in-law. In one of his letters to Kitty, he remarked that they had received two more "books" from George—he meant very long letters—in which he boasted endlessly about the good notices he was getting in the sports columns of the local papers. Teddy, a man with failed baseball dreams of glory in his own past, seems to have been more than a little skeptical of George's ability to reach the majors.

On the other hand, Teddy had grown very fond of his mother-in-law, Mary Fitzmaurice Dolan, whom he called "the Mama." One reason may have been her skill in the kitchen. Several of his letters to Kitty referred to a delicious dinner he had just enjoyed. In fact, Mary was so expert at the stove that Kitty felt intimidated by her, and thus far in their marriage she and Teddy had been eating all their meals on the first floor of 123 Randolph Avenue, while they enjoyed the "rooms" on the second floor, more like star boarders than a separate family.

To Teddy's vast relief, Doc Holland did not lose his nerve in Frank Hague's office. Doc found the mayor surprisingly receptive to his plea to give Teddy the court clerk's job. It was a cause for celebration. "The husband," as Teddy wryly called himself in his letters, had increased his salary by a third and had landed a job that would be more or less immune to the ups and downs of politics.

Teddy was still doing a lot of umpiring, because they needed the money. Sometimes Kitty went along to watch him perform. They were so in love, she wanted to share everything, even though his attempts to explain baseball to her went nowhere. She still wondered why a man could score from third base on a sacrifice fly.

One fall day in 1924, Teddy was umpiring behind home plate in a game that was a hot contest between the semipro Jersey City "Willows" and a team from North Bergen. A lot of money had been bet and a lot of bootleg bourbon and rye with beer chasers was being consumed in the stands. When Teddy called a Willows hitter out on strikes with two men on base, ending the inning, the Willows fans became incensed. One drunken complainer screamed aspersions on Teddy's legitimacy and the legitimacy of all his ancestors back to Saint Patrick's days. Teddy looked over his shoulder and told him to shut the hell up.

The guy jumped out of the stands and came at Teddy with a carving knife as the first North Bergen batter of the inning reached the plate. The batter and the Willows catcher fled. Teddy stood his ground. Dropping his chest protector, he ducked the drunk's slash and knocked him cold with a right cross.

That night Kitty tearfully urged her husband to quit umpiring. Teddy agreed, pretending that she was making up his mind for him. In fact, he had been thinking about it for a year. Umpiring was not a good job for a man who wanted to get somewhere in politics. But Teddy saw it made Kitty feel good to think she was telling him what to do. He did not realize he was creating an illusion of power that she would never possess about anything he considered important.

The good news from City Hall made the Flemings start thinking about another step in their married lives—beginning a family. On their wedding night at the Hotel Pennsylvania in New York, Teddy had told Kitty he was planning to use a condom. "It'd be a shame for us to lose that nice salary you're making," he said. "Let's do it this way for a year or two."

It made sense financially. By this time Kitty was bringing home over $2,000 a year. But this form of birth control was strongly condemned by the Catholic Church. Kitty adjusted her conscience by telling herself it was her husband's decision. Both newlyweds were only nominal Catholics at this point in their lives.

Judging from their letters, contraception did not have any negative effect on the Flemings' love life. Now, with Teddy's promotion, there was enough money to get along without Kitty's salary as a teacher—and she wanted children. Early in 1925, she became pregnant, and immediately resigned from her job. Pregnant teachers were forbidden in the public schools of Jersey City, as well as many other cities. Apparently, the educational powers of the era thought it would lead to children asking questions about where babies came from.

In the late fall of 1925, Kitty gave birth to a girl. Like most women at the time, she had the baby at home. Hospitals were still considered dangerous, germ-ridden places—with good reason. Their family doctor was in attendance, and for a while everything seemed to be proceeding normally. Teddy stayed downstairs with Mary Fitzmaurice Dolan while his sister, Mae, who had already given birth to a girl and a boy, helped the doctor in the second-floor rooms.

Teddy was nervous, but no more so than any prospective father. Kitty's labor pains led to not a few cries of distress, which made him yearn to do something, anything, to ease her ordeal. Mary Fitzmaurice Dolan poured him another drink of the bottle of bourbon he had bought from the Sixth Ward's bootlegger for the celebration.

Suddenly Mae was in the doorway, tears streaming down her lovely face. "Terrible news," she said, wiping her eyes. "It's a beautiful baby girl. But she's born dead."

Teddy was bewildered. He had seen death a thousand times in the Argonne and St. Mihiel. He knew women died in childbirth. But a baby? "What happened?"

"The umbilical cord—around her throat," Mae said.

"How's Kitty? Does she know?" Teddy asked.

"She wants to see you," Mae said.

Teddy bolted up the stairs and down the hall to the bedroom. Kitty was pale and exhausted. The doctor was bathing her face. "I'm sorry," he said. "There was nothing anyone could do."

"You know what happened?" Kitty said.

Teddy nodded.

"Don't you want to see her?" Kitty asked.

"No," Teddy said. He had seen enough death on the Western Front to last him a lifetime. "I really don't."

"I want you to see her!" Kitty cried. "She's on the dining room table. She's your daughter!"

*No she isn't, she's dead*, Teddy thought. He had seen what death did to the living in the Argonne. It turned them to meaningless clumps of flesh. It was demoralizing. It ruined your nerve. It was better to avoid it if possible.

"Go see her. What are you afraid of? She can't hurt you!" Kitty said. "Aren't you a war hero?"

She was almost hysterical. Teddy had no idea he was dealing with a woman who could no longer tolerate disappointment. A woman who felt life, God, fate, owed her recompense for too many years of heartbreak.

With great reluctance, Teddy went into the dining room and gazed for a long moment at the silent little corpse. The child was ugly, blotched with blood; the face had a bluish tinge. For a minute he thought was going to get sick. He thought of the German officer he had killed while he was trying to surrender. Was this payback for that mistake? That made no sense. He struggled to get a grip on his nerves.

Behind him, Teddy heard a sound, something between a sob and a sigh. Mary Fitzmaurice Dolan stood in the doorway. "You'll have another one," she said. "We don't know why these things happen. We have to go on living. I just said the same thing to Kitty."

"You're right, Mama," Teddy said.

He went back to the bedroom and lay down in the bed and took Kitty in his arms. "We'll get through this, Babe," he said. "We'll get through it together."

Kitty did not respond. She could not avoid the feeling that this disappointment was Teddy's fault. She had surrendered herself to him. In her romantic heart, she believed that meant her sweetheart should be strong enough, wise enough, brave enough to protect her against any and all failures. She had hoped Lieutenant Fleming the war hero and future political star would create a life that would enable her to forget Lester Stratton and Tom Connolly and especially Lloyd Harris, the bitterest heartbreak of them all.

Now she saw that Teddy Fleming was unable to work these miracles. He was simply another man who loved her for the time being. Maybe that too would change. Kitty began to wish she had never been born Irish Catholic, never been born in Jersey City, maybe never been born a woman. She found herself yearning for impossible fantastic things, an escape to Paris, Berlin, Hollywood. Someplace where her life would be totally different, where she might even change her name and religion and become another person.

She knew that was not going to happen. There stood realistic Mary Fitzmaurice Dolan in the doorway, a mournful smile of approval on her face. "See how much your husband loves you," she said. "You're going to have more children. You'll forget this ever happened."

No, Kitty thought. She would not forget it. Any more than she would ever forget Lloyd and the dream of escape from her Irish-American identity that he had offered her. Deep in her soul, Kitty rebelled against her mother's hard-eyed realism. Perhaps she knew, or at least sensed, that she was sharing a fundamental emotion with her father. But even as she rebelled, Kitty knew her Jersey City life with Teddy Fleming would continue. There was nothing she could do to stop it.

# 18

# The Birth of the Blues

For a while, Mary Fitzmaurice Dolan's insistence on life's ability to renew love and hope seemed to prevail. Kitty slowly recovered from the sorrow of her lost daughter. She began to enjoy Teddy Fleming's love again. In the fall of 1926 she became pregnant, and on July 5, 1927, delivered a healthy baby boy. To prove her renewed feelings for husband, she insisted on naming him Thomas J. Fleming Jr. and calling him Teddy.

My father wanted to call me David, in tribute to his older brother who had named his first son after him. But Kitty was insistent on making me a "Junior" (and also honoring Tom Dolan) and he let her have her way. I think it was an attempt to convince herself and her husband that her feelings about him had not changed.

I remember nothing whatsoever from the first two years of my life. For Kitty and Teddy Fleming, they were tumultuous times. Politically, the Irish-Americans made their first bid for national power. The governor of New York, Al Smith, won the presidential nomination in 1928. Continuing Little Bob Davis's tradition of partnership with New York's Tammany Hall, Frank Hague had become a friend and early backer of Smith. He had supported him in the 1924 Democratic national convention.

In one of his letters to Kitty while she was vacationing in the summer of 1924, Teddy told her of going to the convention at

Madison Square Garden. Frank Hague encouraged his followers to be part of the cheering crowd during the roll-call votes in Smith's contest with William Gibbs McAdoo, Woodrow Wilson's son-in-law. "You should have seen the demonstration when Smith passed McAdoo, 360 for Smith and 352½ for McAdoo," Teddy wrote. "I thought they would tear the Garden apart. It was impossible to get order for twenty minutes."

Eventually, neither man was able to win the required two-thirds majority and the party settled on a compromise candidate, John W. Davis of West Virginia. The brawl opened deep fissures between the Democratic Protestants of the South and the Irish Catholic backbone of the party in the North. They differed violently over two large national issues, Prohibition and the Ku Klux Klan.

The male Catholics of Jersey City, Boston, New York, and other cities loathed Prohibition, which had closed thousands of saloons and disrupted their social lives. Publicly, the men accepted the law because their priests and women favored it. Privately, they responded by tolerating bootleg liquor and speakeasies wherever they could get away with it. During the 1920s no one who wanted a drink in New Jersey had much trouble finding one. Under Democratic governors the state lived up to Frank Hague's defiant call to make it as wet as the Atlantic Ocean.

About the Ku Klux Klan there was no disagreement. With its "America for the Americans" and its hatred of blacks, Jews, and Catholics, the bedsheet wearers were a revival of the worst side of American Protestantism. With these two handicaps, John W. Davis's 1924 presidential campaign was a disaster of staggering proportions. The Republican candidate, Calvin Coolidge, was able to overcome massive financial scandals in the regime of his predecessor, Warren G. Harding, and win by an incredible eight million votes. Davis did not carry a single state outside the South.

At the 1928 convention, the Irish-led Democrats of the North were able to intimidate the southern delegates with reminders of the 1924 debacle. Al Smith won the presidential nomination on the first ballot. But the ensuing campaign made it clear that the party had not repaired the fissures that were destroying it. In spite of a courageous speech in Oklahoma City defending his Catholicism and calling for tolerance for all religions, Smith was unable to persuade America's Protestant majority that a Catholic in the White House would not be a menace to the Constitution.

The Ku Klux Klan unanimously backed the Republican candidate, Herbert Hoover, though he disdained their support. Pamphlets full of vicious slanders against Catholics circulated by the millions. Over one hundred anti-Catholic newspapers spewed five million copies a week full of venom. Mrs. Ed C. Alumbaugh, sometimes called "the Protestant Joan of Arc," distributed handbills declaring, "To Murder Protestants! And Destroy the American government! Is the oath binding Roman Catholics." A Lutheran minister asked a mass meeting in New York, "Shall we have a man in the White House who acknowledges allegiance to the autocrat on the Tiber, who hates democracy, public schools, individual right and everything that is essential to independence?"

Smith's New York accent and his Tammany Hall background were ridiculed and denounced with equal savagery. Totally dismissed was his progressive record as a legislator and four-term governor of New York. Smith had pioneered laws creating the eight-hour day, the minimum wage, and workmen's compensation. He banned sweatshops and enforced tough safety standards in the workplace. He worked closely with like-minded Jewish and other ethnic Americans to build new schools and hospitals that mitigated the harshness of life in the slums. Yet William Allen White, a normally rational newspaper editor from Kansas, proclaimed, "Tammany is Tammany and Smith is its prophet."

White and millions of other WASPs refused to believe a political organization could mature and pursue new goals. The Kansan insisted the Democratic candidate was threatening "the whole Puritan civilization which has built a sturdy, orderly nation."

In November, Al Smith lost in a landslide almost as big as the one that had buried John C. Davis. He carried only two northern states, Massachusetts and Rhode Island. It was a painful time to be an Irish Catholic Democrat, and no one took it harder than Katherine Dolan Fleming. The election confirmed her already strong suspicion that Irish-American politics was a messy repellent business that would never win the respectability and social position for which she yearned.

Kitty paid particular attention to the attacks on Al Smith's wife, another Katherine, known to friends as Katie. Nasty critics compared her unfavorably to the Republican candidate's wife, slim, attractive Lou Hoover, who was a graduate of Stanford and had accompanied her famous husband all over the world during his business and political career. After five children, Katie Smith had grown fat and she had no instinct for fashion. Like her husband, she also had a lower-class New York accent and downtown social style. One Republican national committeewoman asked a Washington audience to imagine Mrs. Smith greeting a foreign ambassador who congratulates her on her gown. "You said a mouthful!" Katie Smith would reply.

Kitty agreed with the Republicans that Katie would be a disaster as First Lady. When she ventured this opinion at a family dinner party in Mae Fleming Gallagher's house, the Flemings denounced her as a traitor to the Democratic Party. Old Davey Fleming, always inclined to a no-holds-barred argument, pounded the table and reminded everyone that a Republican First Lady, Mrs. William McKinley, used to have epileptic fits at state dinners and they often had to put a napkin over her head. Had any Democratic First Lady ever sunk that low?

Kitty concluded that Davey was the thick mick to end them all. At home later that evening, Teddy Fleming warned her to keep her opinion of Mrs. Smith to herself. His sharp tone was not conducive to a loving good night.

In New Jersey, where the Ku Klux Klan was active in the rural counties, Al Smith lost in a landslide that was closer to an avalanche. Edward I. Edwards, running for reelection to the U.S. Senate, was buried in the disaster, and the Democratic candidate for governor met a similar fate. The state's Republicans, hoping they were riding a wave of anti-Irish-American sentiment, tried to translate the momentum of the state and national victories into an assault on the Hague Organization. With the mayor up for reelection in 1929, the *Jersey Journal* gloated, "Yesterday the whole state turned thumbs down on Hague. Next May it will be Jersey City's turn."

In the midst of this gathering storm, the Fleming family suffered a painful and unexpected blow. In February, Charlie Fleming collapsed with excruciating stomach pains and was rushed to the hospital, where he underwent an appendectomy. This operation was considered major surgery in 1929. Anything that involved penetrating the stomach wall raised the specter of infection and death.

The surgeon issued orders that Charlie was to remain on a strictly liquid diet for several days. Charlie apparently regarded this prohibition as one more solemn pronouncement to be taken lightly. When some friends showed up at the hospital the day after his surgery with a quart of ice cream, he gulped it cheerfully and warned them to ditch the carton where the nurses would not find it. Two hours later, he went into convulsions. By the morning of February 13, he was dead. He left a wife and three children, the youngest only seven years old, whom the surviving Flemings pooled their slender resources to support.

Meanwhile, the mayoralty election heated up. The *Jersey Journal* opened its pages to one of Hague's most savage critics, Dr. Francis L. Golden, who made a specialty of nasty jokes about Hague's growing wealth. Old enemies in the Democratic Party came out of semiretirement, and halfhearted friends, many of them former backers of Otto Wittpenn, switched sides. Soon a fusion ticket of Republicans and Democrats took shape, backed by plenty of money from the state Republican Party. For a while it looked like Frank Hague was in trouble.

The opposition pointed with special ferocity to the mayor's extravagant lifestyle. He had moved into a duplex apartment at 2600 Hudson County Boulevard and bought a $100,000 summer mansion in fashionable Deal, New Jersey. He also acquired a substantial house in Florida and had his picture taken sailing to Europe with his elegantly dressed wife. Where had all this money come from, the opposition cried, on a salary of $8,250 a year?

Kitty Fleming knew a lot about where the money had come from. She had heard her husband tell with wry amusement the story of Billy Black taking the suitcase full of cash to Wall Street. She listened to Teddy talk on the telephone to Doc Holland about certain Sixth Ward employees who had failed to pay the required three percent of their annual salaries to City Hall. She may have heard Teddy and his friends discussing how the big fellow had made a bundle when the Holland Tunnel, which enabled cars to drive beneath the Hudson River between New Jersey and New York, was built in 1927. Through a dummy company, Hague had bought real estate around the Jersey City side of the tunnel and sold it to the tunnel builders for a nice profit. Kitty said nothing in public, of course, but her opinion of Frank Hague sank to a new low.

Teddy Fleming's opinion moved in the opposite direction. He thought Hague was entitled to live well, as Little Bob Davis had done before him. Hague had to operate under the table because he had decided to go it alone, without any of the theoretically legal deals with Protestant Republican businessmen that had made Davis rich. As an Irish-American Teddy admired Hague's nerve. He was risking jail time, if anyone in the know betrayed him. The big fellow was relying on the loyalty of the Organization, something else that stirred Teddy Fleming's deepest emotions.

Hague won the May 1929 mayoral election, but many people thought it was a dubious triumph. His margin of victory was barely 25,000 votes, only half his previous majority. More ominous was the rise of the opposition. In 1925, the Republicans had gotten only 10,000 votes. This time they polled 43,000, almost all from the Protestant and lace curtain Irish uptown wards. Hague's opponents were gleefully proclaiming that they could hardly wait to run against him again in 1933. Rumors swept the city and state that the mayor was planning to flee to Europe with his illicit gains, as more than one New York Tammany chieftain had decamped in earlier decades.

Teddy Fleming and the rest of the Organization were certain that the big fellow would never cut and run. Hadn't Al Smith telegraphed the mayor congratulations for his victory? They looked past the supposedly ominous election numbers to the fact that the mayor had received only 500 votes less than in 1925. His original downtown backers were still loyal and they had proven their political know-how by registering 23,000 new voters from the Italian, Slovak, Polish, and Czech sections of the lower wards.

On the night of the victory, Hague's followers staged a huge demonstration around City Hall. The streets were packed for blocks in all directions. When the mayor arrived in his limousine, he could not get near the building, and he had no better luck trying to squeeze through the crowd. The cheering thousands solved the problem by hoisting the victor on their shoulders and passing him into the building and up the stairs to the mayor's office, where they deposited him on his desk. Hague stood up on the desk and thanked them for winning "a victory for the people."

The cheers all but demolished the building. These were the sons and daughters of the people who had been forced to deny their religion to get a job in Jersey City, who remembered their fathers and grandfathers telling them about Protestants in City Hall sneering, "Irishmen are nowhere." Teddy Fleming told himself those memories created the sort of loyalty that would keep Frank Hague winning elections for a long time.

The exasperated Republicans, who had solid majorities in both houses of the state legislature, appointed an investigating committee that demanded Hague tell them where he had acquired such a large fortune since 1913, when he won his first major public office. Hague grimly declined to answer. He said his personal finances were a private matter, and took refuge behind the constitutional right against self-incrimination.

The mayor's Irish-American followers had no trouble with this answer. But it did not go down well elsewhere. "If Mr. Hague himself would come clean; if he would tell the truth and shame his enemies with the truth, what a triumph would be his," said the *Newark Evening News* in an editorial. "A man who has nothing to conceal, a man whose life is an open book, does not fall back on the right to privacy or other technical safeguards when his reputation is at stake."

I don't know whether Kitty Fleming read those words, but she agreed with the sentiment. Her dislike of Frank Hague deepened—at the very time when her husband's loyalty was growing more intense. To Kitty, Hague was a continuation, even the culmination, of the downtown Irish who had made her ashamed to have a name like Dolan. She was disenchanted with what she saw as Hague's patent lack of honesty and she continued to be repelled by his lower-class argot, which power and prominence had not improved. After she had labored so hard to clean up her husband's grammar, Teddy Fleming had attached himself to a leader who regularly said such things as, "There wasn't no truth to them statements."

Inevitably this gap between Kitty's opinion and her husband's opinion became visible. Teddy Fleming reacted with anger and often with cutting sarcasm—a talent he had not revealed in his courting days. He told Kitty to grow up, to get used to how things worked in politics, especially Jersey City politics. Hague had not invented the three percent contribution from city employees. It was paid in Chicago and

Kansas City and plenty of other places, including Atlantic City, where there was a Republican machine that ran prostitution rings and, on election day, imported floaters by the trainload from the bigger, equally corrupt Republican machine in Philadelphia each election day.

Frank Hague had not invented the idea that the guy who runs things gets a slice of the profits. Tycoons like Henry Ford and John D. Rockefeller walked away with millions of dollars a year. Compared to their swag, Frank Hague was taking peanuts.

Teddy did more than defend Frank Hague. He pointed out the many good things the Organization had done for Jersey City. They had wrested tens of millions in taxes out of the railroads and the express companies and other corporations that had been paying little or nothing for the huge amount of city land they owned. The city now had a decent hospital and a good maternity clinic for poor women. There were dozens of playgrounds and parks on what had been weedy open lots. While mobsters in Chicago, New York, and other cities were shooting people in the streets, Jersey City's mostly Irish-American cops kept the Mafia and other Prohibition-spawned hoodlums at bay.

Kitty listened, disappointment turning her face petulant and stony. For her, the Hague Organization's corruption fatally tarnished its accomplishments, which did not impress her very much in the first place. She did not seem to realize that she was inflicting serious wounds on her marriage. No doubt she felt Frank Hague was inflicting them. Or Teddy Fleming, who persisted in admiring this arrogant, dishonest, uneducated man.

In Trenton, the drama of Hague versus New Jersey's Republicans reached a climax. Summoned before both houses of the state legislature, convened in righteous panoply, Hague still stubbornly declined to answer any questions about his personal wealth. The legislature held him in contempt and put him under arrest. Hague's lawyers appealed to Vice Chancellor John J. Fallon, former Hudson County counsel, one of the many Hague followers appointed by the two Democratic governors the Organization had elected. Judge Fallon issued a writ of habeas corpus, arguing that the legislature, by inquiring into Hague's personal affairs, was usurping a judicial function. The court of errors and appeals upheld him and Frank Hague said he was "very pleased by the decision. It was exactly what I expected."

Still, to the lace curtain Irish of the uptown wards Hague had lost his reformer image. He was receding to the status of a typical political boss, with a reputation for dishonesty and corruption. Again, rumors swirled that he was thinking of fleeing to Europe. He was supposedly being pursued by the IRS for more than a million dollars in back taxes.

If the Republican Party had stayed in power in Trenton and the nation, Frank Hague's reign in Jersey City and New Jersey might well have been on the way to an early and unpleasant end, spelling finis to Teddy Fleming's political career. America was prosperous. President Hoover had gotten elected on the slogan "A chicken in every pot and a car in every garage," and he seemed to be delivering. The stock market was going up and up. Business was booming. Everyone began to think maybe the president was right, America was on its way to eliminating poverty.

On October 24, 1929, the bottom dropped out of Wall Street and Republican prosperity went into a nosedive from which it never recovered. Frank Hague was suddenly transformed from a politician on the defensive to a titan of ever-swelling power. Many of the older Protestant families who had been the backbone of Hague's Jersey City opposition lost everything as banks and businesses collapsed. For thousands of Irish Catholic uptowners, who thought they had achieved the security of the middle class, the raw poverty of their parents suddenly rose, Dracula-like, from the grave of the past to confront them. A city job became not a way out of the slums but a form of salvation, and Frank Hague, the man who controlled the jobs, had to be propitiated and supported, not opposed and voted out of office.

None of these realities was immediately apparent to those who were living through this national trauma. The stock market of the 1920s had dipped before and always resumed its dizzying upward climb. Through most of 1930, there were sputters of revival, followed by more declines. Most people still thought recovery was just around the corner.

The Flemings were absorbed by something more personal than the growing fear of a national economic collapse. Kitty was pregnant again. This time, she told everyone, it was going to be a girl who would replace the baby that had died so tragically in 1925. As the pregnancy advanced, she found herself more and more absorbed in fantasies of how she would raise this daughter. Katherine would be her name—but she would be called Kay. Kitty had never really liked her nickname. She would make sure Kay had a college education. She would insist on renting or buying a summer house at the Jersey shore, where Kay would have a chance to meet Protestant boys, or Catholic boys with a decent education and an interest in a business or professional career.

To make sure nothing went wrong, Kitty decided she would have the baby in a lying-in hospital in the southern section of Jersey City known as Greenville. She went into labor around 5 P.M. on September 14. Teddy happened to get a ride home that night from Gene Ertle, the leader of the Eighth Ward. He was a funny lively man; Kitty liked him. Gene cheerfully volunteered to drive her and Teddy to the lying-in hospital.

Late the next morning, the baby was born. Like many second births, it was a relatively easy delivery. Teddy appeared in the doorway of Kitty's room a few minutes later with a big smile on his face. "Another boy," he said. "If we keep it up, we can start our own baseball team."

Kitty burst into near hysterical tears. Another disappointment! Somehow this one seemed particularly malign. "I wanted a girl so much!" she sobbed.

"Maybe the next time," Teddy said.

"I'm thirty-nine years old. I don't think there'll be a next time."

"Can we name him after Dave?" Teddy said.

"No!" Kitty said. "I don't want him to grow up and marry an idiot like Lizzie."

Her attack on Dave's wife was not really personal; it was an explosion of anger at the way she was involved with all the Flemings, who seemed to bring her nothing but disappointment piled on disappointment.

"I hope you never say anything like that where Dave or one of his kids might hear it," Teddy said.

"Oh, I don't mean it. I wanted a girl!" Kitty wailed.

"Okay. What about Charlie?"

"No. Let's call him Eugene. After Gene Ertle."

"After Gene? He's a good guy but he's not exactly my best friend."

"Eugene," Kitty said. "Eugene David Fleming. That has a distinguished sound. I want him to be distinguished. I want both my children to be distinguished. I want them to be people of importance!"

She was close to raving. She was ready to say almost anything to disagree with him. "Baby," Teddy said, "I don't understand what's going on in your head."

"Of course you don't," Kitty said. For a terrible moment she was tempted to add, *How could an Irish lug like you understand anything that goes on in a woman's head?*

She did not say it. She was appalled that she almost said it. Over the next few days, as Kitty recovered from the birth, she lectured herself on her wayward thoughts. She had to stop thinking them, somehow. She was married to this man. He loved her. Wasn't that the important thing?

Early on the day Kitty was scheduled to leave the lying-in hospital, one of the nurses handed her a letter. Kitty wondered idly who in the world it could be from. She had gotten phone calls and notes from her many friends. She did not recognize this handwriting.

> Mrs Fleming: I thought you'd like to know your husband has developed a wandering eye. He's in and out of Peggy Flanagan's house on Arlington Avenue two or three times a week. She's redheaded and *very* pretty. Her husband lost his job on Wall Street last year and disappeared. She's *lonely*, you know what I mean?
>
> A neighbor and friend

Kitty lay there, propped against the pillows of her bed for a half hour, a woman of stone again. She believed every word of this awful letter. It made horrible sense. She knew when Teddy Fleming used a condom on their wedding night that this was not the first time he had slept with a woman. She had adjusted her mind to that disappointing fact. Men were different. He was thirty-four years old. You couldn't expect him to remain a virgin. But it still bothered her. Now this. Now this! It was the perfect way to get even with her because she did not fall down and admire Frank Hague.

Gene Ertle and Teddy arrived around 4 P.M. to take her home.

Gene was amusing. "I'm really honored that the kid's been named after me. But I'm also nervous. My wife is gonna start checkin' the calendar, trying to figure out exactly where I was nine months ago."

Kitty managed to force a smile. Little Eugene remained asleep for the ride. Up the steep steps to the door of 123 Randolph Avenue Kitty climbed, to be welcomed by her beaming mother. She handed the baby to Mary Fitzmaurice Dolan and Teddy invited Gene to join them for a drink. They had just gotten some good scotch from the ward's bootlegger. Gene said he had better get home and work on an alibi that would convince his wife.

After fifteen minutes or so of cooing and cuddling, Mary Fitzmaurice Dolan gave the baby back to Kitty. His three-year-old brother, Teddy Jr., was taking a late-afternoon nap. Kitty carried the baby upstairs, with her husband solicitously holding her arm. The moment the door closed on their apartment, Kitty turned on Teddy Fleming and said, "You've been seeing Peggy Flanagan. I know all about it!"

She had never seen him so staggered. Not even on the day she had made him look at their dead baby girl. "What the hell are you talking about?" he said.

"I'm talking about adultery," Kitty said. "I'm talking about a divorce! I'm talking about betraying my love! Making a mockery of your wedding vows!"

"Kitty—you really are going nuts. Who told you this?"

"I have a letter from a neighbor who saw you going into that woman's house."

"That's true. She's broke and she's got a three-year-old kid and no husband. She needs a job. She called me."

"You couldn't see her at the Sixth Ward clubhouse? You had to make a *personal* visit?"

"Goddamn it, Kitty. That's all I did. All! I swear on this baby's soul. On little Teddy's soul. I didn't do another thing! I didn't touch that woman beyond a handshake. I'm gonna get her a job at the county courthouse."

"I don't believe you," Kitty raged. "You're a liar like your hero, Frank Hague. You and he and your friends think you can get anything you want, do anything you want, break the law, steal, bribe, be unfaithful to your wives, and lie about it. Because most people are stupid enough to believe you. But I'm not! I'll never believe you again about anything!"

It was catastrophic. There is no other word for it. Kitty's words shredded the fabric of their love, leaving it in tatters. Was Teddy Fleming guilty? Was he lying? Was lying basic to the whole Hague operation, as Kitty claimed? Even if it was, did that mean Teddy Fleming was lying about Peggy Flanagan? I would spend many years of my life pondering those unanswerable questions.

Lieutenant Thomas J. (Teddy)
Fleming a few months after he
won his commission in the battle
of the Argonne

Katherine Dolan in South Plainfield, New Jersey, with her fiancé,
Lloyd Harris, about 1912

A cheerful Teddy Fleming
in Atlantic City on his
honeymoon

Katherine Dolan
Fleming looks
equally happy

Teddy Fleming with his sons, Gene and Teddy Jr., on the beach in Point Pleasant in 1933

Katherine Dolan Fleming with her sons, Gene and Teddy, in Jersey City around 1936

Frank Hague greets Franklin D. Roosevelt at the gigantic rally the mayor staged in Sea Girt, New Jersey, during the presidential election of 1932.

Teddy Fleming (first row, second from the right) takes charge of the Sixth Ward Committee shortly after he became leader in 1933.

Teddy Fleming about 1939, when he was chairman of the Hudson County Board of Chosen Freeholders

David Fleming at the wedding of one of his daughters

Mary Fitzmaurice Dolan (Nana) with Katherine Dolan Fleming at Point Pleasant Beach in the 1930s

Teddy Fleming with Teddy Jr. and Gene, relaxing during a day trip to the Catskills

The Fleming family at home in Jersey City in 1943

Teddy Fleming Jr. home
on leave from boot camp,
with his brother, Gene

Katherine Dolan Fleming on
her way to church at Point
Pleasant Beach

Teddy Fleming takes the oath of office as sheriff of Hudson County in 1945.

Katherine Dolan Fleming in her later years, about 1945

Gil Malmasson returns the ring lost in the Argonne Forest in 1968.

# 19

# Leader

Shake hands like a man. You've got a kid brother now. You've got to set an example for him."

Those words are my earliest memory of my father. The year was 1930. I was three years old. I put my soft tiny hand in his big muscular one and he squeezed it. I yelped with pain.

"Don't you have any sense?" my mother cried. "You could hurt him."

I ran sobbing to my mother and she kissed my twinging hand. Mary Fitzmaurice Dolan, whom I called Nana, laughed good-naturedly. "Come on now. It didn't hurt that much. Don't be a momma's boy."

I had no idea that there was potential trouble in that term, "momma's boy." I only knew it confused me. What was wrong with being a momma's boy? My mother was beautiful and always nice to me, while Nana was old and gray with wrinkles on her face and she often told me to pick up my toys or clean up my room in a voice that sounded unpleasant.

Nana lived on the first floor at 123 Randolph Avenue but she often came upstairs to help my mother clean the house. Each night she cooked dinner for us.

As for my father, I liked him most of the time. But he was big and a little scary. He had a deep voice and sometimes he yelled at my mother and she yelled back. But most of the time he was cheerful and he brought me lots of presents—candy almost every night and at Eastertime a big chocolate rabbit.

For my third birthday my father gave me a baseball glove. He got out a glove of his own and we threw a rubber ball back and forth. I seldom caught it but it was fun anyway. I liked it when he told me I had a "good arm." When I told my mother, she said, "I want you to have a good brain."

My next important memory was two years later, when I was almost five. I had my own bedroom, just off the dining room. My two-year-old brother, Gene, slept in another room off the kitchen. I liked the location of my bedroom. Never a good sleeper, I often stayed awake and listened to what my parents were saying at supper.

They usually dined late, because my father was often delayed at the Sixth Ward Democratic Party clubhouse, where he was the assistant leader. Sometimes I crawled to the end of the bed and peered into the dining room to make a remark on what I had just overheard. In May of 1932 I did this at the wrong time.

"We're not going to the shore this summer," my father said.

"Oh! Why not?" my mother cried.

It was already hot. Peering out, I noticed that my mother's thick dark hair was damp with sweat. Some of her hair spilled over her high white forehead. She sat very straight, like Nana, who was not at the dinner table that night. She was probably visiting her cousins, Lee Shanaphy and his sister, Minnie, who called her "Aunt Mary." They lived on the west side of Jersey City.

"Can't we go even for two weeks?" my mother said. "I can't stand a summer without the beach."

"You're gonna have to," my father said.

"Don't say 'gonna.' 'Going to,'" my mother said. "I don't know why you still say that."

"I don't give a damn how you pronounce it," my father snapped. "We're *going* to stay right here. The most we can manage is maybe four or five day trips."

He leaned on the "ing" in "going." I missed the sarcasm, of course. Teddy Fleming was telling Kitty he was no longer interested in her grammar lessons.

"I want to go to the beach!" I cried. I loved digging in the sand and running down to the water and racing back as a big wave broke. Last summer my mother had taken a picture of me sitting in a hole my father had dug for me and filled with water. She wrote on it, "Teddy's ocean."

"Go to sleep!" my father said.

"We can't rent a house even for a week?" my mother said.

"We can't afford it," my father said. "They're cutting everybody's salary in half."

"Why?"

"We're in a goddamn depression. Haven't you noticed? In the big one in 1893, the Flemings almost starved. This one's worse. The country's flat on its back!"

"I bet the mayor isn't cutting his salary."

"I'm not the mayor!"

I had no idea that the conversation had veered into dangerous territory. Teddy Fleming was not inclined to tolerate Kitty's opinion of how Frank Hague ran Jersey City. He was even less happy to be reminded of the days when the Flemings were the poorest of the poor.

"I want to go to the beach!" I yelled, crouching at the foot of the bed, close to the door.

Suddenly my father loomed over me. "I told you to go to sleep!" he said.

"Why can't we go to the beach?" I said, kneeling up, an impudent smile on my face.

His hand came out of the shadows. It did not seem to move more than six inches. It cuffed me in the face and I went flying backward the length of the bed and clunked my head against the headboard. Did it hurt! I howled.

"Oh! What did you do? What did you do?" my mother cried as she rushed into the bedroom. She picked me up and held me against her. I could feel her breasts. Her delicate fingers, which could riffle the keys of a piano so beautifully, probed my blond hair.

"He's got a bump the size of a baseball!" she cried. "He might have a concussion!"

"I told him to go to sleep," my father said. "Why the hell don't you teach him to do what he's told?"

"It's all right, dear," my mother said, kissing the bump. "Mommy will make it all right with lots of kisses."

But it wasn't all right. It kept hurting. I kept howling.

"Put him to bed, for Christ's sake, and let's finish dinner," my father said. "Why the hell don't you close the door so he can't listen to us?"

"Because he's afraid of the dark."

"That's ridiculous!"

Teddy Fleming, the man who had survived a month of deadly nights in the Argonne, found it hard to believe he had a son who was afraid of a dark bedroom.

My mother ignored him. She got me a glass of water and sat beside the bed, rubbing my head until I went to sleep. My father must have finished his dinner alone and headed for the Sixth Ward's club-house.

The next day was Sunday. When I got up my father was reading the newspaper on the sunporch. He was in his undershirt. I stared at his big reddish hands and wrists and thick pale arms, with their ridges and slopes of muscle. I remembered how I had hurtled backward down the bed from that slap. I wondered what would have happened if he had hit me with his fist. I might be dead like the orange cat that lived next door. He had gotten hit by a car. I had found him in the gutter a few days ago.

My father folded the newspaper and smiled at me. "How's the old noggin?" he said.

I frowned.

"Come here."

He sat me on his knee and felt my head. "That's a big bump," he said. He gave me two pennies. "Buy some candy after lunch. It'll feel better."

"Thanks," I said, although I did not feel very grateful. The bump hurt when I pressed it.

"Are we still friends?" he said, holding out his hand.

"I guess so," I said. I put my hand into his big one. He gave it a light squeeze.

Two years after the explosive day when Kitty had brought my brother, Gene, home from the lying-in hospital and flung the accusa-

tion of adultery at Teddy, along with her rampant disillusion with
Frank Hague's political organization, they were still married—and
most of the time they seemed to have put that ugly scene behind them.
Teddy had apparently convinced Kitty that the anonymous letter was
a lie. Red-haired Mrs. Flanagan had conveniently vanished from the
scene. Teddy had gotten her a secretarial job with the Internal Revenue Service in Newark.

But the wound that scene inflicted on their marriage never really
healed. An undercurrent of antagonism flickered every so often in
their conversation and in their attitudes toward many things in their
lives. Teddy Fleming was largely unbothered by these clashes. He had
grown up with a father who had an explosive temper and a mother
who laughed away his tantrums. He had no idea that a flippant or an
angry remark damaged Kitty Dolan's vision of marriage as a kind of
permanent lovefest between two perpetually adoring sweethearts.

I gradually realized that my mother and father treated me very
differently. My mother called me "Teddy-boy" and was always giving
me hugs and kisses. My father seldom if ever touched me, except for an
occasional handshake, and he never called me Teddy-boy. He called me
"kiddo" or a nickname, Butch, that my mother deplored and never used.

When my father played with me, the games were often rough. He
spent a lot of time showing me how to box, ignoring my lack of enthusiasm for the sport. "Keep your guard up," he'd say and then demonstrate a "combination" in which his fists moved so fast you didn't know
what was happening until one of them tapped you on the jaw. He
bought me an inflated punching bag on a stick and showed me how to
keep hitting it so rapidly that it made a rat-tat-tat sound like a machine
gun. I never learned to make it do that.

My mother said she didn't want me to be a boxer. She thought it
was a stupid sport—and dangerous in the bargain. My father disagreed. "If you know what you're doing, you won't get hurt," he said.
"Anyway, I'm not trying to make him a boxer. I'm just showing him
how to throw a punch. It's something he ought to know."

Teddy was drawing on his memories of Davey Fleming teaching
him how to survive on his newsboy's corner on West Street. Kitty
knew no more about that part of his past than I did. "I don't want him
to be a bully," she said.

There was nothing in my comfortable, protected life to make throwing a punch seem necessary. Pretty soon the punching bag stood in a corner, abandoned, and I didn't have to defend myself against any more combinations.

I soon noticed another difference in the three most important people in my life. Someone had taught Mary Fitzmaurice Dolan (Nana) to look people in the eye. I found her bold stare a bit unsettling. She often seemed to be silently saying I had done something wrong, although most of the time she said nothing. She seldom hugged or kissed me. I somehow sensed that inside Nana was a mysterious sadness.

My mother hardly ever looked you in the eye. She did not seem to think she was good enough, or smart enough, or pretty enough, even though she was all three. Instead of looking hard at you, my mother talked. She had a lovely voice and most of the time she was very cheerful. She talked mostly about herself, her memories, her experiences, her friends.

My father avoided your eyes in a different way, as if he did not want to look too hard at you, because he might get mad. That was my first conclusion. Later I sensed something more complicated, for which my boyhood vocabulary never found a word. Now I would call it diffidence.

He hardly ever got mad at me or my brother, Gene, but he often got mad at my mother, especially when she bought a new dress or hat. "How much did that cost?" he would say. When she told him, he often said, "Jesus Christ!"

As a rule, he did not talk nearly as much as my mother. Most of the time he listened to her—although sometimes he did not pay attention. Often he would pick up a newspaper and read it while she was talking. That annoyed her. She would stop and cry, "Teddy! Are you listening to me?"

My favorite among my father's friends was Dutch. He was a big brawny guy who was full of fun. He called me "Tiger." I could not understand why my mother did not like him. When he visited, Dutch used to play rough games with me. He'd throw me up to the ceiling and catch me coming down. My mother would make exclamations of alarm but Dutch ignored her. I thought that was why she did not like him.

Dutch and my father would go out on the sunporch and close the door. One day I opened it, hoping Dutch would throw me around some more. They had a pile of money on a small table. "Close that goddamn door!" my father said.

"I'll be with you in five minutes, Tiger," Dutch said with a big grin.

Suddenly Dutch stopped coming around. I asked my father what happened to him. "He moved away," my father said.

"Far away," my mother said. She seemed glad about it.

My father gave her an angry look. But he did not get mad, which was a relief. I never asked about Dutch again.

When I was eight or nine, my mother announced she didn't like her nickname. She told my father she especially disliked his version of it, "Kit." She wanted everyone to call her Kay. No one, especially my father and her own mother, seemed to pay the slightest attention to this attempt to change her name. Only a few women friends obliged her with "Kay."

My mother's strong opinions about nicknames may have contributed to my dislike of the one I had: Teddy. A motion picture, *Theodora Goes Wild*, was a big hit in the 1930s. At St. Patrick's Parochial School, some wiseguys in my class made fun of "Teddy." They started calling me "Theodora." I got so mad I wanted to slug them. I found myself wishing my mother had let me take boxing lessons from my father.

One day around this time my father showed me his gun. It was a big black shiny Colt .45. Just looking at it was scary. He had gotten it when he was promoted to lieutenant in the army. He let me point it at the living room wall. He told me that you never pointed a gun at anybody, even if you thought it was unloaded. You always acted as if it were loaded.

He pointed it at the ground and showed me how you fired it. You didn't pull the trigger, you squeezed it very slowly. He showed me how to do it.

The gun went off with a tremendous crash. I jumped at least three feet in the air. My father grabbed me and shouted, "Are you okay?" It was the only time I saw him scared. I nodded, although I was shaking all over.

My mother rushed into the room, her eyes wild. She did not calm down when my father assured her no one had been shot. "I told you I didn't want that thing in my house!" she cried.

My father said he would get rid of the gun. A few weeks later, he told me to get his wallet out of the steel filing cabinet in his bedroom. I opened the top drawer and saw the .45. It was as big and black and shiny as ever. It dawned on me that my father was not in the habit of doing what my mother told him about a lot of things.

Something else I noticed in the file drawer around the gun was a surprising number of watches—six or seven or them. I asked him why he had so many. "I used to sell them," he said. "Before I went in the army."

"Did you make much money at it?"

"I did okay," he said. "But I thought being a salesman was for the birds."

"Why?

"You had to kiss too many asses."

"Teddy!" my mother exclaimed. "You shouldn't use such awful language to a child."

"What would you call it?" he snapped.

"He's too young to understand the idea," my mother said.

"I don't think so. Do you get it, kiddo?"

"Sure," I said, though it took me several more years to really get it.

Sometimes on a rainy Sunday, my father would play cards with me. I liked poker and so did he. We played for nickels and dimes. Usually he let me win fifty or sixty cents. Sometimes he would win it back on the last hand. He would shuffle the cards and deal himself four aces and give me nothing but twos and threes.

"You cheated!" I would shout, as he raked in the coins.

"What do you mean?" he would say. "Did you see me do anything?"

"No, but you must have cheated!" I would insist.

"Okay. We'll play another hand."

He would shuffle the cards while I fixed my eyes on the deck. It looked like perfectly ordinary shuffling to me. But when I picked up my hand, I would have the same twos and threes—and he would have four aces again!

"You shouldn't be teaching him how to cheat!" my mother would complain.

"I'm not teaching him any such thing. I'm only telling him never to bet on a hand you haven't shuffled yourself," my father would say.

I begged him to tell me how to do that trick shuffle. He shook his head. "That's a quick way to get your block knocked off," he said.

I liked the idea of my father winning a bundle at some card game with his trick shuffle. I was pretty sure that no one would ever knock his block off, even if they figured out what he was doing. It was a thrill to think your father was smart enough and tough enough to pull a stunt like that.

By and large, I liked having Teddy Fleming for a father. The memory of his slap faded away. It was the only time that he ever hit me, and when I got a little older I decided I had been a brat that night and probably deserved it.

One of the people who helped me realize my bratty potential—and severely checked it—was Mary Fitzmaurice Dolan. One winter day when I was eight, I was heading out to the backyard to play after school. Nana told me to wear my rubbers, because the ground was muddy. "Oh, get lost, you old rat," I said. "I'm tired of you telling me what to do."

I zoomed out the door before Nana could react and played in the backyard with neighboring friends for an hour or so. I returned with very muddy shoes. Nana was still in the kitchen. "Come over here," she said.

I realized, too late, that she had a washcloth wrapped around her hand. *Whap! Whap! Whap!* I got it in the face three times. I was so stunned I didn't cry. "Don't you ever say anything like that to me again," Nana said.

I never did.

Beyond my small world on Randolph Avenue, large things had been happening in Jersey City and the nation. As the Great Depression lacerated the body politic, the standing of the Republican Party among the voters sank toward zero. To the exultation of everyone in the Hague Organization, it became obvious that the next president would be a Democrat.

In 1932, the Democratic Party nominated Governor Franklin D.

Roosevelt of New York for president. In his acceptance speech FDR called for a "New Deal" for Americans reeling from the massive unemployment of the Great Depression. A longtime foe of Tammany Hall, the nominee was not inclined to be friendly with Frank Hague, who had backed Al Smith at the Democratic convention. At one point the mayor had assailed Roosevelt as a lightweight who would not be able to carry a state west of the Mississippi.

Hague was demonstrating one of the fundamental principles of Irish-American politics, loyalty. He had the emotional endorsement of Jersey City's downtown Irish for this stand. They identified totally with Al Smith's boyhood poverty, his rise from Manhattan's slums through Tammany's ranks to governor of New York. They felt the traduced and slandered "Happy Warrior" deserved another run for the White House. But Roosevelt had put together a formidable coalition that won him the nomination handily.

Frank Hague was nothing if not a realist. He told FDR that he (Hague) had been beaten in a fair fight, and urged Roosevelt to let him prove his loyalty to the Democratic Party. If FDR opened the presidential campaign in New Jersey, Hague promised to stage the biggest political rally in the nation's history. A former Smith man, James A. Farley, was running Roosevelt's campaign, and he persuaded FDR to accept the offer.

The Hague Organization went to work. In an amazing display of their efficiency (aka power), on August 25, 1932, they shipped more than 150,000 Democrats from Jersey City and the satellite towns of Bayonne, Hoboken, Union City, and North Bergen to Sea Girt, site of the summer residence of New Jersey's Democratic governor, A. Harry Moore. The travelers went free of charge and got a box lunch and plenty of beer and bootleg booze en route. They thundered cheers for FDR as he spoke from a platform set up on a drill field used by the New Jersey National Guard.

That display of political muscle impressed Roosevelt. When he won the White House in a landslide, he let Jim Farley designate Frank Hague as the party's spokesman in New Jersey. Soon the federal government began creating millions of jobs through the Works Progress Administration and other agencies. The Hague Organization had the final say on who got these jobs in New Jersey. The numbers were awesome—97,000 in the WPA alone. Every job was handed out with a warning to the recipient to vote the straight Democratic ticket to show his gratitude.

In the ward clubhouses in Jersey City the job seekers lined up by the hundreds. In the Sixth Ward, Doc Holland and Teddy Fleming did their best to help them. My father started calling it his "night job." He spent the day at the Second Criminal Court, where he often sat as acting judge when the appointed judge, the spokesman of the city's Polish voters, Louis Saturniewicz, was busy elsewhere. He doubled as Frank Hague's secretary.

Doc Holland was soon a very tired man. He was in his fifties, and not in good health. He and Teddy Fleming also had to turn out the expected maximum vote for the Organization on election day, or City Hall wanted to know why. Before the election there were the usual parades and rallies at which the Sixth Ward's turnout was carefully tallied, along with the showings of other wards. Then there was the ward's annual boat ride on one of the Hudson River dayliners. This was another big chore, an all-day marathon of handshaking, eating, drinking, and eating some more with two thousand people on the packed decks.

On the night after the 1933 boat ride, Teddy Fleming went to bed a tired man. He was awakened by a phone call around 2 A.M. A shaken voice told him Doc Holland had suffered a heart attack and was dead. Grief was deep and widespread. Doc was a father figure to many people in the ward. Who would replace him? A leader had to come from within the ward. It was not a job that could be handed to an outsider. Frank Hague thought it over for several weeks and summoned Teddy Fleming to City Hall.

In the mayor's cavernous office, Hague sat at a huge mahogany desk. He told Teddy he was considering him for Sixth Ward leader and what the arrangement would be. "All the money from the card games, the numbers, the racing and sports action comes to City Hall. You don't get a cut. I let Doc have a cut because he owned the ward before I arrived. Now I own the ward. Do you buy this?"

Teddy Fleming did not like it but he had no choice. He nodded. He bought it.

"We'll run you for the board of freeholders next year. The salary is five grand plus. You've got to live on that. Can you do it?"

Teddy Fleming said he could do it. Hague put out his hand. "Then you're my guy in the Sixth Ward." As Teddy responded to the mayor's shake with a bonecrusher of his own, they both knew they were signing a contract that was more binding than anything that could have been devised by the smartest lawyer in New Jersey. It was written in their Irish-American souls.

This was clearly not a meeting between equals. Although Teddy was now forty-four years old, he was still the younger generation as far as the fifty-seven-year-old Hague was concerned. Teddy was unbothered by that aspect of the meeting. He still had no reservations about Frank Hague. He deeply admired him and even more deeply appreciated this promotion to the top ranks of the Organization. There were only twelve wards in Jersey City. Two of the large uptown wards were "splits," with two leaders for different sections. This still added up to only fourteen leaders. To be chosen for this elite group was a tribute to how hard Teddy Fleming had worked for Frank Hague for the previous thirteen years. He was proud, pleased, grateful.

Back on Randolph Avenue, Teddy was astounded to discover that Kitty's reaction to the deal was lukewarm. "I was hoping you'd get out of this awful ward so we could move to a decent address," she said. "Did you talk to him about running for the state senate or maybe for Congress?"

"Jesus Christ! Do you know how many people in this city would kill to get this job?" Teddy roared.

"I suppose you're right," Kitty said sulkily.

"You suppose I'm right? I *am* right!" Teddy snarled.

I overheard this conversation but understood very little of it. A week later, Hague announced his decision. Teddy Fleming's picture was in the *Jersey Journal*, the *Hudson Dispatch*, and other newspapers. Beneath it was a story about Mayor Frank Hague selecting him for the job. I read it with no difficulty. My mother had taught me to read at five, a year before I entered St. Patrick's Parochial School.

I was impressed to see my father in the newspaper. So, apparently, was my mother. She clipped out the story and put it in a scrapbook. "It pays to learn good English," she said, as she pasted it onto the black page.

"There's a hell of a lot more to it than your goddamn grammar lessons!" he roared.

"Don't swear in front of the children," she said.

I sat there, baffled. My brother, Gene, three, was totally puzzled. He was too young to have even a clue about what they were talking about. I at least knew it had something to do with saying and writing things the right way. But I could not figure out why my father was so angry about it. I knew nothing about Kitty Dolan's grammar lessons before and after their wedding.

Meanwhile, Frank Hague was making sure that the emergence of Teddy Fleming as a leader was more than the mere matter of a press release from City Hall. The voters must see him as a man who rose from the party ranks surrounded by an aura of enthusiastic popular choice. When Hague nominated him for freeholder, every ward club in the city applauded and bombarded City Hall with approving letters and telegrams. A testimonial dinner attended by three hundred party leaders backed Teddy Fleming as "a coming man."

The climax was a huge rally in the Sixth Ward, with a two-mile parade of some ten thousand marchers, a show that newspapers declared the largest single ward demonstration in the city's history. As many of these marchers as could squeeze into a mass meeting in the auditorium of Public School 22 were greeted by the beaming mayor, who began, "I wonder if Teddy Fleming can live up to the reputation of that great friend of yours and mine. I was never so shocked as I was at the sudden death of Doc Holland. Embedded in his soul was a sense of loyalty deeper than that of any man I ever knew."

In spite of this passing doubt, Hague told the cheering audience he was choosing "this young man" to succeed Doc. The mayor urged them to "give him the same loyalty that you gave Doc Holland. I hope he has all the qualifications that his predecessor had—I know he has the loyalty. I want loyalty, I want honor! I want men who represent their constituents well, who set an example to all the young men in their wards. I have surrounded myself with such young men. I'm proud of them. I'm proud of Teddy Fleming."

In November Teddy Fleming and the other Hague candidates for the board of freeholders were elected by massive margins. It was a delicious time to be a Democrat in Jersey City. The Republicans were nowhere. On election night my father gave the first of many victory parties for his relatives and several hundred friends.

A few weeks later, I discovered that having an important father did not make life more enjoyable. Several of my playmates or their older brothers sneered, "Hey, dere's Fleming. His old man's a big shot now."

Two brothers named Goggin, who lived across the street from us, seemed to take my father's local fame particularly amiss. The Eighteenth Amendment, prohibiting the sale of alcoholic beverages, had just been repealed, making liquor legal again. The less affluent bought liquor in small "nip" bottles, which cost far less than a pint or a quart. Thousands of these things accumulated in garbage cans. They made very handy missiles, which the Goggins became expert at throwing at stray cats and occasionally at other kids.

One day it snowed. I went out in my galoshes and overcoat and mittens, expecting to have a good time. The Goggin brothers started calling me names. I tossed a snowball at them. The older brother retaliated with a nip bottle, hitting me in the forehead.

Fortunately the bottle did not break. That did not prevent me from running screaming to my mother. She charged into the frigid street and pursued the fleeing Goggin brothers to their house. Kitty rang the doorbell and Mrs. Goggin appeared. She was a fat round-faced woman with a short haircut that made her look mannish. She quickly took the same viewpoint toward the Flemings as her sons.

"What are you gonna do? Get your big-shot husband to put my kids in jail?" she sneered.

That night at dinner my mother expressed her outrage and demanded that my father do something. "Forget it," he said.

"Forget it?" my mother cried. "When they could have blinded Teddy-boy?"

"They didn't blind him. I'm telling you to forget it," my father said. "There's about fifty Goggins in the ward. That's a lot of votes."

"As for you, kiddo," my father said, glancing at me with a rueful smile, "the next time, duck!"

In December of that year I opened the newspaper and saw a picture of my father and two or three other men standing in the middle of a lot of upright paper bags. Underneath the picture, the caption said, "Sixth Ward Leader Thomas J. (Teddy) Fleming and his committeemen will distribute almost fifteen hundred Christmas baskets this year. Fleming says the requests from poor families are double last year's totals. It is a grim commentary on the downward spiral of the American economy."

I asked my father what a Christmas basket was. "A turkey and all the fixings," he said.

"Why do people ask for it?" I asked.

"Because they're broke. They can't afford to buy one."

"Do you pay for it?"

"No. The Organization pays for it."

"What's the Organization?"

"It's me and lot of other guys behind the leader, Frank Hague. We get out the vote each election day. We get our guys elected and we run things here and all over the state of New Jersey. We hand out jobs to people who need them."

"Do you have to be a Democrat to belong to the Organization?"

"You bet," my father said. "It's us against the Republicans. The poor guys against the rich guys. What's up? You thinking of becoming a politician?"

"I hope not," my mother said. "He's got too much brains. He's going to be a college professor, I'm sure of it."

"College professors are lucky if they make three grand a year," my father said. "I hope he can do better than that."

"People look up to them. It's a respectable profession," my mother said.

"Jesus Christ!" my father said.

I must have looked scared. I thought they were going to have another fight. Instead, of getting mad, my father put his fist under my chin and made me look him in the eye. "A politician isn't such a bad job," he said. "When I was your age the boss was a guy named Robert Davis. You know what he was worth when he died?"

I shook my head.

"Eight hundred thousand bucks. Keep politics in mind, kiddo."

"I'd like to help people," I said. "That must make you feel good."

"Sometimes," my father said.

The Great Depression began grinding Jersey City's poor unto

desperation. Ignoring my mother's complaints about never seeing him, my father spent his afternoons and evenings in the Sixth Ward's clubhouse, talking to the long lines of men who begged him to find them jobs.

One night he came home to dinner and took a pistol out of his pocket. It was smaller than his army .45. Just behind the barrel was a bulging place where you put the bullets. It looked like some sort of insect.

"Where did you get that thing?" my mother said.

My father told us that a man with a Polish name had pleaded for a job in an especially frantic way. Teddy realized he had already seen him several times and had told him he had nothing to offer. This time he decided to call in a favor he had done for a local labor leader. He told the man to go down to the docks for a shape-up the next morning. My father would make sure he got picked for work as a stevedore.

The man burst into tears. He took the gun out of his pocket and laid it on my father's desk. "If you say no job again, I vas goink to kill you," he said.

My mother was appalled. "What are you going to do with it?" she asked.

"Keep it in my desk, loaded," my father said. "If anyone else has that idea, I'm going down shooting."

"That's horrible!" my mother cried.

"It's life," my father said.

I began to think they saw almost everything differently. I also understood what my father meant when he told me helping people gave you a good feeling—sometimes. I was beginning to realize things were much more complicated than my mother thought they were.

I was naturally interested in my father's job as a freeholder. I asked my mother what a freeholder did. "Whatever Mayor Hague tells him to do," she said.

I asked my father and he said, "We run Hudson County. The jail, the hospital, the county police force. We decide who gets taxed for what."

I did not understand either answer. I decided it was an important job because freeholders got a black Cadillac limousine and a chauffeur to drive them around. I noticed that Teddy Fleming did not sit in the back like millionaires in the movies. He sat up front with the driver and called him by his first name. I gradually realized this was affluence with a democratic touch, essential in Jersey City.

On Sundays, my father took the wheel and we drove to various scenic parts of New Jersey, such as the Delaware Water Gap. One Sunday I asked my father if two or three kids on the block could join us. "Sure," Teddy Fleming said. There was plenty of room in the car. On the way back we stopped at a roadside diner and he bought us ice cream, soda—whatever we wanted. The kids thanked me extravagantly for the ride. I went to bed that night one of the happiest boys in Jersey City. It was my first taste of the pleasure hidden inside the word power.

Teddy Fleming was tasting the same thing in a much bigger way. When he walked into City Hall to see the mayor or one of the commissioners, a lot of people, from the gigantic cop at the door to the head of the tax department to old friends like Billy Black, greeted him by name and shook his hand if he stopped to talk with them. He was a big deal now. He could get favors done. Of course he stayed cool and carefully avoided anything that suggested a swelled head. Nothing was more fatal to an Irish-American politician. But it was still a nice feeling for a guy who had grown up in a tenement without running water and had been warned by Monsignor Meehan that he was on his way to becoming a tramp athlete.

There was only one thing wrong with his life: his wife couldn't or wouldn't see any of this. Why? What the hell was wrong with Kitty? He could not figure it out. Teddy tried but he could not figure it out.

## 20

# Two Circles of Love

Teddy Fleming was leader of the Sixth Ward for only a few weeks when he got a message at the ward clubhouse that Monsignor Meehan wanted to see him. He wasted no time getting down to All Saints rectory. The Mons was still the unofficial boss of the ward. If he wanted something done, the leader had better get to work on it, fast.

In the same office where Teddy had gotten his behind paddled thirty years ago, the Mons was starting to look his age. Deep crevasses ran down both cheeks; his hands had acquired a tremor. But he managed to pour them both a bourbon and gazed at Teddy with what passed for satisfaction in his imperious style.

"So you're the leader," he said. "You're going to run things."

"It looks that way," Teddy said.

"You're going to work your head off, if I know you. Day and night, listening to everyone's troubles."

"That goes with the job, doesn't it?" Teddy said.

The Mons leaned toward him to drive the words home. "Well, let me tell you something you should never forget. Jesus Christ Himself couldn't keep these people happy."

"I'll keep that in mind," Teddy said with a grin.

"I mean it!" the Mons said. "I told Doc he took it too seriously. Look how it got to him. Here's another piece of advice. Don't let

Frank Hague push you around. Push back. Stand up to him. He's not as tough as he looks."

"I'll keep that one in mind too," Teddy said. They sipped their bourbon for a while and talked baseball. The Mons thought the Giants would beat the Yankees this year in the World Series. Then he turned serious again.

"The archbishop is trying to pull a fast one. He sent orders for every priest in the diocese to make a will, leaving all their assets to him. I just wrote him a letter. Would you like to hear it?"

Teddy nodded. The Mons pulled the letter out of his desk and read: "Dear Archbishop Walsh: All the money I have ever had in this world was left to me by my father. If you look in the diocesan archives, you will see how many thousands of dollars he gave to the church each year while he lived. My inheritance was once several hundred thousand dollars. It is now down to sixty thousand dollars. Most of the difference went to fellow priests who were trying to build churches and schools. I have a niece of whom I am very fond; she is my only living relative. She has no husband and no prospects of getting one. I am leaving my remaining money to her in my will."

The Mons put the letter back in the desk. "I thought you should know about it, in case it gets in the papers when they probate the will after I croak. Explain it around the ward. Protect my reputation, such as it is."

"What's this stuff about croaking? You'll bury all of us," Teddy Fleming said.

The Mons just looked at him. They finished their drinks and Teddy went back to running the Sixth Ward. They understood each other in a new way. They both worked for authoritarian organizations, but a man could fight back, if he had the nerve.

When my father told me about the Mons's advice, many years later, he made it sound wryly amusing. At the time, I suspect he found it about as funny as Meehan's pronouncement that he could not hit a curve. Becoming the leader of a ward involved a lot of headaches and challenges that came at you from unexpected directions. Monsignor Meehan was not kidding when he told Teddy Fleming to keep calm and stay realistic.

Letters constantly arrived from City Hall with a note from the mayor's secretary: "Please take care of this" or "Handle this as best you can" or "Do not fail to acknowledge this." One woman wrote to the mayor complaining that she could not get her job back at the city hospital because her ward leader, "Theodore Fleming," would not "vouch" for her. She menacingly noted, "There are eleven votes in my family, all in the Sixth Ward." Another man wanted a job in the city parks for his unemployed brother. He too noted how many votes there were in his family—ten. A Sixth Warder named Charles Ethridge wanted $2,500 from Mayor Hague to perfect his research on the "secret of blood and the secret of disease." He assured the mayor the motion picture rights alone were worth a million dollars. The wife of a saloonkeeper complained about a man named Duke Beagins who had taken a hate to the saloon and broken her husband's windows four times. Another lady candidly noted that people were constantly knocking on her door and urging her to vote the straight Democratic ticket. If her vote was worth so much trouble, how about giving her a job at City Hall to guarantee it?

Then there were the backstabbers. Vincent Ferro, the head of the Vincent Ferro Association, wrote to the mayor proposing a statue to the memory of "our late beloved leader," Doc Holland. He went on and on about how much everyone in the ward missed Doc and noted that his replacement, Teddy Fleming, did not seem to know how to win the hearts of the people in Doc's fashion.

Another group coalesced around James Creegan, who threatened to run in the next election to prove Teddy Fleming had no following in the Sixth Ward. Also heard from in a long earnest letter were four gentlemen who spoke for the Slovaks of the Sixth Ward. They claimed their countrymen were ignored by the Hague Organization and demanded a job for James Sachek, a resident of the Seventh Ward, as proof that City Hall cared about them.

All these people had to be mollified, if possible, with a job or the promise of one, or some soothing solution such as urging them to form a Slovak-American Democratic Party Committee to help get out the vote on election day. (And explaining to them that you didn't write from the Sixth Ward to get a job for someone in the Seventh Ward.) The police had to be prodded to do something about saloon window breaker Beagins. Someone with a voice of authority at City Hall had to be persuaded to tell troublemakers like Ferro and Creegan that they were not going to get anywhere with collision tactics. If they could demonstrate that they had a following who voted the straight ticket, maybe something could be done for them.

The solution or semi-solution to each of these problems had to be reported to City Hall. No detail was too small for the Hague Organization to worry about. Every vote had to be counted and had to be courted, one way or another. Meanwhile, the head of the Meseck Steamship Line wanted Teddy to let him know in January the date of the annual boat ride, scheduled for May. The annual dance to raise money for Christmas baskets had to be organized and as many as two thousand of these politicized gifts delivered to the ward's poor. The thirteen districts in the ward each needed a full-time committeeman and committeewoman to canvass the voters as an election approached. If any of these people got sick or took to drink the leader had to find reliable replacements.

What was Teddy Fleming doing? Basically, he was running a regiment in a political war. He had gone from lieutenant to colonel. He had a second in command, a big easygoing man named Johnny Duff. After him came stocky no-nonsense Arthur Foley, a policeman. Next in line was a genial ex-trucker, another big man, Arthur "Lige" Petrie, and his chunky pal "Georgie" Jamison, a cheerful joker. All these people and their friends and relations had to be treated well. They had to make some extra money on election day from the four or five thousand dollars that City Hall sent to the ward to buy votes where canvassing and persuasion had failed.

Among my father's papers I found a folder marked "Interesting Speeches." One of the most interesting was a talk he gave to the committeemen of the Sixth Ward not long after he became leader. The tone was remarkably self-assured. Teddy Fleming obviously had no doubt about his ability to handle the job. After telling everyone that he wanted to get to know them well on a personal level, he made it clear that this was a joint enterprise. "In assuming the leadership of this ward, I have determined that all of you who work earnestly and faithfully for me, shall not be forgotten when the opportunity arrives for me to be of service to you. On the other hand, no man or woman can expect to be rewarded who continually shirks his or her duty and does not give me the full cooperation and support that I expect."

As Frank Hague became a power in state and national politics, he left the day-to-day chore of running the Organization to a man who had been his devoted sidekick from the day he began his political career by winning election as constable in the Second Ward. His name was Johnny Malone, but his fellow Irish, with that unerring eye for the right nickname, called him "Needlenose." His proboscis not only looked the part—the moniker perfectly fit his temperament.

Malone's chief talent was saying no, often in the nastiest way. He had few if any friends in Jersey City, outside Frank Hague, who reportedly admitted, "I know Johnny's a son of a bitch. But he's *my* son of a bitch." Along with the other ward leaders, my father learned to detest Malone. He was the man a ward leader had to see when he was pushing one of his people for a new job or a promotion. Teddy soon decided it was smarter to wait until Hague was in town and get an appointment with him.

Face-to-face in the mayor's office, Hague discovered that he could expect loyalty from Teddy Fleming, but not subservience. When it came to battling for promotions for police and firemen and other Sixth Ward jobholders, Teddy was tough. In later years, he told me with considerable pride about his first test case. "I had one of my guys up for police lieutenant and Hague passed him over. I went down to the Hall to see him. He said no. I went back a second time. He said no again. They told me nobody ever went back three times. I did. Hague blew his top, and I blew mine. We called each other all the names you can imagine. But my guy got the job."

A few days later, friends at City Hall told Teddy that after Hague calmed down, he growled almost admiringly, "That Teddy Fleming. He's one in a barrel."

"After that," my father said, "they knew the Sixth was *my* ward. No one pushed me around."

The ward leader was never away from his job, even when he was asleep in his bed. One night the telephone woke me up. I heard my father answer it. "Yeah, this is Teddy Fleming," he said.

"Where did it happen? The Seventh Precinct? I'll be out there in a half hour."

I soon heard my father's footsteps on the stairs. In the morning, my mother looked cross. My father was still asleep. "He can sleep late," she said as she served my Rice Krispies. "I've got to get up and send you to school."

"What happened?" I said.

"Somebody got arrested for drunken driving in the middle of the night. Your father had to get him out of jail."

"Why?"

"Because he's a Democrat," my mother said. Her tone of voice suggested she did not think this was a good reason to get someone out of jail.

All this led to a conclusion I arrived at early in life: the term "political machine" so beloved by the newspapers was a meaningless misnomer. There was no such thing in Jersey City or New York or any other city where the Irish-Americans organized things politically. "Machine" suggests some effortlessly functioning entity that grinds out votes willy-nilly by turning Americans into submissive robots. For anyone who saw how things worked from the inside, the opposite was the case. A political organization was a churning mix of ambition and resentments and inertia over which leaders presided only by constant effort.

For Kitty Fleming, politics remained an unpleasant word. She did her best to keep it out of our home. My father conceded that there was something to be said for this idea. When I answered the telephone and a voice asked, "Is your father there?" I was supposed to say, "No," even though Teddy Fleming was reading the newspaper in the living room, only a few feet away.

For a while this caused me considerable mental anguish. I was a very devout student at St. Patrick's Parochial School. The Baltimore Catechism, which I took very seriously, stated that it was a sin to tell a lie. When I brought this up to my father, he said, "Let me see that thing."

He opened the book, essentially the same one he had studied at All Saints Parochial School, and started asking me to recite the answers to various questions. I knew them all. But he kept insisting I had them wrong. "It says right here that God's name is Franklin D. Roosevelt," he said. "How come you don't know that?" He asked me if I was scared of the Holy Ghost. My mother overheard this game and rushed in crying, "Teddy, you should be teaching him to respect the Catechism, not make fun of it!"

"I don't want him to think every breath he takes is a sin," my father said.

Pretty soon I noticed that my mother also told telephone callers my father was not home while he was sitting in the living room. Apparently it did not bother her conscience. In fact, she often hung up with some sort of curt comment about people bothering my father when he was at home. This sometimes led to an angry inquiry from my father about the identity of the caller. "Jesus Christ," my father would often say, and would call back within five minutes. Kitty's desire to keep politics at bay was not even a forlorn hope in Jersey City. It was a flat-out impossibility.

Two years after my father became Sixth Ward leader, we sold the house on Randolph Avenue and moved to a one-family house about two blocks away, on Arlington Avenue. The street was a mix of flats and one-family redbrick row houses and several two- or three-family houses like the one we had left behind. Aunt Mae Fleming Gallagher and her husband, Al, and their children, my cousins Marie and Buddy, lived less than a block away. Our house was not especially big or grand. It was a rectangular two-story box, with three rooms on the first floor and four bedrooms on the second floor. It also had a roomy cellar and a big backyard.

My mother spent endless hours—and a lot of money—decorating the house. She had the sliding doors that separated the living room and the dining room and the hall torn out and replaced with arches. She had the living room walls done in a stucco finish with panels of gold wallpaper. I thought it was beautiful.

Not long after we moved into the house, my mother and father started arguing angrily in front of me and my brother and my grand-mother, who had moved in with us. It was different from the brief exchanges I had heard and worried about on Randolph Avenue. Maybe they had argued this way behind closed doors in earlier years. But now the arguments broke into the open.

The quarrels were usually about money. My father seemed to think my mother spent too much. She said he did not give her enough to run the house. But Kitty often admitted to Nana that when she went shopping in New York, she lost control. A bill from Macy's or Saks would trigger cries of woe when she opened it.

Even at nine, I sensed there was more to the arguments than money. It had something to do with what my mother expected to happen now that my father was a man of importance. She seemed to taunt Teddy Fleming with some of her remarks. Gradually I began to sense something deeper was wrong, but I had no idea what it was.

"I thought by now we wouldn't have to worry about this sort of thing," my mother would say when my father complained about her household bills. Sometimes she would add, "I bet the mayor's wife isn't on a cheapskate budget."

These jibes infuriated my father. He raged that she didn't know what she was talking about. He was not going to "ruin things" so she could waste money in Macy's and Saks. I did not understand how things could be ruined by my mother spending too much money. The arguments troubled me a great deal. I would lie awake at night wondering why my father could not give my mother more money. He always seemed to have a lot of money in his pocket. Sometimes, when he gave me a dollar for a good report card, he would take out a roll of bills two inches thick.

Only much later did I realize that my mother was trying to force my father to break the promise he had made to Frank Hague to live on his freeholder's salary and take nothing from the ward's bookmaking, numbers, and card games. Perhaps Teddy tried to explain it to her; she was probably not impressed by a promise of that sort. How was the mayor going to know if he took an extra two or three thousand a month? Kitty Dolan Fleming had no idea how much keeping a promise like that meant to Teddy Fleming's self-respect.

My father spent money freely on us in other ways. We started going to the Jersey shore each year for the entire summer. He chose Point Pleasant, a middle-class town. Mayor Hague's mansion in fashionable Deal was about forty miles north of us. My mother thought we should rent a house there or in almost as fashionable Spring Lake. My father curtly informed her we were staying in Point Pleasant. He knew what the working-class Sixth Ward would think of him if he started hobnobbing with the mayor and his circle, or with the uptown doctors and lawyers and contractors who went to Spring Lake.

We had a nice life in Point Pleasant each summer. My father came down weekends. Gene and I pitched horseshoes on the lawn and threw baseballs and footballs with him. He was not much good with a football—it was not a sport of his youth—but he could still throw a baseball hard enough to tear your hand off. I used to love the crack it made when it hit my glove. I even liked the sting. I threw it back as hard as I could. Sometimes I had to quit because my hand hurt too much. But most of the time I stuck it out, because of the story he had told me about his boyhood baseball days, how they used to cut the centers out of their cheap gloves to make sure they could catch the ball.

"Didn't it hurt?" I asked incredulously.

"Sure," he said. "But you didn't make many errors."

I got the basic idea. A guy should be ready to take some pain when necessary if he wanted to accomplish something.

My brother and I soon learned how to swim and spent hours in the water. My father seldom went near the beach, and when he ventured into the water he did what he called "the dead man's float" in Jenkinson's saltwater pool, where we had a bathhouse. He would put his face in the water and just lie there.

The first time he did it I got scared. I thought he was drowning. But he pulled his head up and took a breath when he needed it. I gradually realized that he was trying to avoid letting us know he could not swim.

Among the people who came to visit was Tom Fleming, my father's first cousin, who had grown up in the Fleming family. Tom now owned a liquor distribution business in Jersey City that was making him rich, in spite of the Great Depression. My father had obtained the deal for him when Prohibition was repealed. No doubt Tom paid plenty to the Organization off the books. One day Tom inadvertently told me why my father could not swim. "Remember the time we went out to the Kill Van Kull and someone dared you to jump in?" Tom said. "You went down like a rock. That guy jumped in and dragged you out just in time."

Tom grinned at me. "Sometimes your old man had too much nerve for his own good."

"More nerve than brains, I'd say," said Tom's wife, Bess, a blonde ex–chorus girl, who looked and dressed like a moll in a Hollywood gangster movie.

My mother thought Bess was "common." But she laughed heartily at this wisecrack. I could see my father was not amused. "I didn't jump in, I fell," he said. "The riverbank gave way. The guy didn't save me. I was getting out okay until he jumped on top of me."

"That's not the way I remember it," Tom said.

"After a couple of drinks you can barely remember your own name," my father said.

At the time I thought this was family conversation, Fleming style. Much later, I realized Tom's version of the story was true. But my father was not going to let Tom make him look bad in front of me and my brother.

When I was ten or eleven, I started asking my father about his army days. One of the first books I had read, *A Child's History of the World*, had a battle on almost every page. It was amazing and thrilling to realize Teddy Fleming had been in one of these great clashes that had changed the course of history. He responded with funny stories, at first. He told me about Sergeant Major Cruickshank and about Harry Ross marching the company out the gate of Camp Restless (but he didn't tell me where they were going), and about saving the wandering major's life in the Argonne. Gradually, the stories got more serious. He told about the time the captain of his company ran for the rear and about the guy who lost his legs and the lieutenant who ordered him out of his foxhole under bombardment and a direct hit killed the man seconds later. "Were you scared?" I asked.

"In a battle you don't have time to get scared," he said. "You trust in your luck. I never went into action without these."

Out of his pocket he took a pair of dice. "Roll them," he said.

I did. They came up seven every fifth time. "They're loaded," he said. "I took them away from a wiseguy in our company when I caught him using them on the troopship."

I later found out from Aunt Mae Gallagher the real origin of these dice. That was not the point, anyway. Even at the age of ten, I was dimly aware that the centrality of luck in my father's view of life did not jibe with the Catholic religion I was imbibing at St. Patrick's

School. None of the black-robed nuns who taught us in the classroom nor the parish priests who lectured us from the pulpit on Sunday ever mentioned luck. It was God on whom you depended for loving protection. My father never said a word about Him.

My passion for war stories led me to glimpse a side of my father few people ever saw. One day when I was twelve or thirteen—the age when boys are naturally bloodthirsty—I asked him, "Did you ever jump into a trench and stick a bayonet into a German's guts or his heart?"

To my amazement, the blood drained from my father's face. He literally trembled from head to foot. "I don't want to talk about that," he said. "Don't ever ask me about it again."

Only many years later, when I was a man, did he tell me how he had killed the surrendering German lieutenant in the trench fight on Talma Hill.

Another glimpse of this concealed Teddy Fleming was on the wall in his bedroom. It was a framed copy of a poem, "My Buddy."

> *Who was it met me with a smile,*
> *And stayed beside me all the while,*
> *And helped me o'er each weary mile?*
> *My buddy.*
>
> *Who used to help me out at drill,*
> *And sat and talked when I was ill,*
> *Who carried my pack up many a hill?*
> *My buddy.*
>
> *Who used to cheer me with his song,*
> *When everything was going wrong,*
> *Whose faults were short, and friendship long?*
> *My buddy.*
>
> *Whose name is ever in my heart,*
> *Who makes the tears oft' want to start,*
> *Who from me, even death, can't part?*
> *My buddy.*

"Did you have a buddy who got killed?" I asked my father.

"I had a lot of buddies who got killed," he said.

I got a third glimpse of this concealed Teddy Fleming on the way home from a family visit to the U.S. Military Academy at West Point, where we had lunch with one of his friends from officers' candidate camp who had stayed in the army. We stopped in a veterans hospital in northern New Jersey. It was a huge place, with towering ten- or twelve-story buildings. One section contained men who had gone crazy during the war. They were out on porches on each floor, with iron bars and wire mesh to keep them from escaping.

"The war's over!" one screamed when he saw us. "Over the top!" howled a second man. Others shouted unprintable things about the kaiser.

My mother grew exasperated. "What's the point of coming here?"

"I've got some friends in those buildings," my father said. "Not everybody could handle combat." I had a feeling he wanted me to know this. I wondered if some of these crazy men had been among his buddies.

More than once, when we talked about the war, my father went out of his way to say he was not a hero. "I never won a medal. Most guys never won a medal. I'm not trying to take anything away from the guys who did. They usually deserved one. But I saw an awful lot of guys get killed doing things they never got medals for."

"What were they doing?" I asked.

"Trying to help a buddy who'd been hit."

For a long time I brooded about that idea. Jesus, talking about His sacrifice on the cross, said, "Greater love has no man than he who lays down his life for his friend." Was it possible that ordinary men did that sort of thing in a battle? Much, much later, after I had written a history of West Point and talked to a lot of soldiers, I concluded the answer was yes.

I had no idea that these thoughts and conversations were bonding me to my father in a deep and lasting way. They took place outside the circle of love that my mother never stopped trying to weave around me. I valued her love. I value it today. Kitty was always urging me to read more books, to memorize poems and recite them for her friends. She praised my school compositions and my high marks. She bragged about my supposed brainpower to relatives and friends.

I never dreamt that these two circles of love would clash in ways that would almost break my heart.

# 21

# Street Angel, House Devil

During these early-1930s years I also got to know my grandfather. I called him Dadda. Davey was nearing eighty and lived down the block on Arlington Avenue with Aunt Mae Fleming Gallagher. He was a hulking old man with a huge head and massive shoulders. His brogue seemed to have grown thicker with age. Often I could not understand a word he said. He walked on a cane and always seemed mad about something.

My mother told me Dadda would not let Aunt Mae use Lipton's tea because Sir Thomas Lipton was an Englishman who sailed around the world in an expensive yacht. Dadda did not like rich Englishmen. He thought they had stolen a lot of their money from the Irish. Kitty thought this was silly.

Dadda also would not allow insurance men in the house because they had cheated him and a lot of other poor people, years ago. Kitty thought this was silly too. She said it was Dadda's fault. He was too stupid to keep track of what he owed the company. ·

Aunt Mae had long since forgotten her girlhood vow never to pay a cent to an insurance man. She told her Equitable agent to come when Dadda was on his daily visit to nearby Arlington Park, where he sat and talked with other retired oldsters. One day it rained. Dadda stayed home and Aunt Mae forgot the insurance man was coming.

Dadda answered his knock on the door. "Equitable Life!" chirped the innocent imminent victim.

*Wham!* Dadda belted him with a roundhouse right, knocking the poor man down a flight of stairs, dislocating his shoulder. After that, Aunt Mae met him on the corner.

My mother was horrified by the demolition of the Equitable man. She called Dadda the thickest mick in America. She told me, with scorn in her voice, that he could not read or write. That made me feel sorry for him. Already I was reading seven or eight books a week from the local public library. I could not imagine being unable to read. With renewed scorn in her voice, my mother also said that when Dadda first went to work at Standard Oil, his pay was fifty cents a day.

I could not believe it. I often spent fifty cents in an ice-cream parlor, knocking down two chocolate frosteds. "What did he do?" I asked.

"Rolled barrels, I suppose. Something that didn't take any brains."

Kitty could not restrain her low opinion of the downtown Irish Flemings. She did not seem to realize that her concern with social niceties did not make the slightest impression on me. I kind of liked the way Old Davey belted the insurance man down the stairs, even if I did not understand it. I was a boy, after all.

My father called Dadda "the old gent." I remember being impressed by this because almost every kid on our block referred to his father as "the old man." I always heard an edge of hostility, even contempt, in that phrase, which I never used. Was it because some of these fathers were out of work? Or they were too strict? Or they quarreled with their wives the way my father did? I sensed that in some way I could not yet understand, my father admired—or at least liked—his father, in spite of his bad temper.

When I was eight, Dadda produced a poem that he wanted me to memorize and recite for him. He said he'd give me a nickel for every stanza. It was called "Why I Named You Patrick." It had fifteen four-line verses. My father said he'd give me an extra dollar if I memorized the whole thing.

I went to work. It wasn't very hard. I already had a good memory from reciting the Catechism each day in school. In a week I had the whole poem down and recited it for Dadda when I met him in Arlington

Park. He gave me sixty cents and my father gave me the dollar. The poem was about Saint Patrick bringing the true faith to Ireland. The last stanza was the one that Dadda liked best.

> *When you wear the shamrock, son,*
> *Be proud of your Irish name.*
> *No other one I know of*
> *Can stand for greater fame.*

Dadda liked jokes about fighting Irishmen. One of his favorites was about the Celt who got shipwrecked and drifted up to the shore of an unnamed country.

"Is there a government in this place?" the castaway asked the natives.

They said yes.

"I'm agin' it," the Irishman said.

Except for the poem about Saint Patrick, Dadda never mentioned Ireland. Nor did my father. He often referred to himself and others as "Irish," but he apparently had no interest in the country. It took me many years to find out why: their disgust with the Irish civil war that followed the break with the British in 1921. It alienated millions of Irish-Americans for another thirty or forty years.

In 1936, Dadda was coming out of St. Patrick's Church on a snowy day. He slipped on the steps and went crashing to the bottom, breaking his hip. He lingered a few months but never really recovered. He died that summer at the age of eighty and we all went to the funeral. My father looked sad at the wake. I was scared. It was the first time I saw a dead person in a coffin.

Uncle Dave, as I called the Turkey, entertained everyone with funny stories about Davey. Once he was taken to a Brooklyn restaurant by a Tammany boss for whom he was doing a little "floating" (aka voting) and given a lobster dinner. The meal started off with clam broth, which Davey reluctantly drank. Then came a salad, which was also strange to him, but he ate it. When the lobster arrived, Davey threw down his napkin and said, "I drank your hot wather and I aate yer grass. But I'll be damned if I'll aate that bug!"

I could see why everyone liked Uncle Dave, even my mother. My father especially enjoyed his company. He started smiling the minute he saw him at a party or a family dinner. One night Dave told me about my father's boxing days. After Teddy quit the professional ring, he and the Turkey and Charlie used to go to saloons in other parts of Jersey City or Bayonne or Hoboken and talk up Teddy as a tough character who could, in John L. Sullivan's phrase, "lick any man in the house." A local slugger would frequently accept the challenge and they would retire to a nearby boxing ring for a three- or four-round bout. Charlie and Dave would bet their wallets on Teddy and win.

Around this time, thanks to my ability to read the papers, I realized the world beyond Arlington Avenue and St. Patrick's parish was dangerous. John Dillinger was robbing banks and Al Capone and other mobsters were shooting each other and an occasional innocent bystander in Chicago and elsewhere. This perception became acute when a man kidnapped and killed hero pilot Charles Lindbergh's baby.

Knowing this awful crime had been committed in New Jersey, my native state, made it even more scary. Worse, the newspaper headlines stirred numerous psychos to imagine doing the same thing. My father received a letter demanding big money or I would be the next kidnap victim. For two weeks a plainclothesman followed me back and forth to school. I was told never to accept a ride in an automobile from a stranger.

One night around nine o'clock, my mother heard a noise in the cellar. My father was in the Sixth Ward clubhouse seeing job seekers. Kitty called the police. Their response was, among other things, a demonstration of Frank Hague's achievement in shaping up the force. The mayor had made it a standing rule that all such calls had to be responded to in less than five minutes. Hague often drove to different parts of the city, invited himself into a house, and placed an emergency call to see how the local precinct responded.

In our case, perhaps the name Fleming made the response almost instantaneous. My mother had barely hung up the phone when several huge cops charged in our front door with drawn guns while another squad stampeded down the alley. They found no one. But marks on the cellar door suggested someone had been using a screwdriver or some other pointed instrument in an attempt to spring the lock.

For weeks I slept badly, imagining myself as a Lindbergh replay. My father gave me the loaded dice he carried through the Argonne.

"Nobody will touch you with these things in your pocket," he assured me. I was not completely convinced and still had occasional nightmares. Once I half awoke to find a gigantic snake undulating above my bed.

The apparition may have had something to do with my becoming more and more disturbed by my parents' quarrels. An increment to this rising anger was my mother's brother, George Dolan, whom I saw as a charming dark-haired man with a rakish grin. My father took a gloomier view. George was a romantic loser. His pitching career had fizzled without getting him anywhere near the major leagues. Where-upon he pursued another impossible dream: Hollywood. A half dozen years in Tinseltown won him nothing but chorus parts, most of them amounting to milliseconds on the silver screen.

George returned to Jersey City penniless in the middle of the Great Depression and my father got him a job as a stevedore. One day the police, acting on a tip, found a half dozen typewriters and similar valuable items in George's locker. He was arrested for grand larceny.

My father rushed to the police station where George was being held and asked the captain to see the arrest record. He thumbed through it and coolly ripped it to shreds. "Release him in my custody," Teddy said.

"Fleming," the captain said, "I'm gonna get you if it's the last thing I do on this job."

"Go to hell," Teddy said.

This was nerve in action and then some. My father came home in a fury. For the time being, the police captain's challenge was the focus of his rage. "We'll see who's got the clout," he growled. My mother could only wring her hands and beg him to keep George out of jail.

"It's going to cost money," my father said.

"How much?" my mother asked.

"A hell of a lot more than we've got," my father snarled.

How could my father get money he did not have? From a bank? When I asked about it, my mother said darkly, "He can get it if he wants to get it." This left me even more baffled. How could he get it? Steal it? I did not know he—and she—were talking about dipping into the ward's gambling take, which was supposed to go untouched to City Hall, breaking his promise to Frank Hague.

In the Irish-American code of ethics, a family emergency could override such considerations. My father had no doubts about George being an emergency. It would not help his political career if a story appeared in the *Jersey Journal* about the brother-in-law of Freeholder Thomas J. Fleming getting five years in jail.

I followed the rest of the story from my mother's reports. The police captain wrote up a replacement arrest record and George was indicted. My father asked the key witness against him—a police informer—how much he wanted to leave the state for a while. The man said two thousand dollars.

My father met him on the steps of City Hall with the money. The informer said he had changed his mind. He wanted four thousand dollars. My father knocked him cold with one punch and headed for the mayor's office. Soon the informer left town without the money. My father's clout with Frank Hague trumped the police captain's clout. Without the informer the charges were dismissed. George did not go to jail.

Not surprisingly, this imbroglio did not endear George to my father. Teddy Fleming told Kitty he did not want to see his brother-in-law in our Jersey City house—or at the shore. For a while Teddy was barely civil to Mary Fitzmaurice Dolan. As a superstitious man, he may have begun to wonder if marrying into the Dolan family was one of his better moves. They seemed to bring him nothing but bad luck.

One cold winter evening in 1937, when I was ten, the doorbell chimed. I opened the door and confronted a gaunt white-haired man with no overcoat, in spite of snowflakes whipping around him.

"Is your mother home?" he asked in a hoarse voice.

I rushed to the kitchen and told my mother and grandmother about this apparition. Nana looked very sad. My mother hurried to the door and spent about five minutes in the vestibule with the man. When she returned to the kitchen, she told me that was her father's brother, Bart Dolan. He had been a successful men's tailor in New York. But he drank too much and lost his business.

"I gave him some money," she said. "Don't tell your father."

A week later, there was a small story on the back page of the *Jersey Journal*: MAN FOUND FROZEN TO DEATH IN ALLEY. It was Uncle Bart. Would my mother have been able to persuade my father to help Bart if George had not messed up? I doubt it. Growing up downtown,

Teddy Fleming had seen too many drunks ruin their families' lives before dying in the gutter. He had no sympathy for them. If he knew about Tom Dolan's drinking sprees, he would have been even less sympathetic to Bart. I doubt if my mother ever confessed the Dolan family weakness to him.

The irony of all this is rather large. Kitty Dolan, the woman who yearned to marry into a better social strata, preferably Protestant, compromised and married a downtown Irish Catholic with bad grammar and barely discernible class. She turned out to be the one with the disreputable relatives, while the Flemings all stayed off the booze, went to work every day, and did their utmost to rise in the world. Obviously, God had no interest in drawing in straight lines.

After my father showed me the loaded dice that had gotten him through the Argonne, I began noticing that he was incredibly superstitious. Once I picked up a pair of shoes and put them on my bed. He swept them off with a roar: "That's bad luck!" He refused to light three cigarettes with the same match. He was leery about doing anything important on Friday the thirteenth.

My mother laughed at these fears. She bragged about how many thirteens she had in her life. She was born on Friday the thirteenth. She married Thomas Fleming, a man with thirteen letters in his name, and the number of our Arlington Avenue house was 256, which added up to 13. My mother made the appalling (to my father) claim that for her, 13 was good luck.

One night at dinner my mother told us how she found out my father was superstitious. On one of their first dates, they had strolled to a nearby movie theater. Suddenly my father started walking faster and faster. Soon my mother was gasping to keep up with him. "What's wrong?" she cried.

He pointed across the street at a black cat that was keeping pace with them. "I'm not going to let that thing cross in front of us," he said.

I could see my father didn't like the story. But he did not get mad at Kitty, for a change. "I'd still do it," he said, looking at me as he spoke. "There's nothing more important in life than good luck."

I knew what he wanted me to remember. The lieutenant in the foxhole, with nothing left of him but a piece of his raincoat. I sensed he had told me something special—something he could not share with my mother.

A few months later, my father took me to see the St. Louis Cardinals play the New York Giants at the Polo Grounds. The Cardinals were known in those days as "the Gas House Gang." They were fond of picking fights with umpires and opposing players. My father admitted to me that he liked their style—implying that he might secretly be rooting for them against the Giants.

Almost everyone in Jersey City was a Giant fan. In the Sixth Ward, thanks to the influence of Monsignor Meehan, anyone who rooted for the Yankees or the Dodgers was in danger of serious injury, not to mention virtual excommunication from the Catholic Church.

The Cardinals' burly left fielder, Ducky Medwick, was a classic Gas House brawler—and a terrific hitter. At the end of the first, scoreless inning, Medwick trotted back to the dugout. My father said, "Watch what Ducky does with his left foot."

I watched. Medwick carefully planted his left foot on third base bag as he reached the infield. "That's good luck," my father said. "He does that every time he goes out and comes in from the field."

In his first at bat, Medwick belted a screaming triple into the left field corner. "See what I mean?" my father said. I was impressed.

I was impressed in another way a few weeks later when my father introduced me to Frank Hague outside Jersey City's Roosevelt Stadium, after watching the Jersey City Giants play Newark, a rival in the International League. That was the day the mayor mashed my hand and told me my father was a hell of a guy. How many other kids had that kind of father?

This mayoral endorsement and Uncle Dave's stories of my father's boxing prowess inclined me to become friends with some of the wilder characters in my class at St. Patrick's Parochial School. At the head of the line was Billy Braitsch, who had been left back twice, mostly for bad conduct and a general refusal to look at a book. "Braitschy," as we called him, was naturally bigger than the rest of us and quick with his fists. He lived near me and we often walked home from school together. Billy had a terrific arm; with the right coaching he might have become a major-league pitcher. In a snowball fight he was a great ally and a deadly enemy.

One day we started winging snowballs at Jimmy Matthiesen, who was on the other side of Arlington Avenue. Jimmy ducked one from Braitschy that would have taken his head off and it smashed the window of the house next door to ours. Braitschy and Matthiesen ran but I stayed and confessed. I thought my father would be furious but he paid the damages with little more than a growl about having better aim the next time.

This largesse won Braitschy's heart. When elections were held to decide who was going to be president of our fifth-grade class, Billy announced I was his candidate and any male who didn't vote for me was likely to end up with a fat upper lip. I won in a landslide.

My mother thought this wasn't "right" and wondered why the nuns did not stop Braitsch's reign of terror. She also wondered why I hung around with mugs like Braitsch. My father said nothing but I had a feeling he liked Braitschy, as long as Billy didn't do something that attracted the cops in our direction. I suspect Teddy Fleming was already worried that I was going to turn into a momma's boy and considered Braitsch a good sign that I might escape this (to him) appalling destiny. I can see now that I was trying to straddle my mother's goody-goody view of things and my father's streetwise ways.

Another close school friend was Billy Gannon, a husky wildman who more than matched Braitsch in his disinclination to look at a book. Throughout our grammar school years, nuns frequently berated him. "William Gannon, if you'd only study, you could get marks as high as Thomas Fleming." One of the most inveterate ranters was Sister Stella Agnes, our broadbeamed seventh-grade teacher, whose covert nickname was "Dynamite Aggie." By that time I sensed this was exactly what Billy wanted to hear. Let Fleming study his brains out and get high marks. I'll have a good time.

Billy frequently brought his good-time approach to the classroom, sailing paper airplanes when Sister turned her back to write on the blackboard and once rolling several marbles down the aisle, hoping Dynamite Aggie would step on one and fall on her face. Inevitably, one of the girls snitched and Aggie punished Billy with ferocious whacks on the back of his legs with a yardstick. Billy took his punishment with a smile. Nothing could make him cry.

I thought of my father taking similar whacks from Monsignor

Meehan and admired Billy—though I avoided doing anything that stirred Aggie's wrath. I was not at all sure I could take twenty-five whacks without wailing.

On the way home from St. Patrick's School, I often stopped at Aunt Mae Gallagher's house for tea and cookies. I liked her almost as much as Uncle Dave. Sometimes when I got there she would be talking on the telephone to Charlie Fleming's oldest child, Alice, advising her on what to do about her no-good husband, Bill Nagle. Aunt Mae would fill me in on this character, who regularly beat up Alice and her kids. Charlie's widow had married a man named Thomas Freeman and we had lost touch with her and her younger children, Charles Jr. and Raymond.

By this time Mae had lost her good looks. She had gotten fat and her breasts were too large for the rest of her short body. Her shape and her lower-class accent made her the total opposite of my elegant mother. But I remained oblivious to such social distinctions. Besides, I liked the tea and cookies Mae gave me without stint.

On most days she reminisced about growing up in downtown Jersey City, with my father the hero of many of her stories. This was where I heard about the high-collared clerk who wanted to know if you were Protestant or Catholic. She shared her memories of the Black Tom explosion and her plot to match Teddy Fleming and Kitty Dolan. It was marvelous stuff for a future novelist to imbibe.

On other days, while I slurped and chewed, Aunt Mae pumped me, not too subtly, about my parents' stormy marriage. Looking back, I can see she was worried that it was heading for a divorce court. She was more than ready to intervene on Kitty's behalf. Though she liked my father enormously, she did not worship him, and gender was definitely stronger than brotherly love.

Ironically, Aunt Mae's marriage was not a model of tranquillity. Al Gallagher was a soft, spoken, easygoing man, a reader and a thinker. He often discussed national politics with me, something my father seldom did. He read the *Saturday Evening Post* and similar magazines, which never appeared in the Fleming household.

Uncle Al worked nights at the Hudson and Manhattan Tubes. He kept their large three-family house in good condition and drove a nice car. Nevertheless, Aunt Mae seemed disappointed in him. She frequently berated him on matters large and small. I suspect it was because he had no interest in a political career. To her, Teddy Fleming's rise to prominence was the stuff of romance. When Al declined to imitate him, he acquired an aura of failure in her eyes.

One day my mother told me Al had warned Mae, "If you talk that way to me again, I'm walking out of here and I'm not coming back." According to Kitty, that was the day Mae learned to control her temper.

My mother sided with Al, who was her first cousin. She portrayed herself and him as peace-loving people who had married Flemings, a tribe that enjoyed losing their tempers and screaming at their loved ones. She said the Flemings proved the accuracy of the old Irish saying, "Street angel, house devil."

My adult heart still goes out to Kitty, like my boyhood one. But I have never stopped wondering why she could not see that her attitude toward the Fleming family and her husband's career was inflicting a sense of inferiority on Teddy Fleming that made him deeply, dangerously angry. In the name of love she was asking for impossible changes that slowly turned love into something very close to hatred.

# 22

# One True Faith

Election day was the most exciting day of the year in our house. It topped Christmas, Easter, and the Fourth of July. By the time I was ten, I was a complete convert to the Hague Organization's politics. I fervently believed it was the Catholic Democrats of Jersey City against the Protestant Republicans in the rest of New Jersey. These Protestants used to run Jersey City before Mayor Hague took over. They did not care if Catholics lived in tenements with no running water or only cold water. They lived in big houses in the suburbs and owned railroads and banks and factories where they paid Catholic workers as little as possible.

The Republicans were out to get us. They called Mayor Hague a crook. They accused him of stealing votes to elect Democrats. In 1937, the year I was ten, a Protestant minister named Lester Klee ran for governor of New Jersey. Here, certainly, was proof that these heretics owned the Republican Party. It was a very close election, which the Democratic candidate, A. Harry Moore, won only by a few thousand votes, to my great glee.

An infuriated Reverend Klee accused Mayor Hague of stealing the election and a Republican judge sent the New Jersey State Police to seize the ballots in the Hudson County Court House. Mayor Hague ordered a small army of county cops to confront the state cops on the courthouse steps. The state cops went away without the ballots.

The by now almost maniacal Republicans sought the help of the courts. Alas for them, the man who heard their case was Chief Justice Thomas Brogan, whom Mayor Hague had had the forethought to place on the state supreme court several years earlier. Justice Brogan, formerly Jersey City's corporation counsel, listened to stories of Republicans being terrorized into fleeing polling places and men voting from graveyards and mental hospitals and ruled under the great principle of the law, *quod non apparet non est*, that there was no evidence of corruption in the election and therefore no reason to grant a subpoena of Hudson County's voting records.

This was exciting stuff for a ten-year-old. I presumed the Republicans were liars and expressed outrage to my mother at the awful names they were calling the Hague Democrats. "They're telling the truth," Kitty said. "The Hague machine steals thousands of votes each election day."

I was stunned. "Do they steal them in the Sixth Ward too?" I asked.

"Probably more than in the other wards. The Sixth Ward has more stupid people," she said. "They do what they're told. They vote two or three times and the Republican poll watchers look the other way. They know the cops will beat them up if they say anything."

I yearned to ask my father whether this was true. But I was afraid he would get mad at both me and my mother. Was breaking the law like this another way of proving you had nerve? My mother obviously disapproved of it. But my father had more or less broken the law to keep Uncle George out of jail and Kitty had not objected to that. In fact she had begged him to do it.

The year after the great clash with Lester Klee and the Protestants, we confronted another enemy in Jersey City—Communists. They were atheists—making them even more dangerous than the Protestants, who at least claimed to believe in God. Communists were not even loyal Americans. They owed their allegiance to Josef Stalin, dictator of Soviet Russia. This was why Mayor Hague condemned them.

The Communists who invaded Jersey City in 1938 were in something called the CIO—the Congress of Industrial Organizations—and they tried to persuade the factory workers of Jersey City to join their unions. They soon discovered that Mayor Hague did not tolerate these disturbers of the peace in our city. Police regularly arrested CIO men when they tried to speak to workers without a permit. They confiscated their literature when they tried to hand it out at factory gates.

When the CIO held a big rally in Journal Square, they got pelted with rotten eggs, while the cops stood around beaming approval. When prominent liberals such as Norman Thomas, the leader of the Socialist Party, invaded Jersey City to speak on the CIO's behalf, the police unceremoniously deported them back to New York on the first available ferryboat.

My mother seemed to approve of Mayor Hague's determination to bar Communists, aka CIO men, from the city. She had become more and more religious since I started parochial school and we had to go to Mass every Sunday. Apparently she felt atheists deserved no quarter.

No one said a word about the days when Hague had waged war against strikebreakers and prevented violence in disputes between business and labor in Jersey City. The CIO triggered strikes marked by violence everywhere and often displayed a swaggering contempt for local police forces. The mayor may also have been personally offended by the numerous Communists in the CIO's ranks. They violated his vision of Jersey City as an orderly Catholic city.

To my surprise Teddy Fleming was not enthusiastic about suppressing the CIO. "We're getting terrible stuff printed about us in the newspapers all over the country," he said. "That's going to hurt us up the line. We should have let them organize the unions and cut a deal with them to guarantee they'd vote our way on election day."

I was too young to appreciate it, but this was statesmanship. The CIO imbroglio convinced the New York newspapers that Frank Hague was a dangerous man, and they proceeded to demonize him. They seized on a remark he made while trying to prevent a juvenile offender from being sentenced to jail. When the court told the mayor they were only following the law, Hague roared in his best give 'em hell style, "I am the law in this case!"

Connecting this remark to his assault on the CIO, the newspapers began calling him Frank "I am the law" Hague. In one sense it struck me as not far from the truth. The mayor was the law in Jersey City when he wanted to be. He had what counted: clout. He may have been sowing the seeds of future grief for himself and everyone else in the Hague Organization. But for the moment the big fellow looked invulnerable. He was reelected for the sixth time in May of 1937, 110,743 to 6,798.

The people of Jersey City seemed totally devoted to Frank Hague, as far as I could see. He was providing them with a crime-free, vice-free city with clean streets and a slogan, "Everything for Industry," that attracted big companies to build factories in the city. Looming above the skyline was the ultimate source of the average voters' loyalty, the immense hospital complex Hague had built with WPA money, the Medical Center. The mayor spared no expense to staff it with the best doctors in the country.

Beside the Medical Center loomed a separate skyscraper, the Margaret Hague Maternity Hospital, which guaranteed every woman in Jersey City the right to have her babies in first-class medical surroundings. The mayor had named it after his mother, who had delivered her children on the kitchen table of their Second Ward tenement. Of the more than six thousand mothers admitted in 1936, only twenty died, a mortality rate of one-third of one percent, well below the national average. Infant mortality was equally low. Best of all, for those who could not afford to pay, the Medical Center and the Margaret Hague were free.

Election night always meant a party. Hundreds of Sixth Warders poured in and out to shake Teddy Fleming's hand and congratulate him for another Democratic victory. The Sixth regularly had turnouts of over ninety percent, often the best in the city. This was a testament to the ward leader's popularity, some thought. Others hailed it as evidence of his ability to "organize" the ward, to have hard workers in every district knocking on doors to persuade people to come out and vote.

My mother never looked happy at these parties. The next morning at breakfast, if my father was sleeping late, she would sigh and say, "Another night with the lowbrows." She did not think much of the citizens of the Sixth Ward.

One of my mother's favorite verbal targets was Mae Morrisoe, the woman leader of the district in which we lived. When the Nineteenth Amendment became law in 1920, the Hague Organization had appointed women in every district to get out the female vote. Tall and homely, Mae talked very slowly. She worshipped my father; every time she looked at him, her face all but glowed with admiration.

Mae's grammar was atrocious. She said, "I thought we wasn't gonna win this time" and "Them Republicans got taught a lesson, ho-ho-ho." This consigned her to the lower depths in my mother's opinion. Kitty occasionally made even more fun of Mayor Hague's grammar, especially the time he called Jersey City "the most moralist city in America."

In spite of my mother's negative attitude, I enjoyed the election parties. It was fascinating to see the range of characters my father had assembled to help him run the ward. Assistant Leader Johnny Duff's grammar was also pretty bad. But I could not help liking him. He knew everything worth knowing about the New York Giants baseball team. He had been to many World Series games and saw my favorite player, Mel Ott, belt more than one home run.

A frequent election night visitor was Abe Stein, a big balding guy who ran a diner near the Junction, where three main streets met in the Sixth Ward. He and my father would exchange ethnic insults that would get them condemned for political incorrectness by today's liberal thought police. "Is it true what I hear—every hebe in the ward voted the straight ticket?" my father would say as they shook hands.

"Sure," Abe would say. "We charged Duff twice the going rate and he never noticed. You micks are too dumb to add straight."

A lot of the revelers had names that ended in "ski" and "o" and "a"—Pilsiduski, Krasko, Perella. The Sixth Ward was a veritable league of nations, with some streets all Polish, others all Italian, others all Slovak. Two of my father's most ardent supporters were Greek Orthodox priests who had a congregation in the ward. Teddy Fleming gave them all the same firm handshake. They were all his people. I never heard him say a word against any ethnic or racial group.

Another election night regular was a short, slim, curly-haired man named Johnny Smith. "Smitty," as my father called him, was not a member of the Sixth Ward Committee. He worked as a bus driver and had a lot to do with fighting corruption in the drivers' union.

When the union bosses hired goons to discourage the reformers, my father loaned Smitty his army .45. Smitty drove with it under the seat, with a bullet in the chamber. Late one night two big guys got on the bus. Smitty did not like the way they looked him over. He concluded they were planning to beat him silly when he reached the end of the route. Smitty called one of them to the front of the bus and unlimbered the .45. "If I were you and your buddy, I'd get off at the next stop," he said. They did.

"I forgot to take the bullet out of the chamber when I gave the gun back to your father," Smitty told me. "I heard he almost shot your toes off with it. He said a few things to me on the phone that guaranteed I never made that mistake again."

It was a thrill to think I had handled the gun that saved Smitty's neck—even if I almost lost a toe doing it. My mother called these guys lowbrows. I enjoyed their company. They treated me like I wasn't just a ten- or eleven-year-old kid. I was Teddy Fleming's son. That was a great feeling, no matter how many votes they stole.

Another attraction of election night parties were the overheard stories—the sort that never got into the newspapers. That was where I heard about Billy Black taking the suitcase full of money on the Hudson Tubes. My father told the story. Everyone roared with laughter. They seemed to think it was a riot that Mayor Hague had so much money, he sent it to New York in suitcases. I noticed my mother did not laugh at this story. Did it have something to do with the money she and my father argued about so often?

Another story my big ears picked up on election night concerned my uncle, Al Gallagher. Al went to Mass every Sunday and often received Holy Communion, something I never saw my father do. Someone remarked that Al was doing a great job on the grand jury, as usual. "I don't know what we'd do without him," my father said.

The next day, I asked my mother for an explanation. How did someone do a great job on the grand jury? "Al is City Hall's eyes and ears," she said. "He gets put on the jury almost every year. If he hears about somebody getting prosecuted that could make trouble for the mayor, he tells your father and he tells City Hall."

My mother shook her head with frowning disapproval. "If poor Al ever got caught, he could go to jail. It's against the law to tell anybody anything about a grand jury."

Uncle Al apparently did not care two pins about breaking his grand jury oath to keep City Hall alert to storm signals. Apparently he too saw Jersey City politics as an us Catholics against the Protestants struggle. Why didn't my mother understand this?

Johnny Smith told me another election night story that quickened my pulse—and inadvertently explained what had happened to my father's friend Dutch. Back in 1932, Prohibition still reigned and tons of illegal booze flowed through New Jersey to the speakeasies in New York. Hague made it clear to the bootleggers that he would do no business with Mafia mobsters. Why should they get a cut of the profits? The Organization would protect all the hooch and get a slice of everything that was sold.

"Your old man had a pal named Dutch," Smitty said. "He was a bootlegger with an okay from City Hall. One day Dutch told your father the mob was planning to unload a big shipment of Canadian booze from freight cars in the railroad cut that ran under Journal Square. Your father passed the word to City Hall and Hague invited him and me and a couple of other guys to join the showdown."

At about 3 A.M., Smitty said, while the hoods were busy unloading their stuff, floodlights blinked on from all sides of the railroad cut. Hague put a megaphone to his mouth and roared, "Okay, you assholes! You got five minutes to get in your cars and get the hell out of Jersey City. Leave the hooch where it is. We'll take care of it. If I see anyone take even a bottle with him, you're all gonna wind up in the morgue."

The mafiosos fled without even a murmur of resistance and the Organization acquired a half million dollars' worth of booze. Hague gave my father a five-thousand-dollar bonus, which he split with Dutch.

"Unfortunately," Smitty said, "Dutch had a big mouth. He bragged to the wrong people about pulling this thing off." One night as Dutch drove a truckload of illegal scotch down a deserted county road outside Secaucus, a blast of gunfire shredded the windshield, killing him instantly.

That was how I found out why my mother did not like Dutch—and what she meant when she said he had moved far away. I also realized my father thought it was a rotten thing to say. I regret to say I thought so too.

I picked up a lot of random information about Jersey City politics on election night. Italians, for instance, were "bullet voters." They tended to forget their allegiance to City Hall when they saw a

Republican with an Italian name on the ticket. Bullet voters were considered a plague by my father and his workers in the Sixth Ward. You could not reason with them—or threaten them.

The good Democrat was the man or woman who voted the straight ticket. This was the apotheosis of loyalty. Never mind if you didn't like everyone on the ballot. The Organization needed those straight ticket votes to intimidate the opposition, inside and outside Jersey City. Frank Hague was never satisfied to win. He always wanted to win big. Even in primary elections, when he only needed six or seven hundred votes to get on the ballot, Hague insisted on the Organization delivering over a hundred thousand.

Another interesting election night discovery was the "No-Show" job. A certain number of these were handed out to each ward leader. That meant one or two members of the ward committee were carried on some payroll in the city or county but spent all their time in the ward on political matters. No-Shows were considered a sign of the ward leader's favor, and those who got them stirred not a little envy in the hearts of those who had to go to work every day. A No-Show was still snoozing while the lesser breeds were toiling.

Of course the envious conveniently forgot that the No-Show, if he was doing his political job, also worked very late—usually until the bars closed at 2 A.M. In the Sixth Ward, Johnny Duff had the premier No-Show job.

Another thing I picked up during these parties was my father's role as the no-nonsense boss of the Sixth Ward. Woe to the man who did not produce a good turnout in his district. They came into the house tentatively, eyes wary and anxious, and approached him with muttered apologies.

Typical was a committeeman named Swifty Moran. He was a flashy dresser and a lover of horseflesh. He put more time into playing the races than into politics. "Teddy, I don't know what happened. I had promises from at least fifty people. They all welched," Swifty whined one night.

"You want to place any more bets on those nags, you better find out what happened," my father growled.

I soon discerned that underneath a lot of the camaraderie there was a layer of fear, especially when someone screwed up. One night another committeeman proudly announced he had carried his district 868 votes to none. "You idiot!" my father roared. "There were two Republican poll watchers!" They had to concoct a story about one of the Republicans becoming ill and the other one rushing him to the hospital. There was no fear of contradiction. The Republican Party in Jersey City was a totally cowed fiefdom of Frank Hague's imperium.

I was more interested in noting that my father was not always a nice guy down in the Sixth Ward, any more than he was at home. In both places, he was a tough mick with a quick temper. But he got the job done. The Sixth's great turnouts gave him a lot of clout at City Hall, when it came to getting jobs and promotions for his people. Frank Hague ran the Organization like a business. If you got results for him he delivered results for you.

I picked up a surprising amount of information about major political figures at election night parties. A. Harry Moore, who became both a U.S. senator and the governor of New Jersey with Hague's backing, was regarded as a dimwit who barely knew what day it was without checking first with the mayor. Hague needed Moore's Protestant image to win big elections. Moore personified the dilemma of most Irish-American political organizations—their candidates did not play well outside their city or at most their state limits, as Al Smith had dolorously demonstrated.

Election parties were not the only memorable nights in our house. On New Year's Eve my father often threw a party for the family. All the relatives from both sides of the marriage would crowd into the house—Greens, Gallaghers, Flemings, Shanaphys, O'Neils (cousins of the Flemings), and Uncle George Dolan until he became an exile by my father's wrathful decree.

At these parties, Dave Fleming was in his element. He called my father "the Commissar," because he was always bossing people around. Everyone looked nervous, knowing Teddy's temper. "Some people need bossing—and that includes you," my father would growl. Dave just grinned at him.

Later in the party Dave would sidle up to my mother and say, "One of these days, Kitty, you're gonna wake up and find my shoes under your bed."

My mother would giggle girlishly. My father would frown but he let Dave get away with it. I was too young to get the real innuendo but I grasped the general idea that Dave would marry her if my father wasn't in the way. Also in the way was Dave's wife, Lizzie, of course, whose smile always looked goofy because she had lost most of her teeth in seven pregnancies and had not bothered to replace them. If Mae Morrisroe's grammar was bad, Lizzie's was in some subterranean zone below atrocious. She said "We was" and "You ain't" and "Them don't." My mother could only shake her head in despair and wonder why Dave had married her.

After a few drinks, the family parties always turned into songfests. My mother played the piano quite well. She would take over the baby grand in the corner of our living room and they would sing old favorites, many of them Irish or Irish-American songs, such as "I'll Take You Home Again Kathleen," "Danny Boy," and "The Sidewalks of New York." I got a glimpse of the Fleming-Dolan-Green clan's Irish past. The songs obviously meant a lot to them. Sometimes husbands and wives would take hands as a sentimental song reached a climax, as in another favorite, "Nelly Kelly."

> It's the same old song they sing:
> I love you.
> The boys are all mad about Nelly,
> The daughter of Officer Kelly.
> So it's all day long they bring
> Flowers all dripping with dew,
> And they join in the chorus of Nelly Kelly,
> I love you!

After the group singing, solos would be requested. Uncle Al Gallagher invariably gave us a rendition of "Old Black Joe," in which he hit some marvelously deep bass notes. Others sang old favorites, such as "Moonlight Bay." Finally, Aunt Mae would ask my father to sing. He would invariably shake his head. No, no, no, he'd say, as my mother sat with her fingers poised over the keys. Finally, Mae would badger him into submission. No one else had the nerve to try it.

My mother would riffle the keys and my father would reveal a marvelous baritone voice. I could not carry a tune. The first time I heard my father sing, I felt a special pang of envy. Why hadn't I inherited that voice?

He always sang the same song: "Let Me Call You Sweetheart." He sat beside my mother on the piano bench and sang it in an almost meditative way, his head slightly lowered to the right, not looking at anyone, carefully enunciating each word.

> Let me call you sweetheart,
> I'm in love with you.
> Let me hear you whisper
> That you love me too.
> Keep the love light burning
> In your eyes so blue.
> Let me call you sweetheart,
> I'm in love with you!

As he sang the last note in that mellow baritone, my mother kissed him. Aunt Mae beamed. Everyone applauded.

I watched this performance with a painful mixture of amazement and sorrow. My father really seemed to mean those words. My mother seemed to mean that kiss. How or why could they have so many angry arguments if they loved each other that way? Of course I had no inkling of the special meaning the word "sweetheart" had held for them back in the 1920s.

Maybe it was a performance for the benefit of the family. But I didn't think so then, nor do I now. Their early letters prove they had experienced genuine love. There were moments when they both reached back to it, hoping for some kind of magical transformation. But the odds against such a miracle were growing longer with every passing day.

# 23

# I Can't Live with That Man

**M**y parents' mysterious love life was not my only worry. As I reached the age of eleven or twelve, I began to suspect my father did not believe in God. This was serious. My belief in the Catholic Church was as intense as my embrace of Frank Hague and the Democratic Party. I especially worried about Teddy Fleming's apparent indifference to going to church on Sunday. The nuns and priests told us it was a mortal sin to miss Sunday Mass. I feared my father was going to hell. I begged God to persuade or frighten him into going to Mass.

I contrasted my father with my friend Henry Mullaney's father, who was a daily communicant. He took up the collection at Sunday Mass. I sometimes had dinner at Henry's house and stayed overnight. Mr. Mullaney talked about God and God's will all the time. He was a tall, rather prissy man who worked as a clerk in City Hall. I didn't particularly like him but I envied his devoutness. I wanted to stop worrying about my father going to hell.

During the summer, Teddy Fleming drove us to church from our cottage in Point Pleasant and told us he would stand in the back during the Mass so he could have the car ready for a quick departure, avoiding the usual traffic jam in the parking lot.

For a while I glanced over my shoulder during the ceremony to see if he was in the back. I seldom saw him, but when I asked him where he had been, he solemnly assured me he had retreated to the vestibule because the back of the church was too crowded or too hot.

Sometimes, seized by doubt, I asked him what the sermon had been about. "Money, as usual," he said. He was almost always right. The Catholic Church of those days was not shy about demanding an open wallet from massgoers. When the collection was being taken up, the pastor of the church often abandoned the ritual of the Mass to turn and shout, "Did I hear the clink of a coin in that basket? I don't want anything but the rustle of *bills*."

One day I asked my father why he didn't go to Mass. "The people who don't go are a lot better than the people who go," he said. "Like Timmy Mullaney, that draft dodger."

I did not know what he was talking about. He told me that he had gone to grammar school with Mr. Mullaney. He said nothing about terrifying him into replacing Teddy Fleming at midweek Mass at All Saints; Aunt Mae told me that story a few years later. Apparently Mr. Mullaney had gotten married to avoid the draft when World War I began. While Teddy Fleming was ducking bullets in France, Mullaney stayed home and went to communion every day. I stopped envying his devoutness. I also decided I would never be a daily communicant.

I began to realize that my father lived by a different set of rules. One day after Mass in Point Pleasant, a man called to him as we walked to the car. Teddy Fleming talked intently to him for a few minutes. As they parted, the man held out his hand. My father started to take it, then pulled back his hand and said, "I told you I'd do my best."

I asked him why he hadn't shaken hands. "The guy is looking for a better job," he said. "If I'd shaken his hand, I'd have to move heaven and earth to get it for him. I'm not sure I can do it."

That was where I learned the centrality of a promise in my father's code. A promise sealed by a handshake could never be withdrawn. A politician's word was something he never broke. It was his stock-in-trade, his bond of trust with the voters—and with fellow politicians. I was impressed.

I gradually stopped worrying about my father getting sent to hell for not going to Mass—or for stealing votes. The Catholic Church did not seem to disapprove of Frank Hague. One day, the front pages of the local newspapers had pictures of the mayor giving Archbishop

Thomas Walsh of Newark a check for $1 million to help build a new seminary. The archbishop said all sorts of nice things about the mayor.

Mayor Hague also gave $50,000 for an altar at his parish church; the pastor accepted this largesse with a smile as big as the archbishop's. The church's blessing seemed to remove or at least diminish the impact of my mother's remarks about stealing votes and her complaints about my father being a street angel and a house devil.

In Point Pleasant, my father added to our pleasures by buying a rowboat and a three-horsepower outboard motor. We named the boat *Sandy*, after our Welsh terrier. We were soon spending many hours in it on the Manasquan River. I never dreamt this innocent past time would trigger another violent disagreement between my mother and father.

We had an especially good time aboard *Sandy* when we went crabbing. My father nicknamed the crabs as we caught them. "Let's call him Wee Willie Keeler," he would say of a small one, after the famous baseball player of his youth.

"Let's call him Bronco Nagurski," he would say when we got a big one. Bronco was an all-star football behemoth.

We anchored the boat on Lake Louise, only a block from our house. It was a saltwater pond, an arm of the Manasquan River. One Saturday in 1939 we set out on another crabbing expedition and discovered the motor would not start. My father pulled the cord again and again. *Cough cough chug blug*. It was a hot July day. My brother Gene and I sat watching sympathetically. *Cough cough blug*.

From the shore of the lake came a yell: "Hey Fleming! Get a canoe!"

It was August Klinger, a wealthy German-American jewelry manufacturer from Brooklyn. I hung around with his youngest son, George. The father was a born loudmouth who specialized in razzing people. He was renting a house on the lake. For a half hour, Teddy Fleming tried to start the motor while Klinger yelled derision and his weekend guests sat on the terrace, laughing at us.

Cursing under his breath, my father rowed back to shore. We put the motor in the trunk of the car and drove to a nearby boatyard for repairs. "Don't say a word about this to your mother," he snarled. He obviously did not think Klinger's shouts were amusing. I was puzzled by the apparent connection in his mind between the razzing and my mother.

A week later, Mr. and Mrs. Klinger appeared at our door for a Sunday afternoon social call. My mother was obviously thrilled and I soon saw why. Mrs. Klinger was very different from her loudmouth husband. She was genteel, with a sweet, delicate face and dignified, reserved manner. She was the kind of upper-middle-class woman that my mother wanted to associate with—instead of the ungrammatical Mae Morrisroe types that politics required her to ingratiate in the Sixth Ward.

My father was taking a nap. My mother sent me rushing into his bedroom to tell him the Klingers were here. She sat on the porch, conversing eagerly with them. Finally footsteps announced my father's arrival. My mother's face fell. Teddy Fleming was wearing the same dirty tan slacks he had worn at breakfast. Above them was his white tank-top underwear. He had not even bothered to put on a shirt. His hair was uncombed. Two buttons on his fly were open.

My father conversed genially enough, laughing away more taunts about the cranky outboard motor. But the Klingers stayed only a half hour and never called again. My mother was furious with my father. When she asked him why he hadn't dressed decently, he snapped, "The less I see of Augie Klinger, the better. He's a windbag and a Republican in the bargain."

At the time, I was baffled by my father's conduct. He had a closet full of creamy white summer suits. Why hadn't he put one on? Now I understand what he was thinking: *Treat me like a mick and you get a mick*. As for my mother's yearning to socialize with Mrs. Klinger—that was her problem.

Pretty soon I began to think they disagreed about everything. I tried not to take sides, but it was almost impossible to control my feelings. I wanted to love both of them, but how could you do that when they obviously no longer loved each other?

On our Sunday rides during the winter months, my mother would often try to talk my father into buying us dinner in some roadside eatery. He would resist, claiming it was a waste of money to take kids to a restaurant. They never ate what they ordered, which was unquestionably true of me and my brother Gene.

One day we were in heavy traffic on Route 9W and they started arguing about dinner. I was in the front seat beside my father. He turned his head to give my mother a sharp answer and the car ahead of us stopped short. We plowed into the rear of it and my face smashed the windshield. I had cuts under each eye, a big one on my chin, and another big one on my forehead. My mother sobbed that I was going to be scarred for life.

My father lifted me out of the car and sat me on a boulder on the side of the road. I was in a daze. He exchanged insurance information with the people in the car he had hit and an ambulance arrived. An intern stitched my cuts and we drove home. I was still in a daze. My mother moaned about my future scars.

That night, my father came into my bedroom as I was going to sleep. "I'm proud of you," he said.

"Why?" I asked.

"You didn't cry." he said. "Those cuts must have hurt like hell. But you didn't shed a tear."

Was he telling me I had nerve? Or just that he hoped I had it? Either way, it made me feel better about my aching face to know that my father thought I was a man.

When I was about eleven, I started playing sandlot baseball. In our case it should have been called cinderlot—our infield was thick with cinders from a nearby railroad line. But I liked the ballfield's name: the Happy Nines. I liked it even more when I found out my father had played on it when he was a kid. I usually played third base, although I did not have the arm for the long throw to first base. My father had told me third had been his favorite position.

There were two teams in the neighborhood, big guys and little guys. I was one of the little guys. Occasionally, the big guys would play with us. Late one spring day, I was playing third when Joe Keller, who was a high school star, came up to bat. He hit a terrific shot at me. It took a bad hop and smacked me in the teeth.

I ran home with the salt taste of blood in my mouth. Who should I meet in front of our house but my father, just getting into his limousine on the way to a political rally. He was dressed in one of his best dark blue suits, with a grey homburg on his head. I was trying not to cry and I tried harder when I saw him. But I was sure I was seriously injured.

He wiped my mouth with his handkerchief and fingered my teeth to see if they were loose. "It's not so bad," he said. "Let's wash it out."

When my mother saw the blood, she wanted to call the doctor or rush me to the hospital. At the very least, I should lie down for the rest of the day. My father ignored her. He ran cold water on his handkerchief and pressed it against my split upper lip. After about five minutes it stopped hurting.

"Come on," he said. "I'll hit you a couple. You can't let this ruin your nerve."

He picked up a bat and ball on the back porch and we went into the backyard. He hung his suitcoat on the fence, loosened his tie, and started hitting grounders to me. Fielding the first couple, I instinctively turned my head away.

"No, no," my father said. "Keep your head down. Don't let one bad hop shake your nerve. They don't happen that often."

For twenty minutes, he hit grounders to me, soft ones at first, then harder and harder ones, until I was fielding scorchers with my head down.

"You're okay now," he said, after I fielded five hot ones in a row. He put on his coat, straightened his tie, and went off to the rally.

The next day Joe Keller hit another shot to me at third base. I threw him out by a step. Nerve! Maybe I had it! I told my father about it at dinner and he was enormously pleased. I felt ten feet tall for a week.

My euphoria did not last very long. My mother and father had a number of nasty quarrels during the next several months. Some were about money, others about a man who was married to one of my mother's oldest friends, Marie Hannaway Farrelly. She was a big smiling woman who talked almost as slowly as Mae Morrisoe, but was smarter. Her husband, Walter, was a fireman.

A wiry man with a rakish smile, Walter Farrelly was a reader and a talker. He had opinions about everything, from the existence of God to the honesty of Mayor Frank Hague. About God he claimed to have "doubts," which my mother seemed to think was somehow daring. About Frank Hague, Walter had no doubts. The mayor was for the birds. This was not a prudent thing to say in Jersey City if you had a municipal job. Hague expected absolute loyalty from everyone who was on the payroll.

Walter called Mayor Hague a dictator and many other uncomplimentary names while he was on duty in his firehouse. The remarks were soon a matter of record in City Hall. The Organization had "ears" everywhere. Walter proceeded to get "the treatment." With no warning, he was transferred from a firehouse on the west side of the city to one on the extreme east side. This involved a lot of packing and unpacking. Firemen lived in their firehouses for days at a time and they had a great deal of clothing as well as equipment to transport from one station to another.

No sooner had Walter gotten unpacked in the east side firehouse than he was transferred to a station in the distant north end of the city. No sooner had he gotten unpacked there than he was ordered to the south end of the city. And so forth. Walter remained defiant, insisting his ordeal only proved Frank Hague was on a par with Adolf Hitler, Benito Mussolini, and other European dictators.

A weeping Marie told my mother all about Walter's troubles. My mother in turn told my father, and asked him to intercede on Walter's behalf. "Are you out of your goddamn mind?" Teddy Fleming roared. "Tell him to shut his stupid mouth or he'll have a lot more to worry about than packing and unpacking his trunk. He'll spend the next six months in the Medical Center getting his face put back together!"

My mother expressed horror at the thought that Walter might get his features modified by a police nightstick. My father told her to "grow up once and for all, for Christ's sake." I listened to this exchange with fascination. To some extent I sympathized with Walter. On the other hand, didn't he understand that it was us poor Catholics against the rich, coldhearted Protestants in a struggle for survival? Why didn't my mother see this, instead of fretting about Walter's exhaustion and Marie's tears?

This fight got really nasty when my mother announced she was inviting Walter and Marie to dinner. "The hell you are!" my father roared. "What in Christ are you trying to do, ruin me?"

My mother wanted to know why she couldn't have one of her oldest friends for dinner. "Because her husband's a goddamn idiot!" Teddy Fleming bellowed.

"Walter is not an idiot. He's one of the most cultivated, well-read men I've ever met," my mother said.

"He's a cultivated idiot!" my father raged. "Tell him to get a job teaching in some college where he can sound off to his heart's content."

My mother sulked for days and kept asking my father why she could not have Walter and Marie for dinner. Walter claimed to be unrepentant, but after ten or fifteen transfers he had decided to stop saying nasty things about Frank Hague. My father still balked. "I don't like the guy," he snarled.

"I don't like a lot of your friends but I put up with them," my mother said. This was a direct reference to my father's political followers in the Sixth Ward. It sent Teddy Fleming's temperature soaring.

"You goddamn well better put up with them!" he roared. "They help put those nice clothes on your back and the steak and roast beef on your table. You wouldn't have any charge accounts to run up if it wasn't for those guys. If I ever catch you saying anything about them I'll make your life so goddamn miserable—"

"How? By smacking me in the teeth? Becoming a wife beater?"

"You know damn well I'm never gonna do that!" my father roared.

"Stop it, please!" I begged.

Nana and my brother Gene added a silent plea to my words. The combatants desisted but I was left fearing worse was to come. They could not agree on anything.

We were getting closer and closer to the big explosion. I did not know exactly how it was going to happen but I could almost hear a ticking sound, as if there were a bomb in our cellar. I began having the dream of the undulating serpent again. Jersey City was hardly the Garden of Eden but I sensed some sort of evil was heading our way.

A few months later, I got a close-up of the Hague Organization's political discipline. Across the street from us lived a large family I will call the Monahans. The father worked in City Hall. One son, Billy, was around my age. There were three or four older sons and daughters. The father, Pete Monahan, worked in City Hall and was passed over for a promotion. He began talking down Hague in various bars around the neighborhood. Soon the word came from Needlenose Johnny Malone to my father: "Tell Pete Monahan to shut up."

My father asked Monahan to come over for a talk one Saturday morning. He was a big fleshy man, at least six feet tall. He must have weighed well over two hundred pounds. I was in my bedroom reading a book. Suddenly voices rose to decibels far above a conversational level downstairs.

"Don't tell me I can't say what I please about Frank Hague. He's a son of a bitch and so are you," Pete Monahan bellowed.

"Watch who you call a son of a bitch!" my father roared.

I had a vision of him and Pete Monahan slugging it out. I was not at all sure my father would win. Pete outweighed him by at least forty pounds.

An instant later a tremendous crash shook the house. My father shouted, "Kit! Kit! Call an ambulance."

I rushed halfway downstairs, where I had a view of the living room. My mother stood in the hall, wringing her hands. Pete Monahan lay on the living room floor on his back, breathing in a strange noisy way. He sounded like a car that refused to start.

"What happened? Did you hit him?" my mother cried.

"I didn't touch him. He's having a heart attack," my father said. "Call a goddamn ambulance!"

Teddy knelt beside Pete Monahan, trying to unbutton his shirt collar. I retreated upstairs. In five minutes an ambulance clanged to the door. They rushed Pete Monahan to the Medical Center. He was dead on arrival. My father was tremendously upset. He went across the street and spent several hours with the Monahans.

My mother regarded the episode as a disgrace. Coming on the heels of Walter Farrelly's "treatment," she was not disposed to give my father a break. "He's lucky he won't go to jail," she told me. "He would, in any other city."

"You mean you think he hit him?" I said, appalled at the thought of my father being a murderer.

"I don't know what he did," my mother said. "The poor man didn't deserve to be browbeaten that way."

"He didn't hit him," I insisted. "Dad said he didn't hit him."

"Maybe not. But he brought on his heart attack."

About a week later, my father told us he had gotten Mrs. Monahan a job at City Hall. "I was only trying to tell Pete to keep his big mouth shut. I could have straightened things out downtown in a month or two and he would have gotten his goddamn raise. But he was a hothead—"

"You should have kept *your* temper," my mother said.

"Jesus H. Christ, when I want advice from you I'll ask for it!" my father roared. He stormed out of the house without finishing his dinner. A performance, I would realize much later, worthy of Davey Fleming.

Later that night I awoke to hear them arguing ferociously in my mother's bedroom, which was next to mine. "Once and for all will you admit you don't know what the hell you're talking about when it comes to politics?" my father bellowed.

"Sometimes I find myself wishing I could die like poor Pete Monahan when you talk to me this way!" my mother wailed.

"You won't find me crying over you if you do!" he roared.

I pulled the covers over my head but it did not drown out their voices. In the next bed my brother Gene slept soundly.

A few months later, when I came home from school, my mother stunned me with a solemn announcement: "Your father's in the hospital."

"Why?" I asked.

"He's going to have his gallbladder out."

Her tone of voice struck me as strange. There was an almost feverish light in her eyes. I asked for an explanation of how a gallbladder required surgery. I was already working on becoming a hypochondriac. I only had to hear about an illness to be convinced I had it. My mother explained how stones formed in the gallbladder and then got stuck in the duct, causing nausea and pain.

"He's been having some terrible attacks," she said in the same odd voice. "Two nights ago, I watched him crawl out of his bedroom to the bathroom and vomit black bile into the toilet bowl. He was in agony."

I was distressed. I could almost feel my father's pain. "God did it," my mother said. "He answered my prayers. I asked Him to punish that man for the way he treats me."

Once more I was astounded and this time a little frightened. Did my mother have this supernatural ability to invoke God's wrath? I had no doubt that God got angry with sinners. The Old Testament, which we studied at St. Patrick's School, was full of examples of a wrathful Jehovah punishing the sinful people of Israel. But did my father deserve that sort of punishment? Was this what happened when people stopped loving each other?

My father's gallbladder was removed the next day. My brother and I visited him in the hospital a few days later. He was sitting up in bed, surrounded by his committeemen from the ward. He was rapping out orders to check on this labor leader and that lawyer. He wanted a list of every new arrival in the Sixth Ward since the previous election and he wanted it the day before yesterday. Johnny Duff feverishly took notes and kept saying, "Sure, Teddy, sure."

At home, my mother talked about the way the surgery had put a strain on my father's bank account. He had been forced to borrow $500 from his sister Mae to pay the doctor. I was baffled all over again by my father's finances. We seemed to live a lot better than Aunt Mae and Uncle Al. Why did Teddy Fleming have to borrow money from them?

"He could get it from the ward but he doesn't have the nerve," my mother said. "He sends it all to City Hall. Every other ward leader's wife has money coming out her ears. Except me."

I sensed I was getting a little closer to the mystery of the quarrels over money—but not close enough to understand it.

About six months later, Nana died. It was stunningly sudden. During the night I heard a commotion in the next bedroom, where she slept. I drifted back to sleep without finding out that Nana was having a heart attack. When I got up in the morning, my mother told me Nana was dead. It was November 13—Kitty's birthday.

The local undertaker, Alfred Pakenham, set up a coffin in the living room and for two days Nana lay there, silent, her eyes shut. Cousins and friends came and praised her as a wonderful woman. Several people talked about her hard life. That was when I discovered that she had lost three little girls in a typhoid fever epidemic.

There were also guarded remarks about Tom Dolan's "trouble," which had forced my grandmother to open a store at one point in her married life. I asked my mother to explain and she told me rather tersely about her father's drinking problem. I began to understand the sadness I detected in Mary Fitzmaurice Dolan's silences.

On the last night of the wake, George Dolan came to the house. The ghastly white pallor of his face explained his absence on the first night. I soon learned he had Bright's disease, which meant imminent death by kidney failure. George knelt at his mother's bier and wept. I felt tremendously sorry for him.

My mother gazed at George with tears in her eyes. My father said nothing to him. But he arranged for him to go to the County Hospital in Secaucus, where he received decent care. Three weeks later George too was dead. My mother told me that he was so bitter at dying young—he was only forty-six—that he had refused the last rites of the Catholic Church. Apparently, George had continued his father's habit of quarreling with God. Compounding his bitterness was the disappointment of his failed careers in baseball and the movies.

I was getting a graduate course in the dark side of the American dream. Of course, that thought was beyond me at the age of thirteen. I was more inclined to think the Dolans' luck was awfully bad. I began to wonder if my mother knew what she was talking about when she joked about the number thirteen.

During the year after Nana died, the quarrels between my mother and father came to a horrendous climax. Kitty was under a lot of stress. At the age of forty-nine, she had to learn how to cook. Nana had cooked all our meals until the day she died. The results of my mother's early efforts were seldom gratifying. Roasts were burned or underdone, vegetables were cold or overdone. My father never seemed to be satisfied with his coffee. He was equally contemptuous about almost everything Kitty said or did. Without Nana's presence to restrain him, Teddy Fleming's sharp tongue acquired a razor edge.

The climactic fight started when we came home from a Sunday outing in the car. We went up the steps to the front door of our house and my mother fished in her pocketbook for her key. She could not find it.

"You can't remember to take your key with you when you go out?" my father sneered. "Where the hell do you get off claiming you're so goddamn smart when you can't remember something as simple as that?"

He unlocked the door and continued to fling abuse at her in the house. "So goddamn smart you're always telling me what to do and you can't remember your house key!"

"How many times have I told you I won't stand for you talking to me this way in front of the children!" my mother screamed.

"I'll talk to you this way any time I please!" my father bellowed. "Maybe it's time they found out what a goddamn idiot they've got for a mother!"

"And I'll tell them what a double-crossing liar they've got for a father!" she cried.

This was a broad hint that she still nursed doubts about his fidelity. "You can tell them anything you goddamn please. They won't believe you," he shouted. Knowing nothing about the ruinous clash over Mrs. Flanagan, I could only recoil from the violence seething between them.

"Mom, Dad, please stop," I said. They did not pay the slightest attention to me. My brother Gene, who was ten, fled upstairs to his room. I stayed downstairs, pleading in vain while the insults continued to fly. I began to feel like they were throwing rocks, most of which were hitting me.

The fight raged on for another hour and erupted again at the dinner table, when my father said the coffee tasted like swill. "You can't even make a goddamn cup of coffee, much less cook a decent meal!" he roared.

"I can't stand it, I can't stand it any longer," my mother screamed. She ran out to the kitchen and pounded on the red Formica tabletop with her fists. "I'm going to kill myself!" she cried.

My father finished his coffee and went upstairs to begin dressing for his nightly trip to the Sixth Ward clubhouse. In the kitchen, my mother screamed, "You don't love me. You don't love anyone. I can't stand living with you another day!"

I was frantic. I felt I was the only sane person in a crazy house. My brother was too young and too frightened to do anything. I ran out to the kitchen and found my mother on her knees in front of the open oven. "I'm going to do it," she cried. "I'll show everyone what a monster he is. I'll tell the whole world he doesn't love anyone or anything."

She put her head and shoulders into the oven, as if she were trying to see how death would feel. The oven was not turned on. I rushed over to her and tried to drag her out of that gaping black square. "No, Mom, please. No. Don't do it," I shouted.

She shoved me away and lunged toward the stove again, still on her knees. "He doesn't care. I'm going to do it!" she sobbed.

I raced down the hall and up the stairs to my father's room, in the back on the second floor. He was in the process of putting on one of his expensive silk ties. I can still see the color: bright yellow.

"Dad," I wailed. "Mom's putting her head into the oven. She's going to kill herself!"

He flipped the yellow tie one more time and began knotting it. He did not look at me. He looked at himself in the mirror and snarled, "She hasn't got the nerve."

I ran back downstairs and found the front door open. I charged out on the porch. It was December; the temperature was in the twenties. An icy wind whirled along the dark street. Wearing only a housedress, my mother was fleeing down the block like a fugitive.

Without stopping for a coat, I ran after her. She was still in a state of hysteria, half running, stumbling, and running again. "I'm through with him. Through!" she sobbed.

"Mom," I said. "Please come home. You'll get pneumonia."

"I can't live in the same house with that man."

"Yes, you can. Please come home. Please. Gene and I want you to come home. Please listen!" I said, grabbing her arm. She tore herself free and kept lurching down the street, sobbing wildly.

I had no idea where she was going. Now I think she was planning to charge into the Gallagher apartment and denounce her husband in the very parlor where they had met. After about a block, my mother's sobs subsided. She allowed me to take her arm and lead her back down the street to our house. Miraculously, we did not meet any neighbors. In the house my brother, Gene, was in the living room. "Daddy's gone," he said in a scared hollow voice. "It's okay, Mom. He's gone."

That night I lay in bed wondering if I could ever like, much less love, my father again. I was inclined to think my mother was right. He did not love anyone. All he cared about was expensive cars, expensive clothes, being a big shot—and nerve. I didn't know how all that hung together in his head. I only knew I didn't like it.

I cried myself to sleep that night. I felt hurt inside and out. I wondered what was going to happen to us. I wondered if I'd ever understand it. Even today, sixty years later, the memory fills me with muted anguish.

# 24

# All I've Got

After that brawl, my mother and father were no longer lovers—or even friends. For a while, they were very close to enemies. My father did not know what to do about it. He tried to continue operating as if nothing had happened. He came home to dinner. He talked baseball and football with me and Gene. But he had little or nothing to say to my mother. He left the house after dinner for the Sixth Ward clubhouse and saloons and did not come home until 2 or 3 A.M. My mother started calling him "the night owl."

They continued to disagree on all sorts of things. A good example was my graduation from St. Patrick's Grammar School in June of 1941. The graduates had autograph books in which we collected good wishes or words of advice from friends, parents, and relatives. My mother wrote: *Aim High!* My father wrote:

> *Here's to those who are friends of mine*
> *Friends that are good and true*
> *Who like me for what I am*
> *And not for the things I do*
> *There are plenty of fair weather friends*
> *You can find them hereabouts*
> *But here's to the friend that will stick by me*
> *When he knows that I'm "down and out."*

We went to the shore in the summer as usual and my father came down weekends. I noticed that now he usually arrived late on Saturday and went back to the city on Sunday. Sometimes he did not show up at all. I can remember many Saturdays when I left the beach and peered down our street, the Parkway, for a glimpse of his car in the driveway or at the curb in front of the house. I was very upset when he skipped a weekend. For me this was a sign of a widening breach in the marriage.

Meanwhile, my mother started telling me about her grievances, her disappointments, her wounds. I did not want to hear any of it. But I was trapped into being a hapless, often helpless listener. I see now she was doing to me what her father had done with her—set up a rival for a spouse's affections.

My mother was much more angry than pathetic Tom Dolan—and had more dramatic material on which to focus her rage. She began by revealing her explanation of the anger that boiled up about money and other matters, from lost house keys to inadequate coffee—Teddy Fleming's purported infidelity while she was pregnant with my brother Gene. She told me she was now convinced it was true.

"But he said he didn't do it!" I pleaded. I simply did not want to believe it.

"He was lying, I could *tell*," my mother said.

"How? How could you tell?" I asked.

"A woman can tell," she said.

I was baffled by this resort to feminine intuition. She sounded like some kind of sorceress. "Has he—has he done it again? With other women?" I asked.

"I don't know. How do I know what he's doing when he's down in the ward until 2 and 3 A.M. seven nights a week?"

This left me with enough food for thought to give me psychological indigestion. My father's lack of interest in the Catholic religion made me suspect the worst. If he did not believe in God, what was to stop him from breaking any and all moral laws?

Was chasing other women also part of that intimidating word, nerve? Was he a Jimmy Cagney (in his gangster films) type, who loved them and left them and if they complained mashed a grapefruit in their faces? If so, how or why did Monsignor Joseph Meehan, the late pastor of All Saints (he had died in 1936), like and admire him? What about Aunt Mae? I could not imagine her approving of anyone, even her favorite brother, committing adultery.

I wrestled with these thoughts in solitude. How could I discuss them with anyone? I prayed to Jesus to heal this awful tangle of love and hate. I asked Him to do it every time I went to Holy Communion. I made extra visits to St. Patrick's Church on my way home from school. I wondered if I could ask Aunt Mae to help—and decided no.

Externally, I remained a more or less typical American boy. I studied hard and continued to get good marks in the eighth grade at St. Patrick's School. I played baseball and got interested in basketball, a sport that was sweeping the country. In 1941, I graduated from St. Patrick's and was admitted to St. Peter's Prep.

As far as anyone could see, I was enjoying my rather privileged life. My father continued to take us for Sunday rides in his Cadillac. The Hague Organization continued to win city elections by massive majorities. The Sixth Ward performed spectacularly in these local massacres. Teddy Fleming got more than his share of favors at City Hall, including the elevation of his brother Dave to battalion chief in the fire department. Election night parties were as ebullient as ever.

I spent summers at Point Pleasant Beach, far away from Jersey City's stifling heat and humidity. I had a generous allowance. I never had to ask for money to go to the movies or to buy milkshakes and ice-cream sodas. I had the best baseball glove on the block. But inside I was often forlorn. The sadness would hit me when I saw the way my mother and father avoided speaking to each other at the dinner table or on the porch at Point Pleasant. My fervent prayers were not being answered. Worst of all, I felt alienated from my father.

When I was fifteen, I went into the Jersey City Medical Center for a fairly serious operation. I had undescended testicles. Hormone injections had failed to persuade them to gravitate from my groin to my scrotum. The only solution was surgery. Already gifted—or burdened—with a vivid imagination, I pictured myself expiring tragically on the operating table when the surgeon accidentally severed an artery.

In the hospital that night, about an hour after my mother had tearfully kissed me farewell (so it seemed in my jittery state), my father appeared in my room. "Get your clothes on," he said.

Outside, we sped across the city to the Plaza Hotel, the city's biggest hostelry, where I soon found myself mingling with the Democratic Party chieftains of the city and state. They were convening to plan their strategy for the next election.

My father introduced me to Frank Hague and various friends, remarking each time, "This kid's going under the knife tomorrow morning at the Medical Center. How do you like his nerve? He's as cool as a cucumber."

Numerous pols, including the mayor, mashed my hand and said I evidently took after my old man. By the end of the evening, which featured a talk by Hague full of amusing wisecracks about the Republicans, I had begun to believe I really wasn't scared.

Back at the hospital, we found nurses and interns searching frantically for me. My father had consulted no one about taking me out of their clutches for the evening. The floor nurse, a big woman with a horse face, protested his outrageous indifference to the hospital's rules.

"Ah, go to hell," Teddy Fleming said.

We shook hands. It was the toughest handshake my father had given me yet. I gave it right back to him. I slept beautifully all night. The operation was a success.

I still wonder if this was a deliberate intervention to counter my mother's influence or an impulse decision after he got a glimpse of my jitters. Either way, it was an enlightening look at leadership, Teddy Fleming style.

My mother continued to fill my head with stories about her unhappy marriage. I was amazed to discover that two years before I was born, she had given birth to a daughter who had died in the murky (to me at fifteen) process of emerging from the womb. "I made your father go in and look at her. He didn't want to do it. But I made him," she said.

Kitty seemed to think this proved she was braver or stronger than Teddy Fleming—as if in retrospect she was challenging him on his own tough-guy turf.

Next she told me about my father using a condom for the first two years of their marriage. That was a mortal sin, according to the Catholic Church, but she emphasized it was his decision. She was implying that the baby had been born dead because of my father's mortal sin.

Even at fifteen, and still intensely religious, I could not buy this idea. To me the word "mortal" involved something truly awful, such as killing someone. If God had killed that baby because my father had used a condom for two years, Jehovah was playing by a set of rules that struck me as manifestly unfair. It was my first glimpse of the way the Catholic Church messed up the hearts and heads of its believers, especially its women.

As a male, I put myself in my father's place—and suddenly saw why he might not be enthusiastic about going to Mass on Sunday. Every time he showed up, he remembered my mother's accusation about the dead baby. Add to that the accusation that he had been unfaithful, and you had a man in a spiritual trap. No wonder there was a lot of anger bubbling beneath his surface air of authority and power.

These thoughts did not emerge with anything approaching such clarity at the time. I was still deeply sympathetic to my mother's plight as the victim of a man with a terrible temper and dubious morals. I saw far more of her than I saw of my father. Kitty converted me and Gene into weekend companions. We went to the movies in New York and had dinner at a restaurant over there or in Jersey City, where we discussed the film and the actors.

My brother Gene was largely left out of these conversations. There was little doubt that I was my mother's favorite. Like most older brothers, I took this largesse for granted. Mother was unquestionably the chief figure in the foreground of my emotional life.

This meant I got an ongoing earful about many of her friends besides Marie Farrelly and her troublesome husband. In her offhand way my mother was amazingly frank. She also told me about the travails of her friend Mary McNamara King. She was a compact, round-faced, rather attractive brunette with determined dark eyes. Mary looked at me even harder than my grandmother, as if she were sizing me up in some unstated way.

Mary had a pretty, dark-haired daughter, Louise, whom my mother frequently praised as brilliant and suggested we were destined for each other. I got the message early on that Louise had other ideas. I was more interested in Mary and her husband, Fred. He was an odd wispy man with a polite bemused smile on his face most of the time. He had very little to say to me or anyone else.

My mother told me that Mary had had "a terrible time" giving birth to Louise. When it was over, Mary told Fred: "That's it."

"What do you mean?" I asked.

"I mean she told him they were getting separate bedrooms," my mother said. "What else could she do? They were both Catholics."

This revelation took several years to sink in. I was baffled by the way my mother did not seem to think there was anything wrong with kicking your husband out of bed. Only much later did it dawn on me that at some point after they moved into the Arlington Avenue house in 1936, Kitty had done the same thing to her husband. In that house they stopped sharing a bedroom. Kitty had offhandedly explained it by claiming Teddy Fleming snored. She turned her bedroom into a Dolan enclave, with the painting-like photos of her parents on the wall above her bed. Here, I realized when I reached young adulthood, was the explanation for the ferocity of my father's anger.

Mixed in with my mother's semi-revelations were stories that not so subtly denigrated my father. Once, when they were "going together," he had taken Kitty to an ice-cream parlor run by a rotund German. They had a sandwich and a soda and my father paid with a twenty-dollar bill. The German talked jovially to them as he counted out the change. He enjoyed his own conversation so much, he did not notice that he put the change on top of the twenty. My father picked up all the money, took my mother's arm, and escorted her out of the soda shop.

My mother was shocked but my father shrugged off her reproach. "I wouldn't have done it if he was Irish," he said. He might have added that most Germans were Republicans. Having grown up in the moderately affluent Dolan family, my mother had no conception of the us-against-them mentality that occupied a large corner of Teddy Fleming's street Irish mind. Even making that allowance, I was troubled by this story for a long time.

Kitty also told me about South Plainfield, New Jersey, Thornton's Hotel, Aunt Kate, and her daughter Loretta, whose marriage to Lyman Barr had also grown unhappy. I heard how everyone pitched in and enabled Kitty to win the *Courier-News* subscription contest and enjoy six glorious weeks in Europe. Listening, I thought, *No wonder she thinks she's too good for the Sixth Ward.*

Next came the story of her tragic romance with Lloyd Harris. It was heartbreaking but my mother did not tell it as if her heart had been broken. I got the impression that she had never been powerfully attracted to Lloyd in the first place. Only when I grew much older, and had talked to many other women suffering from heartbreak, did I realize the power and importance of the psychological mechanism known as denial. In public and even in private with family members and intimate friends, women often dismiss heartbreak with an offhand tone or a wry remark.

The truth can still emerge at unexpected moments. Only when I began writing this book did my wife, Alice, tell me of a comment my mother made to her mother, when they lunched together not long after we became engaged. Apparently the conversation veered to how they had met their husbands. With no warning, my mother's voice darkened and she said, "He wasn't my first choice."

When I first heard about Lloyd Harris, he did not impress me as a tragic figure. Fifteen-year-old boys are not into tragedy, in the first place. The guy came across as something of a self-pitying wimp. I found myself secretly glad that Lloyd had croaked and I had not wound up with him as a father.

In the midst of my mother's stream of female consciousness, Teddy Fleming still managed to make his presence felt in my life. World War II had begun in 1939. In 1940, Germany conquered France. In December 1941, the Japanese attacked Pearl Harbor and my father tried to get back into the army. They turned him down. They were not interested in 53-year-old ex-lieutenants. But the war became a topic we both read about obsessively and discussed constantly. It revived my boyhood memories of Sergeant Fleming's adventures in the Argonne.

Another topic that we shared was the Hague Organization's brawl with New Jersey's governor, Charles Edison, whom the Democrats had elected in 1940. The son of the famous inventor, Edison was a suave, rather handsome man with a large personal fortune. President Roosevelt had appointed him secretary of the navy, and shortly thereafter suggested him to Frank Hague as a candidate. It was hard to say no to a president, and the Organization had accepted Edison as their man.

It soon became evident that Edison had read several biographies of Woodrow Wilson and was planning to repeat his performance by biting the political hand that created him. He began denouncing "bossism" and declaring he was not going to take orders from Frank Hague. Edison swiftly discovered that Frank Hague was not the aging Newark boss, Jim Smith, whom Wilson had blithely brushed aside.

Mary Norton, the congresswoman from Jersey City, unleashed a withering attack on Edison as an two-faced ingrate. She quoted at length from speeches Edison had made professing his gratitude to the Hague Organization. Hague went to Washington and made sure his federal patronage pipeline was secure. By the time Edison left office in 1943, the governor was a political has-been and the Hague Organization looked more unbeatable than ever.

When his term as chairman of the Hudson County Board of Chosen Freeholders expired, Teddy Fleming became judge of the Second Criminal Court. He had served as the clerk of this court, and that made the appointment logical to Frank Hague. You did not have to be a lawyer to preside over one of these lower courts, where the maximum sentence was a year in jail.

Judge Fleming largely dealt with petty crimes—drunkenness, wife beating, shoplifting. One day a man appeared in his courtroom accused of smoking in the Harborside Terminal on the Hudson River, where tons of vital war matériel were being shipped overseas. The man's superiors said he had been warned twice not to smoke on the job. My father gave him a ferocious tongue-lashing from the bench. The lives of thousands of fighting men were endangered by his carelessness. "Six months in the county jail!" was the sentence.

The story made the local papers and was picked up by the Associated Press as an example of a politician who took the war effort seriously. Hundreds of letters and comments praised Judge Fleming's rough justice. This five minutes of fame renewed my admiration for my father.

My mother continued trying to convert me into a substitute husband. My marks in St. Peter's Prep were astronomical. I seldom got anything below a 95. My excellent memory enabled me to do extremely well in Latin and other languages without trying very hard. Mathematics was the only subject that gave me occasional anxiety attacks. The Jesuits rewarded scholastic performance with a plethora of recognitions: monthly gold certificates, annual announcements of class standing.

I saw myself responding to the exhortation my mother had written in my eighth-grade autograph book, "Aim High!" Kitty began to see me as a genius. She quoted my opinions on national and international politics, the progress of the war, the quality (or lack of same) of books, films, and plays. My head inevitably swelled in this torrent of praise and I soon thought I deserved every word of it. I began ordering my brother Gene around and lecturing him on his supposed bad habits. I was in danger of becoming something worse than a momma's boy— a prig.

My father took a dim view of these developments. He began referring to me sarcastically as "the brain" and wondered aloud if I would ever get my nose out of a book long enough to earn a living. Something very close to antagonism developed between us. His gestures of tough affection, shaking hands like a man, relying on nerve to deal with hot grounders and dangerous surgery, began to seem less admirable—or meaningful. Overshadowing everything was my memory of the night when the Fleming marriage had exploded.

In the fall of 1943, when I was sixteen and my brother Gene was thirteen, my mother persuaded my father to take us on a four-day spring vacation to upstate New York's Finger Lakes. As we drove along, I began reading a book. My father wondered with some vexation what the hell point there was in taking me anywhere when I would not even look at the scenery.

"What do you care what I do?" I said. "You don't love me. You don't love anyone."

I thought the next twenty seconds were our last on earth. My father jammed his foot on the brake while the Cadillac was going sixty miles an hour. Tires screamed and the car swerved off the highway, heading straight for a tree. At the last moment my father got command of the wheel and we screeched to a stop.

"What did you say?" he cried. "What did you say?"

He lunged out of the car and stumbled into a field beside the road. I was horrified and bewildered beyond anything I had seen or heard as a son. I leaped out of the car and ran over to my father. There were tears streaming down his face. "You said I didn't love you," he sobbed, pawing at his eyes. "You said I didn't love you!"

"I didn't mean it," I lied. "I'm sorry!"

"You and your brother. You're all I've got. Don't you realize that?"

*You're all I've got.* Those words burned themselves into my brain, my soul. It is no exaggeration to say they changed my life forever. *You're all I've got.* They told me so much about my father's ruined marriage and his career as a local big shot. They forced me to realize the centrality of love in this man's life—which eventually made me realize its centrality in every life.

That night, lying in our room in a hotel in Albany, my brother Gene and I had our first serious conversation about the dismaying fact that our father did not love our mother but he seemed to love us. We offered each other bits and pieces of observation, trying to make sense out of Teddy Fleming—something we continued to do for the rest of our lives.

# 25

# The Guy in the Glass

In a strange way, my father's confession of love intensified my friendship with Bill Gannon, the husky wildman who had been a classmate throughout my eight years in St. Patrick's and had joined me in St. Peter's Prep. Bill too had a father problem—a very different one from mine. His father was a sad broken failure. But I liked him enormously. Bill, in a bizarre (so it seemed at first) reversal, liked my father.

I gradually pieced together William Gannon Sr.'s story. It was very meaningful for someone who was getting high marks at St. Peter's. He had come from an affluent family who sent him to St. Peter's and on to Fordham College and Law School. He was far and away the most brilliant man in his class in each place. He decided, with a nobility that the Jesuits undoubtedly encouraged, that he was fated to drive Frank Hague out of Jersey City and restore something that had never existed—the city's political purity.

It was a doomed struggle, which led to a life of bitter disappointment. He was never able to make a decent living as a lawyer, and he never came close to building serious opposition to Frank Hague's juggernaut. It was David versus Goliath minus the sling and Jehovah's protection.

When I visited the Gannon apartment in the evening, Mr. Gannon would often be drunk. Not slobbering but tipsy enough to slur his words. He was always delighted to see me. My high marks, my presumed love of learning, were a bond. Often he would say, "I was just rereading my favorite ode from Horace. Do you know it?" He would recite the entire poem in Latin, with amazing accuracy. At other times, it would be a passage from Virgil or Homer. He was as fluent in Greek as he was in Latin. I was awed.

His son Bill was no student at St. Peter's, any more than he had been at St. Patrick's. When I met his father, I understood why. Bill thought getting high marks was pretty pointless if you ended up like William Gannon Sr.

I saw the heartbreak in this situation, even then, though I did not brood about it or even mention it to Bill. I had begun to accept heartbreak as par for the course in many adult lives. I was more deeply moved—as well as puzzled—by Bill's fondness for my father. When we went to a Saturday night movie or a basketball game, often he would say: "Let's go back to your house. Maybe your father'll be home."

Sometimes Judge Fleming would be there. He would pour us some beer and Bill would ask him about the Jersey City of bygone years. From these evenings, I learned a lot about the Hague Organization. For instance, how Hague had "cleaned up" the police force—reduced it to obedience to City Hall. How the mayor had attracted the Dempsey-Firpo fight to Jersey City, putting the town in the headlines for the first time in its history. How the central post office downtown opened everyone's mail during a crisis such as the CIO invasion of 1937.

Bill Gannon was finding out why his father had never had a chance against the Hague imperium. It made him angry, not at his father—love did not permit that—but at the idealists who had sent him on his suicidal mission, in particular the Jesuits. Bill studied as little as possible at St. Peter's, basically majoring in football. I could see he admired my father's tough take on life as a struggle in which fists and nightsticks were often more important than brainpower and ideals.

More than once, I sensed that Bill was a better match as my father's son, just as I was a better match for his father. Nerve came naturally to Bill. On the football field he was afraid of nothing. In fact, his readiness to take on players twice his size had him on the injured list almost permanently.

Theoretically, Bill and I should have been enemies. The Hague Organization had ruined his father's life. But we somehow decided when we were still boys that we liked each other and what had happened earlier in our fathers' lives was irrelevant. Was his befriending the smartest guy in the class a way of sending a message to his father? Was my befriending him a way of saying I liked people with nerve? I suspect the answer is yes to both questions, although that was not clear at the time. In a mysterious way, we helped each other affirm the centrality of a father's love in our young lives.

One spring night in my junior year, my father came home from his nightly tour of the Sixth Ward uncharacteristically early. He summoned me downstairs and announced it was time I learned how to drink hard liquor. My mother protested that it would be better if I never touched a drop of the awful stuff. He ignored her as usual and led me out to the kitchen, where he poured me a rye and ginger-ale. There was only about an ounce of rye in the glass.

He poured himself the standard two ounces plus ginger ale and let me taste his drink. "Never drink anything stronger than this," he said. "And never gulp it. The trick is to make a drink last as long as possible. Let the other guys get loaded. Above all—*never* drink booze straight. Always put water or some other mixer in it."

The intense seriousness with which he delivered this lecture was impressive, to put it mildly. It would take me another ten years to realize that in the Irish-American world, knowing how to drink without getting drunk was valuable information. You had to drink if you wanted to retain the respect of your fellow males. But if you succumbed to the booze—like my mother's uncle, Bart Dolan—you were finished in the American world.

Another retrospective thought was the probability that my friendship with Bill Gannon prompted this lecture on drinking. He liked the way I was hanging around with this wild Irishman—it was a sign that I was not going the momma's boy route. But Teddy Fleming knew there were dangers involved in the wild side of our heritage. Booze was at the top of that risk list. Did he know that Bill's father drank too much? In Jersey City, this sort of information was undoubtedly available to insiders. City Hall kept dossiers on all the Organization's enemies.

That summer, I got another glimpse of my father's attitude toward liquor. I was awakened one night by loud voices on the sidewalk. Someone was saying, "Teddy—I didn't mean it. It was only a joke!"

"Get out of my sight," my father roared. "Get out of my sight before I wipe up the goddamn street with you!"

The next morning, my mother told me she and my father had gone out with Tom Fleming and his wife, Bess. At a nightclub in Asbury Park, after a first round of drinks, Tom had gone to the bar and bought another round, paying for it on the spot. When my father tasted his rye and ginger-ale, he stood up and said to my mother, "We're going home. Now."

Tom had tripled the normal two ounces of rye in my father's drink. By this time Tom regularly showed up at our house pie-eyed, hiding out from Bess, who had a fierce temper and threw heavy objects when she got mad. Tom had never seen my father drunk and decided he would try to get him plastered by subterfuge.

Tom came back later in the day, again begging forgiveness. He sobbed like a five-year-old. My father told him to get lost. It took him twelve months to accept Tom's twenty-fifth slobbering apology. I learned from my mother that Tom was now worth several million dollars, thanks to the liquor distributorship my father had obtained for him. It was an awesome glimpse of my father's power in the family, thanks to the sheer force of his personality. It also made me realize just how seriously he took his lecture on how to drink.

Now I think that episode was also a glimpse of how much my father feared the loss of control that went with getting drunk. He had made his way in the American world by fiercely disciplining his body and his soul. He was aware of the free-floating Irish anger inside him and understood the importance of concealing it. For one of his own kind, a cousin, and by coincidence a namesake, to have tried to undo that self-control and threaten him with humiliation or worse was almost unforgivable. Cousin Tom was very lucky to escape without serious physical damage.

Back in Jersey City that fall, my father sent me up to his bedroom to get him a pack of cigarettes. Rummaging in his bureau drawer, I came across a poem, clipped from a newspaper and pasted on a piece of cardboard.

*When you get what you want in your struggle for pelf,*
*And the world makes you King for a day,*
*Then go to your mirror and look at yourself,*
*And ask what that guy has to say.*

*For it isn't your Father, or Mother, or Wife,*
*Who judgement upon you must pass.*
*The feller whose verdict counts most in your life*
*Is the guy looking back from the glass.*

*He's the feller to please, never mind all the rest,*
*For he's with you clear up to the end,*
*And you've passed your most dangerous, difficult test,*
*If the guy in the glass is your friend.*

I was amazed. It never occurred to me that my father had such a profound idea. It was couched in mediocre poetry. But the idea remained profound, especially if you considered the man who was thinking it. Even then I saw it was very different from the way most Catholics thought about themselves. They were always being urged to examine their consciences. But that was a prelude to confessing their sins to a priest, God's surrogate. They worried far more about the priest's and God's reaction to their sins than their own reactions. The guy in the glass seemed to be operating without any reference to priests or God. It was strictly between him and his image in the mirror.

It took me much longer to connect this poem to the idea Teddy Fleming had gotten from Monsignor Meehan: self-respect. A man has to live and work long enough to realize how often the world tempts him to make compromises and even a few betrayals. Only then does self-respect become crucial to his peace of soul.

That night I also noticed some small blue-covered books in the drawer, beneath the poem, "The Guy in the Glass." I had never seen my father reading a book. Curious, I picked one up for a quick glance. *What Is Religion?* by Leo Tolstoy. Amazed, I picked up another one: *What Great Men Said About Women* by Rufus W. Weeks. And another one: *How to Attract Friends and Friendship.* There were seven or eight more of these books in the drawer. I hurried downstairs with the cigarettes and decided not to mention to my father that I'd seen the books. I also said nothing to my mother. They seemed to be my father's very private business. He never mentioned them to me or anyone else in the family.

It would take me a long time to find out more about these books. They were famous in the 1920s and 1930s. The Little Blue Books, as they were called, were created by a man named E. Haldeman-Julius, a socialist and freethinker, whose goal was to spread culture and knowledge to people who did not have the education or the time to wade through large tomes. He undertook to present major thoughts in bite-sized pieces. In twenty years he published a staggering six thousand titles, which sold for five and ten cents each. Gradually I realized the poignancy of my father surreptitiously reading these mini-books in the privacy of his bedroom. Was he trying to keep up with his brainy son and condescending schoolteacher wife? Or was he honestly interested in some of their ideas? I teetered between these two possibilities and eventually decided they both might be true.

One thing was certain: Teddy Fleming was not a stupid man. But he never overcame deep feelings of inferiority about his lack of education. Several times he invited me to political rallies in the ward. Other pols handled most of the oratory. Teddy's remarks were always brief. Invariably, he would begin, "I have neither the talent nor the inclination to take more of your time tonight."

Often he referred to his lack of education as a reason for mediocrity as a speaker. "As a younger man, the opportunity for a professional education was not my lot," he said in one speech. But he was "unashamed" of his long career in the government because to him it was "public service."

Then came the heart of almost every Teddy Fleming speech. "You are my people. Never forget that. If any of you need help, all you have to do is speak to me. I will do my utmost to serve you."

One night in the fall of 1943, I got a glimpse of how much thought Teddy Fleming had given to his primary job, leader of the Sixth Ward. I answered the doorbell and confronted a small snub-nosed man in a velvet-collared coat that had seen better days. He asked to speak to my father. I said I would see if he was at home.

My father was upstairs in his bedroom, dressing to spend the evening at the Sixth Ward clubhouse, as usual. When I told him the man's name, he frowned. "He's the son of the guy that owned the old watch factory," he said. "They went bankrupt a couple of years ago. I bet he's looking for a job."

My father went downstairs. I hung over the second-floor railing above the stairwell, expecting to hear a parable of Irish-American vengeance acted out. Here was my father's chance to even the score for the hundreds, even thousands, of humiliations this man's father had inflicted on the Catholics of the Sixth Ward.

I was totally disappointed. My father greeted the man courteously and they discussed where he might find work. My father finally decided his training as an accountant might win him a slot at the Internal Revenue offices in Newark. He promised to put in a word for him at City Hall.

Stunned, I asked my father why he hadn't made the ruined Protestant scion crawl. Had he forgotten what they made the Irish do at the watch factory? My father looked at me with mild disapproval. "That happened a long time ago," he said. "That fellow didn't have anything to do with it."

I was chastened and impressed. Did my father's indifference to revenge have something to do with the guy in the glass? Or something he read in the Little Blue Books? Both are possible, but a search for a final answer trails off into mystery. Perhaps more important was the way discovering "The Guy in the Glass" and the Little Blue Books helped me defend Teddy Fleming in my mind against my mother's relentlessly negative remarks and revelations. These discoveries stirred a sense of mystery about him that I badly wanted to solve.

Maybe my father was more aware of what was happening than I realized, and sensed the need to maintain a role in my adolescent life. He suddenly volunteered to be my chauffeur. He had to get up early to be in court and offered to drive me downtown to St. Peter's—about a ten-minute ride by car. That was an improvement on a half hour aboard a crowded, lumbering bus. I put out the word about this taxi service to several friends and they quickly arranged to be on strategic corners along the route and join the crowd. Sometimes there were six or seven of us crammed in the front and back seats.

Since Judge Fleming was out late each night down in the ward, he got up at the last possible minute and proceeded to dress in his usual slow, fastidious fashion. This caused flutters of anxiety in yours truly and the other preppies waiting along the route. My father remained unhurried—and unflappable. Sometimes we would get to the Junction (previously mentioned as a point in the Sixth Ward where three main streets met) with only minutes to go before the nine o'clock bell—and St. Peter's still a good mile away.

Lateness at St. Peter's was punished by "jug"—an afterschool session in which the victims copied Latin verbs or some other meaningless mumbo-jumbo for an hour or two, depending on the dean of discipline's mood at the time. My father knew this was something to be avoided at all costs. If we reached the Junction with the light against us, he gave the high sign to the big red-faced Irish cop who was directing traffic. The cop would raise both hands and stop buses, trucks, and cars on all three arteries while we cruised through the intersection. This demonstration of clout was invariably greeted with cheers by us teenage passengers.

Although we sometimes pulled up in front of 144 Grand Street (St. Peter's address) with the nine o'clock bell clanging, never once were we late. My father enjoyed this game immensely. "Didn't I tell you we'd make it?" he'd say as we piled out of the car for the mad dash to our classrooms. My friends puzzled over why he couldn't allow five or ten minutes' leeway. Only I understood that it was another test of nerve—with not much at stake, but still nerve. Playing the big shot at the Junction added to the fun, of course.

At St. Peter's, another drama began developing in my adolescent life. I was singled out by the school's student counselor, Father Francis Shalloe, S.J., as a likely recruit for the Jesuit order. Shalloe (pronounced "Schull-loo") was a hulking, broad-shouldered man with a shock of gray hair and a wide Irish-American face that seemed genial and even kind at first acquaintance. Sitting opposite him, virtually knees to knees in a small office, where he smoked cigarettes until the air was thick with acrid fumes, he was a formidable figure of authority.

My mother thought Father Shalloe was a wonderful man. He had told her I was a wonderful boy—one of the most gifted students he had seen in his twenty-some years at St. Peter's Prep. There were few Jesuits who did not elicit my mother's enthusiasm. The school had a Mother's Club and she became one of its more active members. In my senior year, she was its president. The Jesuits were "such gentlemen," Kitty would virtually croon. The comparison to my father, the hot-tempered Sixth Ward mick, was unspoken but more than audible to my sensitized inner ear.

Father Shalloe was obsessed with sex. He wanted to know whether you touched yourself in forbidden ways—i.e., masturbated. He was especially troubled if he saw you in the stands with a girl at a football or basketball game. That brought a summons to the student coun-selor's office and a demand to know exactly what you had been doing with this female. Had you touched her breasts? Had you thrust your tongue into her mouth? Had you (heaven forbid) had intercourse?

My sex life was virtually nonexistent, except for some mild exper-iments in masturbation, for which Father Shalloe made me feel acutely guilty. I could almost smell the flames of hell broiling my toes. As for doing anything nefarious with girls, I lacked access. Without a sister, there was no likelihood of girls wandering in and out of my house. I went to an all-boys school. The Catholic girls went to all-girls schools, and the twain seldom met.

With me at least, sex was a minor theme in Father Shalloe's dis-course. The subject under continual discussion was the priesthood. Father Shalloe claimed he had a special ability to detect young men with vocations. He had no doubt whatsoever that I possessed this rare gift of God. All I had to do was look into my soul and see it. For the better part of two years, I kept looking but could not detect it. That only caused Father Shalloe to increase our interviews from once to twice a week.

Father Shalloe enlisted my mother in this campaign. She confided to me that she was praying that I would receive the grace from God to become a priest. This information made me acutely uncomfortable. I also prayed to God for help, but I somehow never specifically asked Him for the grace of a vocation.

Father Shalloe frequently asked me to compare the majesty of a love affair with Jesus Christ—the inner life of a priest—and a love affair with even the finest woman. He asked me to compare spiritual glory with worldly glory. My father was an important man. But was he really happy? In retrospect, I'm fairly sure that Father Shalloe was speaking generally, but I immediately suspected my mother had told him about her ruined marriage. This displeased me intensely—I felt it put me at a grievous disadvantage.

My father was a bystander in this spiritual drama. But I soon discovered he was not neutral. One day when we were alone on the porch at Point Pleasant, between my junior and senior years, Teddy Fleming suddenly said, "I hear you're thinking of becoming a priest."

"Father Shalloe thinks I've got a vocation," I said.

"Seems like a hell of a waste of your life to me," he said.

That was all he ever said to me about my supposed vocation. But it carried enormous weight. I did not immediately agree with him. I was still intensely religious. I saw much of life in religious terms. Jesus's call to "Come, follow me" resonated in my soul. I could see the nobility, the idealism, of the priest's life. But I was not at all sure, in spite of Father Shalloe's assurances, that Jesus's words were aimed at me. My father's comment added hugely to my uncertainty.

After that summertime exchange, I went back in Jersey City for more pressure from Father Shalloe. I still took these sessions seriously. One Sunday, I stayed after Mass at St. Patrick's and pondered the huge statue of Jesus on the cross, to the right of the altar. It was a very realistic sculpture, with bloodstains around the nails in the feet and hands. Jesus suffered this transcendent death for me, I thought. How can I do less than offer my life to Him?

Something huge and indefinable started swelling in my chest. The statue blurred. I felt a curious blend of pleasure and pain coursing through my body. Was I having a mystical experience? Was Jesus about to whisper in my soul the decisive words, *Come, follow me?* I half wanted to hear them and at the same time I dreaded them. I no longer seemed to have control of the situation.

A hand tapped my shoulder. I turned to find Bill Gannon sitting behind me, a big grin on his oval face. "What the hell are you doin'?" he said. "The Mass has been over for ten minutes. I hope you're not gettin' religious or something crazy like that."

Mysticism, the wisps of spiritual ecstasy, drained from my body. I was being told to return to being one of the guys, a man among men. I struggled to my feet and said, "What's the plan for the day?"

"I've got a yen to see that new Gary Cooper movie. Does that grab you?"

"Sure."

We strolled out of St. Patrick's Church into the real world of Jersey City. I never had another mystical experience.

Not long after this aborted spiritual voyage, I had my first intellectual experience. My mother subscribed to the Book of the Month Club. One day I saw in the catalog a title that intrigued me: *War and Peace* by Leo Tolstoy. It was the *War* part of the title that attracted me, of course. My mother gave it to me as a Christmas present. When I opened it on Christmas morning, I asked my father if he had ever read it. He thumbed the book and said, "Are you kidding? It's six hundred goddamn pages!"

A few weeks later I came down with a strep throat and was confined to bed for a week. I read *War and Peace* and was transported. Here was a world infinitely different from the one I knew. I was riveted by the battles between the Russians and Napoleon's invading army. It all seemed particularly relevant because similar carnage was being reenacted between the Russians and the Germans in 1943. I was almost as fascinated by Tolstoy's disquisitions on the forces of history. I did not understand them very well. But I felt a semi-mystic identification with the idea that history played a part in our lives, whether we liked it or not. It would take me many years to realize that history was happening to me in Jersey City too. My father, my mother, Frank Hague, all were part of an historical experience summed up in the word *Irish-American.*

When I was seventeen, my father taught me how to drive. It was an ordeal. He insisted on absolute perfection at all times. "Both hands on the wheel," he would bark. "Look in the goddamn rear mirror before you make a turn." If I went five miles over the speed limit on a country road, he would give me hell.

That summer I rode around a lot with friends who had cars of their own. One Friday I was out on Route 35 with George Klinger in his Buick. Traffic was heavy. A lot of people were heading south for a weekend at the shore. "Holy smoke, look at this guy," George said, glancing in the mirror.

A moment later a five-passenger Cadillac passed us as if we were traveling in slow motion. It was going at least eighty miles an hour. The driver was a husky white-shirted man with his tie loosened, his blond hair blowing in the wind: Teddy Fleming. He had only one hand on the wheel.

When I got home that night and told him what I had seen, he denied everything. He said he had not taken Route 35. I realized that for him, lying was a way of keeping things simple. He was not about to get into a discussion of when and where I could speed. That could easily lead to me getting killed. He was trying to get me through adolescence in one piece.

The next day, he let me drive the family to church. "Keep both hands on that goddamn wheel," he growled as we pulled out of the driveway. I put up with it, because, again, I heard behind the tough treatment, *You're all I've got.*

Those words resonate in my mind and heart today, almost as intensely as they echoed in my adolescence. Now I see them in a more complex way, as part of a duality that I struggled to tolerate. I did not want to choose between my mother's love and my father's love. But this is what my mother was asking me to do, again and again, with her attacks on my father. Once more I almost cry out: Kitty, Kitty, why couldn't you see I was a male? Why didn't you realize that destroying Teddy Fleming was tantamount to destroying his son and namesake?

# 26

# You're in the Navy Now

Quarrels always seemed worse at our summer house. The gleaming sea, the bright sun, the warm sand seemed to accentuate their ugliness. A nasty one erupted when my mother's favorite cousin from her South Plainfield days, Loretta Thornton Barr, decided to redeem some of the chits her family held for Kitty's years of free board at their hotel.

Loretta was always described by my mother as exquisitely beautiful in those halcyon days. When she showed up in Point Pleasant, it was hard to discern the youthful knockout in the rolls of fat that encased her. She was about fifty pounds overweight. She brought her two sons, Sonny and Jack, with her, fully expecting to spend the summer or a good part of it. She threw in a sad tale of an abusive husband from whom she wanted to distance herself. My mother's soft heart melted. She opened her arms—and house—to Loretta.

Teddy Fleming's heart had an opposite reaction. He took an instant dislike to Loretta. The spoiled child of older parents, she expected service as well as attention in our beach house. Judge Fleming also sized up Sonny and Jack as serious trouble. Sonny was a handsome charm boy and small-town Pennsylvania football star who had "paternity suit" written all over him. Jack had several screws loose. He had wildly grandiose opinions about everything, especially himself, and was a heavy drinker.

One day Jack got drunk at a bar on the boardwalk and started a major riot. He wound up in jail. My father extricated him only by promising the authorities that Jack would be out of Point Pleasant by sundown. That night, while Loretta was having a midnight snack in the kitchen, my father went to my mother's upstairs bedroom and told Kitty that her old friend also had to depart. If she stayed, Jack was likely to return and another riot might inspire a newspaper story that would connect him to the Flemings.

Kitty refused to ask Loretta to leave. So Teddy undertook the task downtown Jersey City style. In stentorian tones that drifted down the stairwell to the kitchen, he announced that he was not going to put up with a certain freeloader for another day. Loretta departed that very night in tears.

My mother lamented that she would never be able to restore their friendship. She never did. Although Sonny showed up now and then for an overnight stay—my father liked him because he was a good athlete—Loretta never spoke to my mother again. Kitty blamed my father for the loss of Loretta's love. She never seemed to take seriously Jack Barr's potential for raising hell. I succeeded in staying neutral in this collision. Several conversations with Jack had convinced me that he was a nutcase, but I avoided telling Kitty this.

In that same seventeenth summer, I got a job that gave me a new perspective on several things. Point Pleasant's veteran lifeguards were all fighting the war, and Orlo Jenkinson, the tall, humorless proprietor of Jenkinson's Beach, was forced to "rob the cradle," as he put it, by hiring me, my friend George Klinger, and several other teenagers. I was soon meeting a lot of girls, who gravitated to the lifeguard stand as if it were magnetic and they were made of some particularly complaisant metal. It did not hurt that one of my fellow lifeguards, Eddie Klein, had matinee idol looks.

Some of the lifeguards were Point Pleasant natives. While we sat on the stand or lazed around Jenkinson's Pool, we discussed sports and sex, the only two topics they seemed to have on their minds. I was amazed by how far they had gone with various girls. They made me wonder if I was sexually retarded. But I felt no compelling need to do anything about it. I was Catholic—they weren't. I smugly assumed I had higher moral standards.

That did not stop me from thinking very seriously about these mysterious creatures in two-piece bathing suits. For a while I found myself mesmerized by Lillian Grish, a tallish brown-haired girl with mocking eyes and a nice figure. She was a year older than I and therefore barely deigned to give me the time of day romantically. But Lil was a bit of a tomboy and loved to splash water and throw sand—offenses that required outraged males to seize and hurl her into the first oncoming breaker.

The sensations I experienced when I had my arms around that squirming female body were disturbing, to say the very least. It gradually dawned on me that becoming a Jesuit and taking a vow of celibacy was not something that appealed to me.

During that same summer, my father gave me the closest he ever got to a lecture on sex. We were on the porch in Point Pleasant again one night, and he suddenly started talking about the dangers of syphilis. His voice came out of the darkness in an eerie, almost impersonal way.

"The average guy doesn't realize the dangers of the diseases you can pick up if you fool around with the wrong women. Syphilis, for instance. It's the most contagious disease in the world. If you get it, you're as good as finished. You're on your way to some hospital where you go blind and your brain rots in your head. Your nose falls off. You're a kind of monster. It's unbelievable, how contagious syphilis is. You go to a whorehouse and pick up a pen and if there's syphilis on it, and you touch your lips or your eyes, you've got it."

I did not think any of the sweet young things who swarmed around my lifeguard stand had syphilis. I wondered if my father thought they did—or if he just felt I was getting to the age where the lecture was appropriate. I was inclined to the latter opinion. In later years, I realized he was also thinking of the possibility that I would soon be going to war—they were drafting eighteen-year-olds. In those pre-penicillin days, syphilis was still the killer disease it had been for the doughboys in World War I.

I barely knew what syphilis was, at that point. But I soon bought an "Encyclopedia of Sexual Knowledge," by someone with a heavy German name. It described venereal diseases, as well as every sexual perversion and neurosis in the medical vocabulary. I kept it in a bookcase in my bedroom, with the title facing in, so my brother Gene, a mere child of fourteen, would not discover it. Years later, he remarked to me how much he had enjoyed reading it.

When I was in my senior year in St. Peter's Prep, I showed a glimmer of talent as a writer. For one of my weekly compositions, I wrote, "The Fleming Saga." It portrayed the Flemings as a bunch of wild Irishmen who had moved to America after drinking Ireland dry—and continued these habits in the New World. Rereading it recently, the humor seemed heavy-handed. But my father loved it. He had copies photostatted on the forerunner of the Xerox and passed them out to all his friends in City Hall. Did it appeal to the wild Irishman he kept locked inside him? I think so, now.

In 1945, my last year at St. Peter's Prep, a gifted young orator in the class behind me won a national debating prize. Frank Hague decided to make the award personally and half the school streamed the four or five blocks from 144 Grand Street to City Hall for the ceremony.

The mayor was in a cheerful mood. He remarked that he had made a few speeches himself when he was only a little older than the prizewinner but no one had given him any awards for them. "We was fightin' the big shots in them days, and they had the newspapers in their pockets," the mayor said.

The awful grammar made me wince. I could almost hear my mother's sarcastic comments on it. Worse, not a few of my classmates had the same reaction. Around me a lot of guys gave me mocking glances, as if to say: This is the big shot your old man thinks is so great?

I was simultaneously embarrassed for the mayor, and irked at him. Why hadn't he cleaned up his grammar? My father had done it with my mother's help. It would take me several years to realize that no one could have corrected Frank Hague's grammar without risking sudden death.

I left City Hall that day wishing my father was not a part of the Hague Organization. It was a primitive, meaningless resentment. It made me feel guilty. I was simultaneously angry at my classmates, most of them from middle-class families who no longer remembered the downtown poverty that had brought Frank Hague to power—and did not seem inclined to give him credit for his tax victories over the railroads, or the Medical Center, or the election victories that had made Jersey City the most powerful city in New Jersey.

My feelings toward my father were like a stock market chart. They went up and down with time and circumstances. My mother was always in the picture as a witness to his flaws even when she was not pointing them out. After that visit to City Hall, his stock went into a slide. I could not tell him my latest thoughts about Frank Hague, which led me to say little or nothing to him.

My mother added to my emotional turmoil by embarking on a theatrical career. She suddenly volunteered to participate in a variety show staged by St. Patrick's Parish's Rosary Society, an organization she had largely ignored, as part of her general policy of doing as little as possible to help Teddy Fleming's political career. The song she chose to sing had large symbolic meaning to her—and eventually to me: "A Bird in a Gilded Cage."

Kitty went to a lot of trouble to acquire a nineteenth-century costume, complete with floor-length gown, sequins, beads, and a huge flowered hat. She rouged her cheeks and reddened her lips to add to the impersonation of a woman who had sold herself to a rich husband. I can still remember my uneasy sensations when I watched the curtain come up in St. Patrick's auditorium and there stood my mother transformed into a woman from another time. With tragic gusto she began to sing:

> She's only a bird in a gilded cage,
> A beautiful sight to see.
> You would think she was happy
> And free from care;
> She's not, though she seems to be.
> It's sad when you think of her wasted life,
> For Youth cannot mate with Age,
> And her beauty was sold
> For an old man's gold,
> She's a bird in a gilded cage!

It was evident to me, even then, that Kitty was telling herself—and others in the audience who had the requisite information, such as Mae Gallagher—that the song was a commentary, if not an exact replica, of her life. She too had sold her beauty for gold. I did not like it at all. But what could I do about it? I applauded with the rest. I noticed that my father did not come to the show.

Meanwhile, life continued, with its usual mix of school and sports. I played Petruchio in Shakespeare's *The Taming of the Shrew* and for a while talked about becoming an actor. My mother thought it was a wonderful idea, which probably gave my father the bends in private. He could see another George Dolan taking shape before his appalled eyes. On this one, he did not have to intervene. My drama coach, James Maher, was a marvelously wrinkled old retired thespian who had played with all the big names in the theater of the first decades of the twentieth century. When I informed him of my plan to pursue a stage career, he replied, "Come with me."

Maher led me out of St. Peter's Prep and down several disreputable blocks of downtown Jersey City to a bar that was safely distant from the Jesuits. There, he bought me a rye and ginger ale and a double for himself. He toasted my ambition and said, "You're too intelligent to waste your time being an actor."

In the spring of my senior year, I started playing baseball on a field in Hudson County Park, on the west side of Jersey City, far from the dirt-cinder field of my boyhood. The competition was tougher in these games. Players came from all parts of the city.

I still played third, my father's favorite position. One day a batter hit a pop foul. I went after it and caught it seconds before colliding with a wire fence. A jutting piece of wire went through my gum, causing blood to flow. I stayed in the game and got a hit my next time at bat against one of the best pitchers in the city.

That night at the dinner table, my father said, "I liked the way you went after that ball—and held on to it in spite of that fence." Unknown to me, he had been sitting in his car watching the game.

My mother was horrified to hear about my punctured gum and had me swishing an antiseptic around my mouth for days to make sure the nefarious wire had not poisoned me. I was more impressed, and touched, by my father's quiet attendance at the game—and his praise. Nerve, that's what he was saying. Maybe you've got it after all. Suddenly his stock was up again—way up.

My senior year in prep school dwindled down, with Father Shalloe becoming more and more importunate about my stalled vocation. Complicating my problem was Elizabeth Boyle, Bill Gannon's cousin, a redhead who had gotten the highest marks in our class at St. Patrick's

School. After seeing little of her for several years, I suddenly found her conversation fascinating. To my dismay she informed me that she intended to become a nun. She had experienced that mysterious infusion of divine grace known as a vocation.

This led to more soul-searching and additional conferences with Father Shalloe. One day I and several friends went to New York to visit our Latin teacher, Father William Riordan, S.J., in St. Vincent's Hospital, where he had undergone surgery. Riordan was a very different man from Father Shalloe. Balding, with a wry wit that frequently skewered those who lagged behind the learning curve in reading Cicero and Horace, he was not popular with most of my class. But I liked the way he gave our numerous know-nothings a hard time. Everyone who got good marks at St. Peter's was a target of their derision.

While we were in Father Riordan's hospital room, Father Shalloe strolled in. The two priests chatted agreeably for a moment and Shalloe turned toward the door. "Tom," he said, using the nickname I had acquired at St. Peter's, "I hope you're going to make up your mind soon. There's not much time left, you know."

I assured him I was thinking hard. There was a long pause as Father Shalloe's footsteps faded down the hall. "What was he talking about?" Father Riordan asked in his sharpest tone of voice.

I explained that Father Shalloe was urging me to decide to become a Jesuit. Father Riordan sat up very straight in his bed, his already ruddy face a brighter tinge of red. "He has no damn business talking to you about that!" he growled. "That's between you and God—and nobody else."

I took a deep slow breath. Putting those blunt words together with my father's remark about wasting my life, I decided I was not going to become a Jesuit after all.

That still left me with the problem of extricating myself from Father Shalloe's clutches. By now it was the late spring of 1945. The Germans had surrendered but the Japanese were still resisting ferociously on Okinawa and other islands. Tom Sweeney, only a year ahead of me at St. Peter's, the son of one of my father's best friends, had joined the Marines and gotten killed on Okinawa. I had barely known him but he became a semi-legendary figure in the school, especially among his fellow football players. One night I was in a bar with several of these muscular characters and they talked about joining up to avenge Tom, before we got drafted into the army. Everyone agreed that this was the best thing to do, not only idealistically, but realistically. If you volunteered, especially in the navy or the Marines, you could have some say in where and how you served. This proved to be a total myth but everyone believed it at the time.

Suddenly I saw the perfect excuse to finesse Father Shalloe, no matter now much smoke he blew in my face. At our next meeting, I solemnly informed him I was going to join the navy. I mentioned my father's reputation as a hero in World War I and said I could not bear the thought of him thinking I had joined the Jesuits because I was afraid of dying for my country like Tom Sweeney. For once in his life, Father Shalloe was speechless.

The following day was Saturday. With some of the footballers I headed for a navy recruiting office in New York. After the usual stripping and prodding and poking by numerous doctors, we were all accepted. On the way back to Jersey City, we met several girls I had gotten to know at Point Pleasant. They asked me what I was doing in New York. I told them I had just joined the navy. "Oh Teddy, you didn't!" one of them cried.

My St. Peter's friends thought this was hilarious. For weeks they would shrill, "Oh Teddy, you didn't!" when they saw me in the halls. But I think they were secretly impressed to discover I had a contingent of female admirers—something few other members of the class of 1945 could claim.

My mother said almost the same thing as the Point Pleasant girls when I told her I had enlisted. At the time it upset me because I was all too aware of how she was still asking God to send me a vocation. To give her credit, after the initial shock Kitty did not reproach me, even though she must have sensed this was a decisive break with her attempts to make me her life companion. She even said she was proud of me.

At the time, I was far more worried about my father's reaction. He was an Army man all the way. He even rooted for Army's football team against Navy. To my surprise, he barely commented on my decision.

On the day in mid-July 1945 that I left for Sampson Naval Training Station in upstate New York, Teddy Fleming drove me to Pennsylvania Station in New York City. As we sped through the Holland Tunnel, he stared at the car ahead of us and said, "I've always been proud of being an infantryman. But strictly between you and me—I'm glad you joined the navy."

He meant the navy was a lot safer than the infantry. Again I heard the message: *You're all I've got*. We shook hands pretty hard that night.

# 27

# Swabbie

The navy was an experience in freedom at first. I felt liberated from my mother, my father, Frank Hague, and the Jesuits, not necessarily in that order. But I soon discovered all these realities traveled with me, first to the Sampson Naval Training Station, and then to the USS *Topeka*, a light cruiser that I boarded in September 1945 in Portland, Oregon.

Whenever I told someone I was from Jersey City, I got eye-rolling and an inquiry about the infamous Frank ("I am the law") Hague. When I tried to defend the mayor by explaining how the catchphrase had originated, few were interested, and not a few scoffed. I soon stopped mentioning Jersey City, or telling anyone that my father was part of the "Hague Machine," as everyone called it. Most people were satisfied with "New Jersey" when they asked where you were from.

My mother wrote to me almost every day, giving me a running account of the family's doings. I heard all about my father's November 1945 elevation to sheriff of Hudson County, the best-paying job on Frank Hague's patronage tree. She even told me how much the sheriff got—$12,500—which seems a trivial sum these days. But the figure should be multiplied by ten to approximate the dollar in those bygone years.

That suggests a job several notches above the middle class, who were still struggling along on half that amount. She also told me that

Mayor Hague had given my father an inscribed gold ring, with a handsome square-cut onyx in the center of it. It was a gift he reserved for his most loyal and effective followers.

I also heard a good deal about my brother's adventures at St. Peter's Prep. He was three years behind me, in the class of 1948. Gene was developing into a big, good-looking guy, with a lot of talent on the basketball court. One day he was approached by a Jesuit priest who was teaching him Latin. The priest wanted my brother to come up to his room to look at some interesting drawings of ancient Roman ruins. When Gene demurred, the Jesuit put his hand on my brother's arm in a strange way—something between a grab and a caress.

My father's reaction to this attempted seduction demonstrated he did not share my mother's opinion that all Jesuits were gentlemen. He got on the telephone to the president of St. Peter's Prep and said he wanted that Jesuit out of Jersey City in twenty-four hours or he would come down and have a talk with him. The Jesuit vanished on my father's schedule. My mother thought the whole thing was "awful," but she did not object to my father's solution.

Distance from my mother accentuated my feelings of guilt for not becoming a Jesuit and for joining the navy without consulting her. I remember rushing around Long Beach, California, where the *Topeka* was temporarily docked, to find the most saccharine Christmas card in the history of bad taste, a gigantic heart with an oozing sentiment about love and devotion unto eternity. I did not feel an iota of this emotion. I only wanted to offer it to her. Kitty loved it—which only made me feel more guilty.

Another story that invaded my mother's letters was Marie Farrelly's sad fate. She developed cancer and surgery failed to stop its spread. Walter Farrelly nursed her tenderly throughout her yearlong ordeal. They even "abandoned modesty," as my mother put it, giving me a glimpse of her generation's sexual mores. She meant Walter brought Marie a bedpan and changed her nightgown when necessary. It was a touching testament of their love for each other and my mother was deeply moved by it. By this time my feelings about Walter Farrelly were on my father's side of the equation and I found it hard to summon much sympathy for him or his suffering wife.

Meanwhile, I was discovering the sexual mores of the U.S. Navy and the state of California, which made a nice conjunction. The USS *Topeka* was the usual cross-section of young America, with a quota of old navy types, such as our division's first-class boatswain's mate, Ernest O. Homewood. He was a slab of a man with a voice like a foghorn and thirty years of hash marks on his sleeve.

Before our first liberty in Long Beach, California, Homewood gathered our F (for fire control) Division in our belowdecks compartment for a lecture. "This goes for all you guys, not just the boots we got aboard in Portland," he roared. "You're gonna meet a lot of babes on the beach who'll be reachin' for your wallets while you're reachin' for their you-know-whats. If by some miracle you get to the point of makin' out, get this through your %$@&!! heads—put a boot on it! I don't care if her name is Agatha Vanderbilt Rockefeller the Fourth. She can still have the clap and maybe the syph!"

This was a long way from Father Shalloe and almost as far from the innocent eroticism of the lifeguard stand in Point Pleasant. It was light-years away from my mother's ideas about sexual modesty. But it fit nicely into my father's lecture on syphilis. I had no personal problem with Boats Homewood's advice—I had decided to prove to myself and Father Shalloe that I had not refused to join the Jesuits out of a reprehensible desire to get laid as soon as possible. Moreover, the women I encountered strolling the Long Beach Pike, the West Coast's biggest amusement park, were the ugliest whores I had ever imagined seeing.

Boats Homewood had chosen me to become a member of F Division because my navy test scores revealed a high IQ. He ignored other scores that disclosed an abysmally low mechanical aptitude. Fire controlmen dealt with complex computers and range finders that operated the ship's guns—high tech stuff I was unlikely to comprehend. My lack of mechanical skills did not bother Homewood because he too knew nothing about machinery. His job was to make sure we kept our compartment and work stations scrupulously clean, our dress uniforms pressed, and our shoes shined for the perpetual inspections. All the "deck" divisions (as distinguished from the firemen, the "black bang," whom deck sailors considered the dregs of shipboard humanity) had a first-class boatswain who oversaw our shipboard routine, not unlike a sergeant in an army company. It would take me a while to discover

Homewood had long-range plans for me beyond the purviews of F Division and the USS *Topeka*.

After we shoved off for Japan and other points in the Far East, Homewood tried to accelerate my rise in the navy. The first step on the ladder was seaman first class. To pass this test, a candidate had to master all sorts of tricky knots. He had me and a half dozen fellow boots start with class-one knots—bowlines, sheepshanks, and cat's-paws. I was terrible at it, but that only prompted Homewood to give me private lessons. Soon I was tackling carrick bends and timber hitches. I won't pretend to remember anything about these exotic tests of my seamanship. The only one I can handle today is the slipknot, which any moron can tie. This retention may have had something to do with being told that it was the knot you had to know if you fell overboard and someone tossed a line to you.

Homewood soon pronounced me ready for elevation to seaman first class. He overcame the objections of our division officer, Lieutenant JG Otto Zemke, a former enlisted man who had become an officer during the war. Zemke, who looked like typecasting for a German SS officer, ranted that it had taken him four years to become a seaman first class. I had only been in the navy four months.

Homewood told him he did not know what he was talking about, "as usual." The navy had to change a few rules to keep people like me in the service. "Don't talk to me that way!" Zemke raved. "I'm your commanding officer."

"I'll talk to you any way I goddamn please," Homewood said.

I thought we were both going to get court-martialed. But Homewood went back to teaching me how to improve my timber hitch and Zemke clumped out of the compartment. Homewood glared after him. "When that miserable kraut was a petty officer I seen him do things to guys in the old navy that'd make you sick to your stomach," he said.

I was grateful to Homewood. The promotion to seaman first class meant another thirty-two dollars a month. As our friendship grew, I asked Homewood why he had joined the navy. "You wouldn't ask that question if you saw where I grew up in Alabama," he said. "A crummy little two-room shack. My old lady had thirteen kids. My old man kicked us out the door soon as we got outta grammar school. The navy gave me a home, son."

I was back in Aunt Mae's kitchen, listening to her tell me stories of the Flemings' poverty-haunted youth. Even more fascinating for someone who already found the past intriguing, Homewood was a walking, talking history of the old navy, the one that existed before the tidal wave of civilians joined it after Pearl Harbor. He told me stories of his adventures on the China Station and in the Philippines. He knew men who were the leaders of World War II—Ernest King, Chester Nimitz, Bull Halsey—when they were junior officers.

The ancient superstitions of the sea swam through Homewood's head—the albatrosses who settled on mainmasts, guaranteeing a ship's safety in storms or battles, the power of a captain's "joss" (named for the incense sticks Chinese Buddhists burned in their temples), the awful things that happened when a captain lost contact with the good spirits that protected a ship. When it came to luck and what made it or ruined it, compared to Homewood, Teddy Fleming was a rationalist.

I saw another side of Homewood—and the old navy—when we steamed into Pearl Harbor. In California, a lucky sailor might meet some moderately respectable women at the USOs, or pick one up in a bar. In Honolulu no respectable woman went near a swabbie. But that did not mean it was impossible to get laid. Commercialized sex was everywhere. Sailors stood in lines outside of brothels to get two minutes of happiness for five dollars an ejaculation. The U.S. government guaranteed virtual immunity from venereal disease. Navy doctors inspected the officially licensed bordellos every week to make sure the girls were uninfected.

There was nothing wrong with any of this as far as Homewood was concerned. It was life as he had known it since he lied his way into the navy in 1913 at the age of sixteen. I was seeing things I had never imagined in my Irish Catholic ghetto in Jersey City. I found myself yearning to write a frank letter to my father, telling him about it, asking him: was it like this in France? But I was afraid he would think I was trying to accuse him of something. So I wrote wordy letters to my mother instead, telling her about the beauty of Hawaii and the majesty of the Pacific's distances.

On our last night in Pearl, before we shoved off for Japan, I was snoozing in my rack in F compartment when an urgent hand shook me awake. It was Rob Lipscomb, the guy who slept in the rack beneath mine. "Boats needs help!" he hissed. He shook awake two other guys in our vicinity and we pulled on our dungarees and lurched up to the quarterdeck.

On the dock, a riot was in progress. Homewood, totally drunk, was fighting a dozen shore patrolmen. When one of them grabbed his arm, he whirled the man in the air and slammed him to the ground like a toy. Two of them were clinging to his legs, like pygmies trying to subdue King Kong. The others were clubbing him with no visible effect.

"Go get him," snarled the officer of the deck. We rushed down to the dock and Lipscomb begged Homewood to calm down. Whatever had gone wrong on liberty couldn't justify losing his stripes and maybe ending up in Portsmouth (the U.S. Navy prison). Any minute, they were going to summon the captain to the quarterdeck.

The invocation of the captain's wrath worked. Homewood subsided and let us half drag, half carry him up the gangplank. There, he miraculously came to attention, saluted the officer of the deck and the flag on the *Topeka*'s fantail, and let us lead him belowdecks.

It was a fearful struggle, getting Homewood down several vertical ladders to our compartment. As we stripped off his uniform, he babbled about his visit to a Chinese whorehouse. Suddenly Homewood focused on me. "Flem, what the hell you doin' here? You shouldn't be seein' what a bum I am when I get drunk. Didn' mean to get this way, it was goin' to that goddamn Chinese whorehouse. Brought it all back. Little Chinese girl I had in Shanghai in the thirties. Sweetest little thing you ever saw. Had a kid by me, Jesus I was thinkin' of *marryin'* her—goin' Asiatic, you know. Then the goddamn Japs started runnin' wild and they pulled us outta there. I jus' gave her a month's salary and lef' 'thout even sayin' good-bye. Truth is I was afraid to leave the goddamn navy. 'Fraid I'd wind up livin' outta garbage cans. But you got brains, Flem, you don' have t'go my route."

I was very upset by the time we got Boats settled in his rack. I had begun to see what he was doing. He was making me his navy son. I did not like it. I had enough trouble with the father I had left behind in Jersey City.

My service experience could not compare with my father's in most respects. No one fired a bullet or shell at me in anger. The war had ended with the atomic blasts over Hiroshima and Nagasaki a month before I boarded the USS *Topeka*. Oddly, the closest I came to getting killed was a foggy, rainy day in the Sea of Japan, when I was having a conversation about my father. In late December 1945 the Seventh Fleet steamed out of Tokyo Bay for what the brass called war maneuvers. Exactly who we were going to fight was anyone's guess. There was not an enemy warship left on the seven seas.

The assistant commander of F Division, Lieutenant JG Joseph Clark, a chubby redheaded reserve officer, told us the real story. We had to fire away a lot of surplus ammunition, otherwise Congress was liable to cut the navy's appropriation for the coming year. I remarked that I could understand the appropriation politics we were pursuing. In my hometown, one of the goals was to keep as many people as possible on the government payroll.

Clark asked me where I was from. When I told him, he chuckled. "I'm from Bayonne," he said. That was just south of Jersey City on the long narrow ridge that was the chief feature of uptown. Bayonne was virtually indistinguishable from our metropolis. Clark had a younger brother who was going to St. Peter's Prep at that very moment.

"Didn't your old man just get elected to something?" he said.

"Sheriff," I said.

Clark whistled appreciatively and grinned. "Can he get me a job if and when the admirals ever let me out of their clutches?"

As the lieutenant said this, two six-inch shells from another American cruiser somewhere in the murk came whistling through the *Topeka*'s superstructure and exploded a few hundred yards away. The ship took violent evasive action while our captain made sulfurous comments over the TBS (Talk Between Ships) radio about our sister ship's fire controlmen.

At the time, I did not think it was particularly strange to come so close to getting shredded by high explosives while talking about my father. It seemed to fit, somehow, in the scheme of my life. As if Teddy Fleming had invoked some supernatural power to keep me thinking about him.

Another figure who gradually loomed large in my shipboard life was Chaplain Carl Benson, a cheerful midsized energetic man with a small brush mustache. He sent out a call for volunteers to work on a projected ship's newspaper, the *Sunflower*. I was one of the few who showed up for a meeting in Benson's tiny office, which doubled as the ship's library.

Chaplain Benson was a Baptist. At the time I was not aware that most members of that sect tend to a fundamentalist view of the Bible and Christianity. My knowledge of other religions was zero. But Benson was a Baptist from Chicago, and he had an extremely sophisticated approach to religion. He also had a knack for asking the right questions. He soon learned I was a Jesuit boy, and that made him respectful of my supposed intellect.

Benson asked me if I had read *The Quest for the Historical Jesus*. I did not know what he was talking about. He explained that this was a book by a German theologian, Albert Schweitzer, who was a follower of Schleiermacher, another German scholar who had raised serious doubts about the divinity of Jesus. Would I like to borrow Schweitzer?

I spent the next two or three weeks at sea reading *The Quest for the Historical Jesus*. It blew my devout Catholic mind. According to Schweitzer, Jesus was only one of many Jewish prophets who had imagined himself redeeming the corrupted state of Israel from the domination of the Romans. They all thought there was no time to waste because the world was coming to an end at any moment. Most of them had wound up crucified like Jesus.

I had more than a few long talks with Chaplain Benson about Albert Schweitzer. Did he think this German proved that Jesus was not divine or even a particularly original prophet? Benson said he thought you had to take Schweitzer's "modernist" view of Jesus into account when you talked to intelligent Christians. For himself, he had found a solution in another European thinker—a Dane named Soren Kierkegaard.

I had never heard of him either. Kierkegaard believed that faith was not a rational act so it did not matter how many obstacles your intellect put in the way. In fact, the more "absurd" your mind told you Christianity was, the greater (and by implication, more heroic) was your "leap" to faith.

In prostrate Japan I was awed and occasionally horrified at the totality of the war's destruction. Tokyo was a moonscape, with only a half dozen steel and concrete buildings still standing, all blackened by the firestorms created by American incendiary bombs. In the towns around Tokyo, and in the civilian streets around the naval base of Yokusaka, however, relatively normal life continued and U.S. sailors had no trouble finding booze and women.

After a few months in Tokyo Harbor, the Seventh Fleet was ordered to show the flag in Shanghai to bolster the Chinese National-ists in their losing struggle with the Communists for control of China. The *Topeka* tied up at a quay in the Whangpoo River for six weeks and I got a sailor's-eye view of poverty that made the Flemings' struggles in Jersey City seem benign.

The streets swarmed with beggars of all ages, many of whom looked close to death from starvation. I never saw a Chinese passerby give them a penny. They were simply part of the scenery, to be stepped over or pushed aside if they got too demanding. Boats Homewood advised us to imitate the Chinese. If you started giving to the beggars, you would be broke before you got a hundred yards from the dock.

A day did not pass without the body of a baby girl floating by in the current. Female children were considered a liability by the Chi-nese. This was especially true of the people who lived on the sampans that clotted the Whangpoo's banks farther upstream. The newborns were unceremoniously tossed overboard by their disappointed par-ents. One of my friends was Don Schnable, the coxswain of the *Topeka*'s motor whaleboat. At chow he would complain bitterly about the way the officer of the deck forced him to tow the bloated little corpses that got trapped against the ship into the middle of the river to continue their journey to the China Sea.

Boats Homewood said Shanghai was not the city he had known in the 1930s, when every American sailor was a hero. In those day the British had been the ones everybody hated. Now they were gone and the Americans seemed to have taken their place on the foreign devils chart. He advised us not to go beyond the borders of the International Settlement, a sort of white man's city within the Chinese city. Even that was not very safe because it was now policed by the Chinese.

Rob Lipscomb and I found this out when we got into an argument with a rickshaw man about a fare. We went looking for a supposedly great restaurant in the winding streets off Bubbling Well Road, the main drag in the International Settlement. Our rickshaw man got tired, waved vaguely down a side street, and doubled his agreed-on fare. When we told him to go to hell, a huge crowd gathered around us. There were no other Americans in sight and the popular vote was definitely not going our way.

Two Chinese policemen shoved their way through the crowd to regard us with very unfriendly eyes. After the rickshaw man spoke his piece, one of the cops pulled out his gun and aimed it at us. Lipscomb still wanted to argue, but I decided nerve was not the answer to this problem. We were about to become statistics. I paid the doubled fare and we got out of there.

Everyone was happy to leave Shanghai for Manila, which Boats Homewood assured us was one of the greatest liberty ports in the world. I had heard a lot about the Philippines from Father Shalloe and other Jesuits; the order had long sent missionaries there. I was unprepared for the version of the nation I encountered as a sailor. The hundreds of brothels that ringed the Cavite Naval Base did a stupendous business. I was privately dismayed by such rampant prostitution in a country that American Jesuits had been supposedly uplifting and otherwise educating for decades. I was tempted to write Father Shalloe a cynical letter, asking: how come? Not until I did some historical research many years later did I realize the Jesuits were mere bystanders in the very tangled tale of America and the Philippines.

Soon we were at sea again, heading for Guam. Chaplain Benson gave me another book to read: James Joyce's *Portrait of the Artist as a Young Man*. It was my first serious contact with the land of my ancestors. I found the real world of modern Ireland even more riveting than *The Quest for the Historical Jesus*. I was especially fascinated by hero Stephen Daedelus's defiance of the Catholic Church and his determination to forge an identify for himself as an artist, independent of Rome's spiritual domination. Although the chaplain never so much as hinted at his intentions, I now think Benson was hoping I would get this message.

On the voyage to Guam I suddenly found myself under arrest, charged with stealing navy property and facing a possible year in Portsmouth prison. The whole thing seemed unreal to me. My offense had been committed by several thousand other sailors in the Seventh Fleet. In wintry Japan, we had been issued foul-weather jackets to wear over our dungarees while on duty topside. They were comfortable fleece-lined garments. When no one collected them as we sailed from freezing Tokyo and chilly Shanghai to Manila, the scuttlebutt went out to all hands: *Mail yourself a souvenir. Stick your jacket in a box and ship it home. If and when anyone inquires, say you lost it.*

I thought this was a great idea, procured a box from a friend in the mail room, and shipped my jacket back to Jersey City. Unfortunately, when a tidal wave of similar boxes hit the navy post office in San Francisco, some enterprising officer opened a few and decided grand larceny was being committed. Since they could not prosecute everyone without crippling the Seventh Fleet, a select few were chosen to terrorize the rest. My name came up in this game of punishment roulette.

I was ordered to appear at a preliminary hearing before the *Topeka*'s executive officer, a fat pompous character named Osborn. My division officer, Lieutenant Zemke, and his assistant from Bayonne, Lieutenant JG Clark, accompanied me. When I pleaded guilty, the exec looked very stern, gave me a tongue-lashing, and said I deserved a summary court-martial. Where the hell did I get off stealing navy property? He worked himself into a fury while I said no sir, yes sir, wherever I thought it was appropriate.

The exec said he was forwarding my case to the *Topeka*'s captain with a recommendation of a summary court-martial. I still thought the whole thing was unreal. But Lieutenant Zemke's attitude soon convinced me the future was ominous. "If you think I'm gonna put in a good word for you, you're crazy!" he sneered. "You're one of Homewood's pets. Let him get you out of this."

A glum Lieutenant Clark told me this was bad news. Usually, a division officer can recommend clemency for such a minor offense and the captain will follow his advice. But I was caught in the old navy feud between Homewood and the Kraut, as everyone called Zemke.

I turned to Chaplain Benson, who said he would write to the captain on my behalf. A few days later, as the time of my hearing before the captain approached, the chaplain demonstrated what was wrong with Protestantism. He said he had decided he couldn't write to the captain because I had pleaded guilty. I would have to accept my punishment. I recalled my father's exertions on behalf of Uncle George. I remembered him getting out of bed at 3 A.M. to get a Sixth

Ward drunk out of jail. I decided I preferred good old corrupt Irish Catholicism anytime.

Homewood was also not very helpful. He called me a lot of names, "asshole" being the only printable one. But he was out of the loop, as far as having much influence with the officers was concerned. For one thing, his record was so thick with charges for rioting and assaulting shore patrolman, he was hardly the character witness I needed.

Fearing the worst, I appeared at captain's mast as we approached Guam. The captain was not at all like the executive officer. He was much older, with a graying mustache and a surprisingly mild manner. He was almost grandfatherly. Standing by my side were Lieutenants Zemke and Clark. This was standard procedure at captain's mast. Your division officers were supposed to be there to defend you against the captain's wrath. Also present was a subdued, worried Boats Homewood.

To my surprise, after the charges were read, and Zemke said nothing as expected, Lieutenant Clark said he had asked another officer, who had a law degree, to look into the question of charging one man for an offense committed by many. Could he speak on my behalf? The captain gave his approval and Clark ushered this officer into the cabin. Small and dark, he introduced himself as Lieutenant Robert Feder—and gave a succinct summary of the epidemic of vanished foul-weather jackets. No fewer than three hundred had disappeared on the *Topeka* alone. Lieutenant Feder said he was not an expert on navy law, but prosecuting one man for such a widespread offense raised a question of equity—a principle he hoped the navy would not want to violate.

The captain harrumphed and said navy justice was just as concerned with equity as any other legal system. It was evident that I had been unaware of the seriousness of my offense. Although he agreed with the executive officer that the crime, in the abstract, merited a summary court-martial, instead he was going to sentence me to thirty days' confinement aboard ship. Did Lieutenant Zemke, as the division officer, think this was adequate? Zemke glared at Homewood for a moment and said, "Yes, Captain."

Out on deck, Homewood slapped me on the back and called me a "lucky son of a bitch." He had never seen the "old man" (the captain) in such a good mood. I strolled up to the bow with Lieutenants Feder and Clark. "Guess where this guy is from," Clark said, grinning at Feder.

"Where?"

"Hoboken."

Hoboken, just north of Jersey City, had a mayor who worshipped Frank Hague and imitated him in all things judicial and political.

"When Joe told me what a jam you were in, I said we had to get you off or our names would be mud with Uncle Frank," Lieutenant Feder said.

He was talking about Mayor Hague. It was incredible but true. My father's share of Hague's clout had extended seven thousand miles to save me from a navy prison cell.

Confined to the ship for thirty days, I soon discovered Homewood had ideas about how I should spend my time. He wanted me to become a fire controlman third class, a rated man. The problem was my inability to grasp even the relatively simple science a third-class FC needed to know. When I pleaded inability, Homewood told me to memorize the whole %$@# book if necessary. One way or another, I was going to pass that test.

One evening, on the deck outside main forward work station, as the Pacific sky put on its usual display of sunset fireworks, Homewood confided his vision of the rest of my life. "Here's the way to go, Flem. You should sign up for a three-year hitch—and apply for 'Napolis. The navy's got a quota of guys who go from the fleet each year. You get in without kissin' some congressman's ass for an appointment. You'll do great at Annapolis, Flem. You got the brains to go a long way in this man's navy."

Homewood started talking about the navy, not as it existed aboard the USS *Topeka* or any other ship in the Seventh Fleet but as it existed in his heart. He talked about the way it took care of its own, the way it rewarded loyalty and dependability and courage, the way it gave a man a purpose in life. "I feel all that every time I salute that flag on the fantail, Flem. It ain't the lousy civilians I'm salutin', them assholes in Washington and New York who run the country. It's the guys who took it on the chin at Pearl Harbor and Savo Island and Midway, the guys who said navy all the way and meant it. That's the kind of a guy I want you to be."

*Fatherhood*, I thought. I saw that Homewood wanted the pride, the satisfaction, of fatherhood through me. He was telling me his deepest feelings, he was saying things he seldom revealed to anyone. As I write this now, my eyes swim with tears. But in 1946, Homewood was talking to a nineteen-year-old Irish-American who had narrowly escaped a summary court-martial thanks to the U.S. Navy's weird approach to crime and punishment. A nineteen-year-old who had already evaded one attempt to commandeer his life for another large authoritarian organization, the Catholic Church.

"Boats," I said. "I appreciate what you're saying. But I think you've got the wrong guy. I'm not exactly in love with the navy. If I ever get to Annapolis, it'll be to blow up the goddamn place."

Homewood was hurt. For a moment I thought he was going to swat me overboard. But he was a leader of men and he didn't quit easily. In that respect he was the equal of Father Shalloe. "Okay," he said. "But I want you to keep your nose in that fire control manual and make third class. You're gonna be in for at least another year. You got lots of time to change your mind."

Trying to keep Homewood semi-happy, I agreed to study hard for my rate. With my good memory I might be able to fake my way through the exam by parroting the manual even if I did not understand it. My complaisance was also based on the widespread assumption that we latecomers to the wartime ranks would serve a minimum of two years to help Uncle Sam keep the peace. Why not get a rate and a little more money to make liberty more enjoyable?

Veterans of the war, depending on their length of service, were going home at a steady pace. A week seldom passed at Guam without another large departure from the *Topeka*. Several departees were on the staff of the *Sunflower*. One day, Chaplain Benson told me I was now the editor. With a reduced staff, this became virtually a full-time job.

I taught myself to type and spent most of each day in the chaplain's office, writing or rewriting copy. The paper was a weekly. Though it was seldom more than four pages, it was a chore to keep up with the deadlines. I had no time to study for my third-class fire controlman test and was forced to inform Homewood that it would have to wait for a while.

One day, a large red face filled the porthole that brought an occasional whiff of fresh ear into our editorial dungeon, which we had nicknamed the Black Hole. It was Homewood. He glared at me, sitting at my typewriter, and roared, *"Fleming, I can't believe it! You're turnin' into a #$@%@ yeoman!"*

In Homewood's deck sailor universe, a yeoman (aka typist-stenographer) was the lowest form of life in the U.S. Navy, even beneath the detritus of the black gang. Among other things, yeomen were widely considered to be queer, and by deduction, cowards. (Both canards, I should add.) Boats was hoping to shock me out of my defection from his plan for my life. Not many yeomen got into Annapolis.

I was upset and sought out Homewood at chow to assure him I still wanted to make that rate. I wanted to keep his friendship. I was starting to feel guilty about disappointing him—although I had no intention of changing my mind about going to Annapolis. I had conferred with Lieutenant Clark about the idea and he had told me I would go out of my mind in the place. The course consisted of indigestible amounts of math, engineering, and science.

That night, I was back at my typewriter, putting together the next issue of the *Sunflower*. BuNav press releases were a standard part of our news sources. The postwar navy was rife with reorganizations and transfers of ships and men. I glanced at the latest press release on my desk and froze. In language unusually plain for BuNav, it said that everyone who had joined the navy before the war ended would be discharged as soon as possible, probably within the next six weeks. The draft was continuing to supply the navy with a satisfactory number of new men, etc. etc., and President Truman was bowing to the wishes of Congress, etc. etc. I paid no attention to the remaining verbiage. I was going home!

My thirty-day confinement aboard ship had ended two weeks earlier. The next day I took liberty on Guam and headed for the nearest Western Union office. I sent a cable to my father. "WILL BE DISCHARGED WITHIN THE NEXT SIX WEEKS. GET ME INTO A COLLEGE. ANY COLLEGE."

Back aboard the *Topeka*, I broke the news to Homewood. He was very disappointed. "You coulda made admiral, kid," he said.

I did not have the heart to tell him his vision of me was a fantasy. "Boats," I said, "I think I'm going to be a writer. If I make it, I'll put you in a book. I guarantee it." It would take me another thirty-five years, but I kept this promise in my novel, *Time and Tide*.

"You might pull it off," Boats said. "You Irish guys are good at bullshit. But who's gonna read it to me?"

BuNav's announcement proved to be on the money in 14-karat gold. In four weeks I was on a troopship that steamed me and a thousand other sailors back to Long Beach, California, where we boarded troop trains that clanked some of us across the country to a processing center on Long Island. I was able to keep my parents abreast of my schedule and destination with telegrams and phone calls. In exactly six weeks, on July 15, 1946, I emerged from the processing center with my discharge in hand.

Waiting for me was Sheriff Thomas J. (Teddy) Fleming beside a gleaming seven-passenger Cadillac. With a big smile, my father held out his hand. My navy career ended as it began, with one of the toughest shakes we ever exchanged.

# 28

# What's Philosophy?

After a steak dinner at Cavanaugh's, one of New York's better restaurants, my father and I headed for our summer house in Point Pleasant. En route he told me he had gotten me into Fordham College, the Jesuit school in the Bronx. I was underwhelmed. I had no desire for more Catholic education. I wanted to continue the American education I had been getting aboard the USS *Topeka*.

Teddy Fleming sensed my lack of enthusiasm—which I suspect he shared—and explained that time had been short and other colleges did not have a place for me. All the schools were being swamped by a glut of applicants, thanks to Congress's decision to pass the GI Bill, financing higher education for veterans.

I told him not to worry about it. Like most people my age, I wanted to get through college as quickly as possible. I was grateful for the chance to get started without wasting six months or a year working at some zero-minus job. Also, I told myself maybe I would learn something from the Jesuits' philosophy courses that would resolve my by now rampant doubts about the Catholic Church.

I soon discovered nothing much had changed between my mother and father. They were still distant with each other. I never saw them kiss or make affectionate remarks. Kitty had a tendency to say things that were supposedly humorous but were thinly veiled putdowns of her husband, the sheriff. She wryly referred to herself as "the First

Lady of Hudson County." Another gambit was asking me or my brother Gene whether it was better to be a big frog in a small pond or a small frog in a big pond. Kitty claimed she could not decide how to answer that question.

My father seemed to tolerate these remarks. His elevation to sheriff had doubled his salary, more or less removing money as a source of quarrels. Kitty could run up her charge accounts without triggering an explosion. Looking through a pocket diary my mother kept during the forties gave me further insights into their ongoing relationship. The entries are all brief, but none are hostile, and one or two are positive. Both my parents seemed to have realized that if they were going to stay together, there was no point in further brawling.

Beneath this surface politeness, there was still a lot of alienation. I sensed this when my mother tried to resume her life's-companion style with me. She soon realized it no longer worked. I simply was not interested in her chatter about Mary McNamara King and other friends. Nor did I take well to her urging me to tell her "all about" my adventures in the navy in Tokyo, Shanghai, and other ports in the Far East. My now thoroughly masculinized psyche recoiled from the kind of intimacy Kitty wanted to achieve.

Boats Homewood was not someone she would even begin to understand. I was not about to tell her about the lines before the brothels in Pearl Harbor or the orgiastic liberties in the Philippines. My father never asked me a single prying question. Teddy Fleming understood from his own army experience that the navy part of my life was my own business and no one else's.

I had other things on my mind during that first summer home—notably a determination to find out more about Ireland and the Irish side of my Irish-American hyphen. James Joyce's *Portrait of the Artist* had ignited a kind of anger at my near total ignorance about the land of my ancestors. I soon assembled a small library of books and spent much of that summer reading them.

I absorbed in scarifying detail the remorseless English conquest of Ireland, which began in 1170, when an Anglo-Norman lord, Richard de Clare, the Earl of Pembroke, known as Strongbow, an ally of King Henry II, carved out a domain around the city of Dublin. (One of his right-hand men was Baron Amadis de Fleming.) It was the beginning of a long agony scathingly summed up by Jonathan Swift, the great satirist of among other things, England's abuse of the Irish: "Eleven men, well armed, will certainly subdue one single man in his shirt."

I worked my way through the appalling racism of English rule in Ireland, starting with the 1366 Statute of Kilkenny, which one writer has compared to Adolf Hitler's Nuremberg laws segregating the Jews. The statute banned the Irish language in areas ruled by England; equally forbidden was intermarriage with an Irish man or woman; even Irish names were banned. Only English ones were tolerated.

From this subterranean starting point things descended to the penal code of the seventeenth century. By this time militant Protestantism had engulfed the politics of England; the Irish responded with defiant Catholicism. Religion became an even handier tool to reduce the Irish to abject submission.

Irish Catholics were forbidden to vote; they could not hold public office or sit on juries; they could not own weapons, nor could they own a horse worth more than four pounds; a Protestant could buy any horse a Catholic owned by offering him five pounds. No Catholic could attend a university or any other kind of school, nor could a Catholic teach anyone, even as a private tutor. A Catholic could not own land, and when he leased a farm he was obliged to hand over any profit that exceeded a third of his rent. If he failed to do so, the first Protestant who discovered his evasion of the law could take possession of the farm.

It was amazing how much of it dovetailed with the history of the Irish in Jersey City. The war between the two religions had been carried to America virtually intact, and continued the tradition of prejudice, hatred, and oppression.

For a while my favorite writer was the Kerry poet Egan O'Rahilly, who lived between 1670 and 1726, and saw Ireland's dark night of the soul begin under the penal laws. Here is O'Rahilly addressing an English landlord.

> *That my old bitter heart was pierced in this black gloom,*
> *That foreign devils have made my land a tomb,*
> *That the sun that was Munster's glory has gone down*
> *Has made me a beggar before you, Valentine Brown.*

*That royal Cashel is bare of house and guest,*
*That Brian's turreted home is the Otter's nest,*
*That the kings of the land have neither land nor crown*
*Has made me a beggar before you, Valentine Brown.*

That summer I was more Irish than American. When I talked to my father and mother about my discoveries, I saw bafflement in their eyes. They knew little or nothing about the history of Ireland, ancient or modern. For them Irish culture consisted of the songs they sang at New Year's Eve parties and singers performed at parish variety shows. I was especially baffled by my father's lack of interest. Hadn't Davey Fleming discussed his memories with his sons?

At this point I knew nothing about the disillusion with Ireland after the Irish civil war of 1921–24. I was able to read with almost effervescent emotion William Butler Yeats's poem to the 1916 Easter Rebellion martyrs. For years I recited the closing lines to myself before sleep.

*And what if excess of love*
*Bewildered them till they died?*
*I write it out in verse—*
*MacDonagh and MacBride*
*And Connolly and Pearse*
*Now and in time to be,*
*Wherever green is worn,*
*Are changed, changed utterly:*
*A terrible beauty is born.*

My mother, displeased by my withdrawal from her orbit, wondered aloud why she was cooking and cleaning a summer house when all I did most of the day was sit on the porch and read. My brother Gene was no help—he stayed up most of the night listening to big-band swing music and slept most of the day. I now realize he too was in an escape mode. Something close to antagonism developed between me and my mother.

One night after dinner we were in the kitchen washing the dishes. As I handed Kitty the coffee cups, I found myself saying, "I spent a fair amount of time at sea thinking about what you told me about the father and Mrs. Flanagan. Even if it's true, don't you think it's time you forgave him?"

I can see now that after my refusal to share my navy experience with Kitty, these words were a double shock. She heard them not as advice but as rejection, betrayal. For a moment she gazed at me with an awful mixture of anger and grief in her eyes. Whirling, she seized the edge of the sink, putting her back to me. "Get out of here!" she cried. "Get out!"

"I'm only trying to help you see how—"

"I'm not interested in your help if that's what you think!" she cried.

Kitty snatched a handful of silverware and flung it into the sink, smashing a half dozen dishes. Groping for the broken pieces in the soapy water, she gashed her thumb. She held up her hand with the blood drooling down it and said, "See? See what you've made me do?"

I fled the kitchen and never mentioned the subject again.

That fall I headed for a dormitory in Fordham College with some of the sense of relief I felt when I had joined the navy. I no longer wanted to cope with the emotional complications of life in the Fleming family. This collegiate distancing would soon prove as illusory as my naval escape.

I was not happy at Fordham. The Jesuits all struck me as incredibly parochial, compared to Chaplain Benson. They treated us as if we had arrived straight from a Jesuit prep school, humbly eager to absorb their wisdom and accept their discipline. About two-thirds of the freshman class of 750 were veterans, most of them several years older than I was. When the dean of discipline posted a notice saying no one could stay out later than nine o'clock on Saturday night without a letter of permission from his parents, someone surreptitiously stuck beside it a scrawled reply: "Is it okay if I get a letter from my wife?" That summed up the disdain that rapidly accumulated between a hefty majority of the class of 1950 and the faculty.

In one English literature course, the Jesuit professor told us that no Catholic could read the *New Yorker* magazine without risking an "occasion of sin," because the magazine's prevailing point of view was so secular. We literally laughed in the man's face. Some Jesuits, carried away by their huge GI Bill–financed enrollments, saw themselves creating a separate American Catholic culture. Traditionally, they had mostly educated elites. Suddenly they were into schooling the masses. Their vision of the future was wildly unrealistic. American freedom was the driving force in our souls, not a right turn into some sort of authoritarian state within the state.

For the first two years Fordham offered no optional courses. It was the same doses of religion, Latin, English, and math I had studied at St. Peter's Prep. The Latin was taught as grammar without the slightest reference to Roman history or culture. The math was algebra and calculus, two arcanas I could see no point in mastering. After an acrimonious interview with the dean of the college in which I told him I wanted some optional courses and he told me I could not have any, I wanted out of the place as soon as possible.

I told my father I was applying to Princeton. He was perfectly agreeable and said he would talk to a few friends in the New Jersey state government who might be able to put in a word for me. My mother was shocked at my rejection of the Jesuits. She was afraid I would lose my faith at a non-Catholic institution. She called up Father Shalloe, who urged her to send me down to him for a talk. I said no thank you. I had no desire to go near the man.

Meanwhile, Ireland suddenly added another emotional complication. On a gray drizzly Saturday in November 1946, I strolled into my Fordham College dormitory after lunch and saw a short stocky man tacking up a poster on a bulletin board. It advertised a meeting in a nearby parish hall the following day to hear a lecture on "contemporary Ireland."

I arrived in time to get a seat in the first row. The crowd was small—no more than thirty or forty people, mostly young men around my age. The speaker, a big black-haired Irishman with a brogue, got our attention with his opening sentence: "Contemporary Ireland is the last act of a four-hundred-year-old tragedy." After recounting the massacres by Strongbow and other English invaders, the penal laws and the rack rents and the famine of the 1840s, he condemned the British "occupation" of Ulster's six counties for the better part of a half hour. He had equally abusive things to say about the Irish Free State, which had become the Republic of Ireland. They had sold a united Ireland to the British for a mess of "capitalist pottage."

Next he went to work on us Irish-Americans. He denounced our bland indifference to Ireland's plight. Our sheep like acquiescence in the partition of Ireland and our tolerance of, not to say fondness for, the morally degraded government of southern Ireland proved our almost criminal political stupidity. Now that we had gotten the truth from his lips, it should be clear to all of us that our first political loyalty must be to the creation of a united republican Ireland. Anyone who failed to respond to this appeal was "a traitor to his Irish blood."

Perhaps I should emphasize that the speaker was not preaching terrorism. The IRA bombing campaign that ignited the quasi–civil war in Northern Ireland was a decade and a half away. This man only wanted our money to give the republican cause a stronger political voice. Nevertheless, my response was savagely negative. Not only did I refuse to give him a cent, I stalked out of the hall during a question and answer session, declaring my angry indifference to his message.

I made no attempt to analyze my reaction at the time. All I knew was my gut antagonism to that phrase, "a traitor to his Irish blood." How dare this mick with his country brogue and zealot's arrogance say that to me? I had just as much Irish blood in my veins as him. Three of my four grandparents had been born in Ireland and the fourth, Tom Dolan, had an equally Irish bloodline. The implication that he, as a homegrown Celt, had a de facto authority to order me around was infuriating.

At least as galling was his accusation of political stupidity. In Jersey City, being Irish was synonymous with political savvy. No other organization in the country could match the ninety percent voter turnouts we racked up to elect Democratic senators and governors and presidents.

There was another reason why that Irishman infuriated me when he claimed Ireland had first call on my allegiance. I was only three months out of the U.S. Navy. I had come aboard the USS *Topeka* after the shooting war ended. But the aura of victory still pervaded the ranks. When I went ashore in Tokyo, Shanghai, Manila, or any other port of call, I drank with men who had fought and won some of the greatest naval battles in history. Each time I paused on the gangplank to salute the American flag on the *Topeka*'s fantail, I shared some of that victorious pride.

In the dialogue that I conducted in my head as I strode down Fordham Road to the college campus, I also rejected the Irishman's parenthetical claim that I was a typical Irish-American, ignorant of Ireland's culture and tragic heritage. My summer with the literature of Ireland made me confident I knew as much about Irish culture and history as he did, and probably a lot more.

I strode past the Irish-American cops directing traffic on Fordham Road, past the Jewish-run dress shops and jewelry stores, past the Sunday strollers with their medley of ethnic faces, tensely insisting I was not going to let some #$%x&# Irishman tell me I was not Irish because I declined to get involved with the land of my ancestors. This was the moment when I began to feel assailed, almost beleaguered, by an acute awareness of my hyphenated state of mind and soul.

It would take me several decades to recognize this encounter as a turning point in my life. Coming on the heels of my immersion in Irish history and literature during the previous summer, it represented an almost perfectly designed laboratory experiment that demonstrated most Irish-Americans were not and never would be Irish. The radical disillusion with Irish nationalism that Davey Fleming and so many others experienced in the early 1920s was the best thing that ever happened to the Irish-Americans. It cured the Irish of that era of an obsession with the land of their ancestors—a trauma that still troubles too many ethnic Americans.

I studied hard during that first year at Fordham to impress the people at Princeton, and the results were promising. Soon a letter arrived from the famous university, informing me I was accepted. But there was a catch. I would have to start over again in freshman year. Not one course I had taken at Fordham was deemed worthy of a Princeton credit.

There it was, staring me in the face: the old us Catholics against the arrogant white Anglo-Saxon Protestants that had been the political lodestar of my boyhood. It was true! They really did think Catholics were inferior and could be treated with contempt.

I was disgusted—and enraged. The Irish side of my hyphen took charge. I was O'Rahilly lamenting Ireland's fall. I was old Davey Fleming's shipwrecked Irishman floating up to a foreign shore and announcing before he got off his raft that he was "agin' the govern-ment." For a while I was a one hundred percent supporter of Frank Hague's approach to politics.

I decided to stay at Fordham. Youth is a time of impatience, and a year seemed more important than a prestigious diploma. But I vowed to give myself an education that transcended the Fordham curriculum. I began my own reading program, mostly in history, which eventually totaled several hundred books. I was on my way to becoming that most unlikely of creatures for a guy from Jersey City—an intellectual.

This put me on a collision course with Teddy Fleming. On a visit home during my sophomore year in college (1947) I remarked that I was reading a book on modern politics and while I did not agree with the Communists, I could see that their criticism of capitalism had some validity.

My father exploded. The remark confirmed one of his ongoing fears about me, that I was too smart for my own good. He started roar-ing that if I wanted to believe in communism, I'd better get ready to support myself. He was not going to pay to educate someone to betray his country.

I tried to tell him why I thought the Communists weren't so bad. I compared them to the Democratic Party in our native city, which also proclaimed a readiness to succor its adherents from the cradle to the grave. That only made him madder. He was remembering the Hague Organization's much-publicized battle with the CIO in the late 1930s. "Go up to Journal Square and tell people you like Commu-nists," my father shouted. "You'll get a nightstick in the teeth and I won't raise a finger to get you out of jail."

I insisted I was not a Communist, I was only conceding a certain amount of justice to their criticism of naked capitalism. That was not good enough for my father. He roared even louder. "I'm not going to have a Communist in this house, you understand me? No Commu-nists in this house!"

He wouldn't look at me. He just kept roaring: "No Communists in this house!" It was incredibly infuriating and frustrating. I got so angry I almost cried. His voice seemed to spew a kind of willful darkness that lashed me relentlessly. It threw me back to memories of the way he used this tactic with my mother. For a while it was like reliving those nightmare arguments. It was almost as if he were punching me. I felt battered by it.

I hated the way he refused to trust me and my college education. He knew what he knew and he wasn't going to let me change him. I sensed his terrific distrust of the world beyond the boundaries of Jersey City—maybe even beyond the boundaries of the Sixth Ward. I also glimpsed for the first time what my mother must have encountered when she tried to change this ferocious man in ways he suspected or disliked. It made me more sympathetic to Kitty's travails.

Now I see that Teddy Fleming was taking a leaf from Old Davey's book. He won arguments by yelling louder than his wife and/or sons. When in doubt, shout. I can smile wryly about it from a distance of fifty years, but I was not amused while taking the punishment. The experience left me with a strong sense of alienation from Teddy Fleming for many months.

In my junior year at Fordham, I finally reached that supposed intellectual summit of the Jesuit educational system, philosophy. What a bummer. As far as the Jesuits were concerned, there was only one brand of that large word—scholastic philosophy, as taught in the Middle Ages. Modern philosophy—Descartes, Kant, Schopenhauer, Nietzsche, James, Dewey—was out of our league.

I was disgusted. I had already been reading on my own in the subject, with a special interest in the existentialists, so I had some idea of what most of my classmates were missing. Our teacher, David Cronin, S.J., at least recognized the absurdity of the curriculum and discussed modern thinkers in class. But for the final exams, we had to regurgitate the standard answers from the scholastic philosophy textbook.

One Sunday, after spending the weekend at home, my father drove me back to Fordham. I sat in the back of the car with my friend Jerry Long. We had gone to St. Peter's Prep together, where we shared an enthusiasm for the theater. We had jointly starred in Shakespeare's *Twelfth Night*, he as Malvolio, I as Sir Toby Belch. Jerry had become an intellectual at least as pretentious as yours truly. We argued about philosophy, Jerry favoring the textbook scholastics, while I held forth for the existentialists, in particular Chaplain Benson's hero, Søren Kierkegaard.

My brother Gene, a freshman at Fordham (against my advice), was in the front seat with my father. As we crossed the George Washington Bridge and entered the Bronx, my father asked him in a low voice, "What's philosophy?"

At dinner in the dining hall that night, Gene told me about Teddy Fleming's question. I almost wept. I thought of the Little Blue Books in his bureau drawer. I remembered "The Guy in the Glass." My alienation vanished. Oh father, father, I whispered to myself, forgive me.

Around this time, my Uncle Dave died unexpectedly. After his ladder company had extinguished a blaze in the Hudson Tubes at Exchange Place, he had gone down into the tunnel without an inhalator to make a final inspection—an act of bravado (read nerve) that was apparently typical of his style as a battalion commander. The smoke was still thick and some of it got into his lungs. It affected his heart and within a few months he was dead.

My mother met me at the door when I came home from Fordham for a weekend and told me the news. "I don't know whether you should mention it to your father. I've never seen him so upset," she said.

In the kitchen, Teddy Fleming was sitting by an open window, staring into the yard. He barely said hello to me. I decided I should say something. "I'm really sorry—about Uncle Dave," I said.

My father continued to stare out the window. "I really loved him," he said. He brushed at his face. I realized he was crying. "I really loved him."

*You're all I've got.* Except for that moment on the highway, it was the only time I heard Teddy Fleming say he loved someone. It brought back that primary memory with terrific force. Once more I saw the caring man beneath the hard-eyed politician. I loved him again without qualification.

# 29

# Decline and Fall

**W**hile I played intellectual games at Fordham, things were happening in the political world of Jersey City that cast ominous shadows on Teddy Fleming's future. In 1947, Frank Hague resigned as mayor. He was seventy-one and felt it was time to hand on his power to the next generation of loyal Democrats. Privately, the big fellow may have decided his name had become a liability to the Organization. No such thing was ever admitted publicly, of course.

In an emotional farewell in the auditorium of Lincoln High School, only a few blocks from our house, orator after orator extolled the mayor's achievements. I was there for this speechfest, which left most of the listeners in a daze of uncertainty about what was going to happen next.

Power is a seductive drug, and the mayor could not abandon it completely. Critics noticed that he retained his chairmanship of the Hudson County Democratic Party and the New Jersey Democratic Party's committees. He also remained vice chairman of the Democratic National Committee. This meant he still had the final say on judgeships and other forms of patronage that counted most to political insiders. More important from the viewpoint of the average voter, Hague anointed as his mayoral successor his nephew, Frank Hague Eggers, already a city commissioner. Hague had a son, Frank Hague

Jr., but he had striven for nonentity and achieved it. It was not a surprising ambition, with such a ferocious taskmaster for a father. In the mid-1930s, when the Organization was at its zenith, Governor A. Harry Moore had appointed Frank Jr. to a seat on the New Jersey court of errors and appeals "because it will make his father happy." But Frank Jr. had long since resigned and vanished into obscurity.

Frank Eggers was a short, earnest, intelligent man who lived only a block from the Flemings on Arlington Avenue. Most people liked him. I remember sitting next to him at a dinner in the Sixth Ward. He asked me if I was going into politics. When I said no, he warmly approved. "If any kid of mine says he wants to be a politician, I'll knock his block off," he said.

It was a strange attitude for a man who was trying to succeed Frank Hague—and an omen of trouble to come. Eggers was like Al Smith—an Irish-American who thought he could somehow purify Jersey City's version of Tammany Hall, or at least make it less reprehensible to the public.

Behind the political scenes in Jersey City, there were rumblings of discontent. John V. Kenny, the leader of the dockside Second Ward, thought he should have been the mayor's successor. A short, beak-nosed, charming man whose saloonkeeper father, Nat, had given Hague his start in politics, Kenny had many friends in the city and not a few acquaintances in the Republican Party who were eager to encourage a revolt that would wreck Hague's preeminence in New Jersey's politics.

On my visits home, Teddy Fleming did not seem particularly worried about the omens of fratricide in the Democratic ranks. He was reelected sheriff in 1948, running ahead of everyone else on the Organization ticket in Hudson County, including President Harry S. Truman. With that triumph in his pocket, Teddy welcomed me to the traditional election night celebration with almost extravagant cheer. The house was bulging with people. Along with rivers of booze, there was enough food to feed an AEF division.

At one point in the tumultuous evening, I found myself in a corner with my father. We clinked classes and he said, "Have you decided what you're going to be?"

I shook my head, instantly wary. "I'm still thinking."

"Think about becoming a lawyer. I guarantee you that you'll be worth a million bucks by the time you're thirty."

Here was an offer that was hard to refuse. I was getting it from a man who did not give out guarantees (promises) casually. A million dollars in 1948 was a stupendous amount of money, at least ten million in twenty-first-century dollars. I was profoundly touched—almost overwhelmed. But having fought off two previous fathers (Shalloe and Homewood), I was ready for dubious battle with my real one. "What would you say if I decided to be a writer?"

"I'd say you were nuts. But if that's what you want, it's okay with me."

The victory party swirled around us with people burbling political slogans and catchphrases. The two Teddy Flemings were suddenly separated from the whole thing, as if some sort of magical bell jar had descended from the ceiling. In his laconic way, my father had just confessed his dream for me—a vision of megabucks earned with his clout and the brains of a son who was Thomas J. "Teddy" Fleming Jr. It would be his payoff for the years of late nights in the Sixth Ward's saloons and at the clubhouse, listening to tales of woe from the luckless and defeated. This was light-years beyond Father Shalloe's Jesuitical persuasions and Boats Homewood's naval paternity. This was FATHERHOOD, underlined and in capital letters, my father talking to his son.

Yet without a moment's hesitation, without the slightest hint of recrimination or bluster about what he had done for me, Teddy Fleming had surrendered his dream. He was letting me go my American way, without arguments or guilt trips. Why? There was only one answer. Because he had confessed something more important in that moment on the highway when those unforgettable words, *You're all I've got*, exploded between us.

That love meant more to him than the dream of a son dazzling juries and impressing CEOs and political bosses, maybe eventually going for something as big as governor or senator. He was letting this son choose a career he did not even faintly understand or appreciate.

I wanted to say something splendid, or at least clever. One possibility leaped into my head from my first encounter with Frank Hague:

*You're a hell of a guy.* But I settled for the everyday, hoping he would know what I felt. "Thanks, Dad," I said.

Neither of us knew that men and events beyond the borders of Hudson County had been deciding the Hague Organization's fate for the previous decade. The war with Governor Charles Edison had taken a heavy toll on Frank Hague's political resources. The governor's revolt had been aided by a slow but steady population shift within New Jersey. More and more people had moved out of the crowded cities of Hudson County to the suburbs. The same thing was happening in Newark, Paterson, and other cities where political leaders had allied themselves with Hague, thanks to his patronage power and his ability to deliver winners at the state level.

The suburban Democrats privately agreed with Edison about Hague, although few of their leaders had the courage to side with the governor. Many of the suburbanites' neighbors in their supposedly peaceful enclaves were Republicans, or worse, independents—a word that sent chills down every politician's spine. The suburban Democrats had Kitty Dolan's uptown Jersey City reaction to Frank Hague: embarrassment. They soon constituted a movement within the Democratic Party demanding new leadership. The Organization's failure to elect a governor after Edison's term expired was seen as evidence that Hague was on the ropes. They were not impressed by the Democrats' victory in 1948. They gave Harry Truman's brilliant come-from-behind presidential campaign credit for that triumph.

At the heart of the growing malaise was a generational problem. Hague and his circle had been in power for thirty-four years. Younger men were growing impatient for a slice of clout at the top. They were no longer content to let the grim reaper deliver this exhilarating commodity in due course. They found plenty of supporters in the generation that had fought World War II and come home expecting some tangible rewards for their valor.

Hague's instinct in choosing as his successor the much younger Frank Eggers was sound. But the choice was corrupted by Eggers's blood relationship to the boss—and even by his name. Frank Hague Eggers would soon become a ruinous epithet in the mouths of the Organization's enemies. The big fellow's fatal flaw, it would soon become apparent, was arrogance.

It was an understandable failing, when his previous three decades of mostly victorious leadership is included in the mix. But Hague's arrogance and its concomitant flaws—his flashy lifestyle, his unaltered Horseshoe accent and grammar, were combining with the shifts in New Jersey's voters to render him and his followers fatally vulnerable. For Teddy Fleming, this vulnerability coincided with an illness that was ominously symbolic.

In January 1949, I came home from college for a weekend visit to find my father sick in bed. Except for the hospitalization to remove his gallbladder, it was the first time I had seen him ill. He looked haggard, almost desperate, sitting up in his bed massaging his foot. His big toe was apparently infected and was giving him a lot of pain.

That night my father went to the hospital. We learned he had gangrene in his toe. A podiatrist had accidentally cut the toe while clipping his toenails. Gangrene had developed because he had severe arteriosclerosis, a disease about which my brother and I—and my mother—knew nothing. We soon learned that it was life-threatening in its own right. But first the gangrene had to be defeated.

For three months Teddy Fleming lay on the ninth floor of Frank Hague's Medical Center in a special electric bed, which tipped him up and down all night to improve his circulation. The pain of gangrene was horrendous. He told me one night it was like having someone shove a hot nail through the toe every sixty seconds. To dull the pain, the doctors gave him Demerol, a drug that caused severe depression. He told me, on another visit, that he often awoke in the morning and seriously considered pitching himself out the ninth story window.

While Teddy Fleming writhed in torment, John V. Kenny was organizing a revolt against Frank Hague Eggers, who was running for mayor with his uncle's backing. It soon became apparent that "the little guy," as his followers called Kenny (to contrast him to Hague, "the big fellow") was no joke. To bolster his chances, Kenny put an Italian-American and a Polish-American on his five-man slate. The Hague Organization fielded five Irish-Americans, as usual, and confidently announced they would run on their record of achievement.

No one, except maybe children under the age of five, had the illusion that John V. Kenny was a reformer. My father's friend Johnny Smith told me about the time he needed $25,000 to help reorganize the bus drivers' union after he had gotten rid of its corrupt leaders. My father put in a call to Kenny, who said he would be glad to lend Smitty the money.

Smitty soon received directions on the telephone that led him to the New Jersey Central railyards, on the Hudson River. He made his way through a hot cindery wilderness of freight cars and switching engines to a boxcar with its sliding doors open. Outside it, several big, unmistakably tough guys asked him where the hell he thought he was going. When Smitty explained, they hoisted him into the car. There sat Johnny Kenny behind a table, improvised by putting a door over two sawhorses. On the table was a half million dollars in cash, in neat piles by denominations.

It was, Smitty explained to me, "the fruit season." That meant every fruit shipper in the country paid Kenny a handsome tribute to keep things quiet with the trucking and stevedore unions, lest there be strikes and their produce end up rotting under the late-spring skies instead of disappearing down New Yorkers' gullets. This was, incidentally, Hague's way of saying thank you to Nat Kenny's son. No other ward leader was allowed to sequester that much cash in his own pocket.

Introduced by the musclemen, Smitty got a warm welcome from Kenny. Any friend of Teddy Fleming was a friend of his, etc. etc. "Teddy says you need some dough fast," Kenny said. "How much?"

"I was gonna say twenty-five," Smitty said, eyeing the piles of cash on the table. "But we could really use fifty."

"You got it," Kenny said and counted out fifty one-thousand-dollar bills without even taking a deep breath. It was, of course, a loan, which Smitty's union would have to repay within a reasonable length of time or Smitty would have to worry about infirmities like broken arms and collarbones, not to mention kneecaps and legs.

With this kind of money behind him, Kenny was formidable and a lot of people knew it. If Teddy Fleming had been a healthy man, he would have been warning Frank Hague about the ominous comments he was hearing in the Sixth Ward and other downtown wards from ethnic voters, especially those who were World War II veterans. But Teddy Fleming was out of it, and the big fellow was listening mostly to sycophants like Johnny "Needlenose" Malone, whose tiny brain had by this time totally congealed from too many years of power.

Frank Eggers and his fellow Organization candidates orated about the Medical Center, about the city's vice-free image and low crime rate. The Kenny opposition ignored achievements, issues, and political philosophy and blasted only one target: Frank Hague. Their argument was simple: Hague was an evil dictator, Eggers was his stooge.

They endlessly denounced "King Frank's" wealth and royal style. They descanted on how few days Hague had spent in Jersey City in recent years, which made him an absentee dictator. In the ethnic neighborhoods, they told the Italians and the Slovaks and the Poles that Johnny Kenny was an Irish-American who wanted to give them a decent slice of the municipal pie. They called themselves the Freedom Ticket and published a Freedom newspaper to spread their appeal to every district in every ward. In one of their better coups, they got their hands on photostats of Hague's bills at Sulka, one of New York's toniest men's stores, revealing he paid seventy-five dollars for a shirt and twenty-five dollars for silk underwear. Kenny supporters inside the telephone company leaked the astonishing bills Hague ran up each year on collect calls from his Florida mansion to City Hall.

Voters started switching sides. I remember noticing with a shock that a cop in Journal Square, the city's main business district, was directing traffic using a "V for Victory" sign, which the Kennyites had adopted as a tribute to their leader's middle initial. In many wards, saloons put Kenny's picture in their windows.

No such outbreak occurred in the Sixth Ward, but Johnny Duff told me to warn my father that the Creegans and a few other old antagonists were showing signs of restlessness. Johnny assured me that he could handle the problem. I was spending most of my time on the Fordham campus and remained emotionally distanced from the battle. I was far more worried about Teddy Fleming's struggle with gangrene.

As the election roared to a climax in May of 1949, Frank Hague made a fatally wrong decision. He lost confidence in Frank Hague Eggers and his fellow candidates and returned to Jersey City to turn Johnny Kenny's challenge into a personal contest. There was a hint of desperation in his announcement that he was going to stage a tremendous rally in the heart of the Second Ward—where he had begun his political career. Now it was Kenny territory, but Hague was confident he could reconquer it.

On the Friday before the rally, Hague sent letters to more than seven thousand voters in the Second Ward, recounting the story of his association with Kenny. He told how, out of gratitude to Kenny's father, saloonkeeper Nat, he had gotten Johnny his first job and had helped him rise in politics. "If he now betrays me," Hague asked, "how can he be trusted not to betray you?"

On May 3, the ward clubs formed up outside City Hall at about 6 P.M. Orders had gone out to every jobholder in the city to be on hand. Many stayed home, deciding that the loss of a job was less dangerous than the possibility of a fractured skull. Hague, his lined, Florida-tanned face grimly set, escorted Eggers and the other candidates to the front rank of the parade. With long strides, he led them up Grove Street into the Second Ward—and bedlam.

Six deep, the Second Warders lined the curbs, screaming contempt and defiance at the boss and his aging battalions. They pelted the marchers with eggs, tomatoes, stones, and chalk powder. Police had to fight to clear a space in front of the speaker's platform outside Public School 37. The less courageous fled into the school's auditorium. The stalwarts formed up before the flag-draped platform. Around them surged a bellowing mob of thousands, sounding horns and cowbells, waving Kenny placards and streamers.

The police cordoned the platform. Hague, Eggers, and the other candidates stepped out before the crowd. Eggs spattered them. The derision rose to a tremendous crescendo. Eggers tried to speak. He managed a few sentences and gave up in despair. He could not even hear himself. With a shrug he motioned to the others to leave the platform.

The five commission candidates filed off, but Frank Hague did not move. For a moment, he stood alone, his face a mask of fury. Striding to the edge of the platform, he glared down at the shrieking mob. For more than three decades he had ruled people like these. He had fought those who opposed him with ballots and with police clubs and fists. He had won almost every time. Remembering, the crowd went silent.

For a long hushed moment, they faced each other. Then a small thin man in the first row sprang forward, swinging a "Down With Hague" sign on a pole. As it twisted and whirled toward him like a crashing kite, Hague had to step back to avoid it. The man screamed, "G'wan back to Florida!"

Smashing aside the sign, Hague pointed at the culprit. "Arrest that man!" he roared. He was speaking to the police around the platform. In Jersey City, those words had often been the signal for swinging clubs, the crunch of wood on bone. The man fell back, cowering. The crowd held its collective breath. It took another moment for them to realize what was happening. Not a cop moved. Every man was anti-Hague. Quite logically, they had decided they had no obligation to obey the ex-mayor of Jersey City.

The crowd exploded into a howl that dwarfed all their previous vocal efforts. For a moment something very close to shock played across Frank Hague's face. He stalked off the platform. His word was no longer the law in the Second Ward.

In the Medical Center, the scene was swiftly reported to Teddy Fleming by Johnny Duff and other members of the Sixth Ward Committee who had risked their lives to back Hague's aborted rally. Panic was seeping through the ranks. Teddy decided his leadership was vital, no matter what his doctors said. His gangrene was in remission but the toe had not healed. The doctors wanted him to stay in the hospital for at least another month.

That night, Teddy summoned me to help him get home. He wanted his departure to be as private as possible. As we waited for the hospital to check him out, my father confided to me that he thought Hague had made a major mistake by refusing to match Kenny and put one or two non-Irish-Americans on the ticket.

In the Sixth Ward, Teddy Fleming had organized Italian-, Slovak-, and Polish-American committees who were supporting the Organization. Most of the other ward leaders, taking their cue from City Hall, were sticking with the Irish-Americans-at-the-top system that had run the city since 1917. With an irony only those who remembered the Hague Organization's history could appreciate, they wrote off the downtown wards and bet they could win uptown, where thousands of newly prosperous Irish-Americans had moved in the thirty-four years of Hague's ascendancy.

As we walked to his waiting limousine, my father leaned heavily on me. He could not sustain much weight on his bad leg. It was another moment that would haunt me for the rest of my life. I not only accepted the almost dead weight of his pain-wracked body, I became this man who had taught me so much about courage. I forgave him for the pain he had inflicted on me and on my mother. I accepted that part of my inheritance with a kind of fatality that gradually became history in my adult mind.

Teddy Fleming was what he was not only because of the choices he had made within the confines of his harsh world, but also because he loved me, and that reality transcended philosophy, transcended everything, including my disenchantment with Frank Hague, which I carefully concealed from him and everyone else.

> *The kings of the land have neither land nor crown.*
> *Mayo God help us.*
> *Us against them.*

On election day, Johnny Kenny revealed how closely he had studied the tactics of the master. His ward and precinct leaders made the same heroic effort to get out their vote, matching the Organization telephone call for telephone call, car for car, promise for promise. As many as forty-one watchers were on duty at each polling place, making it impossible for the Organization to fall back on rough stuff to intimidate the opposition into staying home.

Most important, Kenny had unprecedented amounts of money to spend. The going rate for a purchased Jersey City vote had long been five dollars. Hague's ward leaders were soon deluged with calls from their district committeemen. Kenny was paying fifteen dollars a vote! The ward leaders called City Hall, where Needlenose Malone was in charge. "Screw'm," he growled. "Just take their names. We'll even the score with them startin' tomorrow."

I stood beside Teddy Fleming as he made one of these calls to Malone. The Sixth Ward, with its ethnic enclaves, including two black districts, was particularly vulnerable to a vote-buying assault. When Johnny gave him the same response he had given other leaders, my father slammed down the phone, called Malone a "total asshole," and telephoned George Ormsby, the Sixth Ward's bookmaker. "Can you get me ten grand right away?" he said.

"Come down and pick it up," Ormsby said.

Before the polls closed, the ten thousand dollars was gone, plus several thousand dollars of Teddy Fleming's money, which he always kept handy at election time. By the end of the long day, my father was an exhausted, very worried man. Calls from fellow ward leaders had him fearing the worst. At nine o'clock the stunning news came over the radio. Johnny Kenny had swept every ward but one—the Sixth.

Downtown, a mob of Freedom Ticket voters snake-danced through the streets, carrying a coffin labeled "The Hague Machine." Kenny and several lieutenants stormed into City Hall, hoping to seize incriminating records. But the Organization had known for hours that the election was lost, and the invaders found nothing but charred scraps of paper in the furnace room. The vault in the mayor's office was empty. Earlier, according to reliable witnesses, two police captains had lugged suitcases full of money to the First National Bank.

Sheriff Fleming remained a very sick man. The gangrene stayed in remission but his circulation was terrible and the doctors continued to fear the disease would recur and travel up his leg. Johnny Kenny urged him to join his coalition. They were eager to incorporate some of the old organization's leaders. As sheriff of the county, Teddy Fleming still had considerable clout.

My father temporized, mostly to keep Kenny at bay. The Organization was down but by no means out. Hague had picked a strong candidate for governor in the fall election, a popular three-term congressman and millionaire chicken farmer named Elmer Wene. If Wene won, he would immediately appoint a Hague man as Hudson County prosecutor. With Sheriff Teddy Fleming in control of the grand jury selection, it would only be a matter of months before most of Kenny's administration would be indicted—and considering what Hague knew about Kenny's take during the "fruit season," the new mayor might well be jailed.

After a long strategic silence, Kenny announced he was for Wene. But there was not an iota of enthusiasm in his endorsement. Meanwhile, Hague, revealing his age and the destabilizing impact of his recent defeat, made an almost incredible blunder in his final preelection speech. "We'll be back in the driver's seat in Trenton in January," he thundered.

Instantly, New Jersey's Republicans seized on their favorite battle cry, "Beat Hague," which Kenny's victory had seemingly defused. The Republican candidate made it the theme of his final campaign speech.

It also gave Kenny exactly what he needed to persuade his Freedom Ticket followers to vote Republican. Wene lost by seventy thousand votes. Hudson County went Republican for the first time since Woodrow Wilson turned off Irish-American Democrats in 1920. On election night, Frank Hague resigned as state and county leader of the Democratic Party. The Hague Organization had become history.

Or had it? In the Hudson County Court House, Sheriff Fleming continued to duck and dodge Johnny Kenny's invitation to get on his team. He used his health, which continued to be bad, as an excuse. Soon messages reached him from New York, where Frank Hague was now residing: another comeback attempt was in the works. My father appointed a few Kenny people to the county payroll and waited for something to happen.

Late one night in the fall of 1950, Frank Hague and a half dozen of his top lieutenants visited our house. I can still see the lined, grim faces, the expensive topcoats and homburgs, crowding down the hall to the kitchen, where my father awaited them. The ex-mayor asked Sheriff Fleming to join him in a last-gasp effort to regain power in the 1951 elections for the board of freeholders and other county offices.

If the gamble failed, Teddy Fleming stood a very good chance of going to jail. The other side had enough inside information to put away almost anyone they chose. My father pointed this out to the big fellow. Hague responded by promising to put $100,000 in a New York bank in my father's name, and buy him a new car. He would need both items if Kenny succeeded in convicting him and he lost his job and his pension. This was enough insurance for Teddy Fleming to take the gamble. They shook hands.

I was not part of the conference but my father had told me what was in the wind. I came downstairs and found the sheriff alone in the kitchen, fingering a drink. "You said yes?" I asked.

"Yeah," he said.

I knew what my father was risking for his loyalty. By now I also knew the real test was not only loyalty, it was nerve. In spite of gangrene and Demerol he was demonstrating that he still had it. I held out my hand and said, "I'm proud of you."

A light broke over his ruddy face. "Thanks," he said. For the first time I think I mashed his hand harder than he mashed mine. I meant those words. In the morally gray world of Hudson County politics, there was no ethical difference between Johnny Kenny and Frank Hague. That left me free to admire my father's stubborn adherence to his Irish-American code of honor.

Hague's counterrevolution made headlines for a while. My father fired the Kenny men on his payroll and appointed Hague loyalists. But the odds were against the coup from the start. Whoever controlled Jersey City's City Hall had too much muscle for the rest of Hudson County to ignore. Kenny cut deals with the minor power brokers in Union City, Hoboken, Bayonne, North Bergen, and West New York and Hague threw in his cards. He had promised my father to spend a million dollars in the campaign. He did not spend a tenth of that sum before he gave up. Kenny won the election, and this time Frank Hague was finished.

That left Sheriff Fleming out on a very precarious political limb. But Johnny Kenny decided it would not look good to incarcerate the man who had been the biggest vote-getter in the county when he ran for sheriff in 1948 and carried his ward in the mayoralty brawl in 1949 (and in the 1951 comeback try). Johnny was an Irish-American too, and understood why my father stayed loyal to Frank Hague. Also, Johnny and my father remained friends. The new leader let Sheriff Fleming retire on a decent pension at the end of 1951. This amnesty enabled Frank Hague to decide he could forget the promise to put $100,000 in the bank in Teddy's name. But the big fellow bought him a new car—a handsome gray Oldsmobile.

By this time I was a married man, living in Yonkers, working as a reporter for the local paper. I visited my father not long after he left the Hudson County Court House for the last time. I was surprised to find him in an upbeat mood. Now I realize the emotion was relief. He had survived thirty-five years in Jersey City's politics without a jail sentence.

"What are you going to do now?" I asked.

"As little as possible," he said. "I've finally gotten one."

"One what?"

"A No-Show job."

# 30

# Heartbreak House

$A$round the time that the Hague Organization started to unravel, my mother discovered a lump in her left breast. Her doctor told her it was a benign tumor but advised her to watch it carefully. The tumor started to change color and grow, but Kitty ignored it for over a year. When she finally saw the doctor again, he rushed her into the hospital for a mastectomy. After the operation, he told my father the cancer had spread and she had a year to live at most.

My father summoned me and my brother, Gene, who was still at Fordham College, to our house to tell us the news. After reporting what the doctor had said, he struggled to his feet and cried, "I never touched another woman. So help me God. I never touched another woman!"

He limped down the hall to the kitchen, leaving Gene and me sitting there, stunned and appalled. Years later, my brother and I discussed my father's declaration of innocence. Gene was inclined to think he had lied. He was afraid that my mother would accuse him again on her deathbed and he was trying to defend himself against the loss of our love by making a preemptive strike.

At the time I was inclined to agree with Gene. It reminded me of the lie Teddy Fleming had told me about speeding down Route 35 long ago. Lying about certain matters did not bother him if the stakes were high enough. In this case, the stakes could not have been higher: the possible loss of his sons' love.

The Hague Organization's puritanical style, the knowledge that
the mayor had decreed anyone caught chasing a skirt was in deep trouble with him, now inclines me to take Teddy Fleming at his word. This
conviction was deepened by reading the love letters he and Kitty
exchanged in the first years of their marriage, and my father's belief
that a promise once made was an irrevocable obligation. What
destroyed their marriage was much more complex than simple
infidelity.

One weekend after World War II, my brother Gene went to a
sheriffs' convention in Atlantic City with my father. Johnny Duff, the
assistant leader of the ward, came along. For Johnny, who was a bachelor, my father arranged a visit from a lady of the evening, supplied by
the hotel as an unspoken part of room service. My father paid for "the
lassie," as he called her. But he did not order a lassie for himself.

Fidelity, I thought, when Gene told me this story. I contemplated
a picture of Teddy and Kitty in Atlantic City on their honeymoon.
Only now did I see how the word became synonymous with heartbreak. It encompassed my father's fidelity to Frank Hague and the
promise he made to the big fellow and my mother's readiness to mock
that fidelity and simultaneously insist on a marital fidelity that gradually transcended the literal meaning and became a demand for an
impossible permanent romance.

With the aid of a team of nurses, Teddy Fleming cared for my
mother as she slipped toward death. A residual tenderness emerged as
he tried to help her cope with the dehumanizing pain. He called her
"Kit" and sat beside the bed, holding her hand. When she died, he
wept and cried, "Oh my sweetheart, my sweetheart!"

I visited my mother frequently during that last sad year. My wife,
Alice, and I spent much of the final summer of Kitty's life with her at
a house in Mountain Lakes, New Jersey. At her insistence, my father
had sold our summer house in Point Pleasant in 1949, and we spent
the next two summers in rented houses in this pleasant suburb. It was
a sad attempt to experience the lifestyle for which Kitty had yearned
all her life, far from Jersey City's political streets.

For a while I wondered if my mother had committed a kind of
unconscious suicide. I saw her wishing for death because I had rejected
her love and sided with my father. In her mind, I was convinced, she

had envisioned a drama of reconciliation and remorse. As she died of cancer, my father would nurse her tenderly, as Walter Farrelly had nursed Marie—and as she died Teddy would beg her forgiveness. Her favorite son would join this chorus of contrition and Kitty would forgive us both with her last breath.

This final act of tragic romance was betrayed by reality, like so many of Kitty's visions. She died unexpectedly one morning in January 1953, without exchanging any final words with her husband. I was at work in New York. My absence only accentuated my guilt.

This suicide-by-cancer version of her story was terribly, horribly plausible to me at the time. I have since been told by cancer specialists that a reluctance to face the possibility of having the dread disease is widespread, and that my psychological theory, though possible, was by no means necessarily true. Despite these assurances, for many years I was periodically assailed by a morbid, mindless guilt. I loved my mother and I hated the thought that I had disappointed her. It was not easy to accept the hard truth that love can be a devouring as well as a sustaining force in our lives.

Over the years, fidelity-as-heartbreak swelled in my mind to encompass my mother's whole life. I realized that it is a mostly feminine experience. For a man, matters of the heart are important, but so is his career. He can derive satisfactions from his work that override the heart, at least for a time. But for a woman, the heart is primary.

This was especially true of the women of Katherine Dolan's generation, who had very limited career opportunities. For those with high intelligence, like Kitty, careers that fulfilled their minds and utilized the full range of their abilities were even fewer. This enlarged the primacy of the heart and worsened the potential for heartbreak. In Kitty's case, her vulnerability was intensified by the crushing disappointment of her ruined romance with Lloyd Harris.

Not long after my mother died, several ulcers appeared on Teddy Fleming's right calf. They were potentially gangrenous. For a while his doctor recommended a treatment that seemed left over from the Spanish Inquisition. He told my father to pour boiling water on the sores. Only someone who saw dealing with pain as proof of his manhood would have tolerated such an ordeal. Worse, it did not work. The pain of gangrene began pulsing, not merely in his toe, but in his entire leg. Sleep became an impossibility. A consulting surgeon decided to remove his leg below the knee.

I stood beside my father's bed in the Jersey City Medical Center after the operation, sadly pondering his fate. For a man who had been an athlete, a soldier, a leader, the loss of a leg would have to be demoralizing. I braced myself to deliver all sorts of consoling nostrums.

He came out of the anesthetic and recognized me. He nodded and I smiled tentatively. "It's good to see you," he said.

He lay there for another silent minute. I waited tensely for a lamentation. I realize now I dreaded seeing him feel sorry for himself. I should have known better.

"Teddy," he said. "I've been a son of a bitch all my life. From now on I'm going to try to be different."

"Let's shake on that," I said.

It was a pretty good handshake for a man just off an operating table.

At first I found Teddy's SOB confession amusing. But as I grew older and began thinking about my father's life, it became serious and revealing. It was sobering to discover how aware he was of the tough-guy-leader role he had chosen to play in life. What is more startling in retrospect is the realization that it did not come naturally to him. Beneath the tough guy was the sensitive man who kept a poem to his lost buddies on his wall, shuddered at the memory of killing that German lieutenant—and worried about what the guy in the glass thought of him.

My conclusion is supported, I think, by some of the pictures in this book. Often, the camera catches Teddy Fleming with his eyes cast down, thinking somberly about his life. In the full-faced photo he used in the newspapers during his years of power, half of his face is in shadow. There is an aura of tough worldliness in the half that is exposed to the light. With the flesh of middle age on his cheeks, at first glance he could be a Mafia boss.

But a second glance conveys another impression. There is an unexpected sensitivity around his mouth. The overall effect is thoughtfulness. He was not simply an order taker or giver. Here was a man who had examined his life. There is even, in the shadowy half of the picture, another unexpected quality: resignation. There is scarcely a glimpse of the ferocity of the street slugger—or of the buoyant 1920s skier in Central Park.

By the mid-1930s my father was aware of his life's limitations. He knew he was never going to be more than a powerful local politician. That had its rewards. But it also had its frustrations, even if we omit the sense of inferiority my mother imposed on him with her unrealistic aspirations. Frank Hague's organization did not give an intelligent man much chance to grow, to act independently. It was run from the top down much of the time. A ward leader spent his life dealing with people considerably less intelligent than he was. Although my mother turned this task into a black mark against her husband, there must have been times when he agreed with her about the voters of the Sixth Ward. Teddy Fleming was often a lightning rod for their discontents and frustrations.

A week after my father lost his leg, he was about to leave the hospital when he suffered a massive heart attack. Only desperate procedures kept him alive. When I arrived the next day, he was in a fury at the hospital, the doctors, the nurses, and everyone else in sight. The idea of death sneaking a punch like that, after he had sacrificed a leg to elude his scythe, enraged him.

"Tell that goddamn nurse I need a bedpan," he snarled.

I rushed into the hall. The floor nurse was nowhere to be found. I rushed back to tell him and he said, "Then you get me a bedpan, fast."

I found a big aluminum pan under the bed. "Get me up on it," he said.

It was a terrific struggle to hoist his thick torso, an almost dead weight, onto the pan. I finally managed it and with a grunt he evacuated his bowels. "The same feeling as a heart attack," he said. "In case you're interested. Get rid of it."

Again I had to imitate Sandow the Strong Man to get the pan out from under him. I stumbled back with the thing in my hands and stared down at the biggest blackest turd I had ever seen.

I looked away, not simply because it was ugly and foul-smelling. I kept looking away as I walked to the toilet to get rid of it and realized what I was feeling. Even now, evacuating death from his body, he was my superior. I would never produce a turd that big. A despair swept over me that seemed to infect the very idea of my manhood.

*Never never never*, sneered a voice, as I dumped the turd into the toilet and watched it spin down the flushing pipes. *No matter what you become, he will always outshout, outshit you.*

"Sorry about that," he said when I came back with the emptied bedpan.

He really was trying not to be a son of a bitch. My spasm of inferiority did not seem to have any profound effect on me. I was already into achieving things with my brain, not my brawn.

The ex-sheriff spent a month or so at home regaining his strength. To learn how to walk on an artificial leg, he moved to our New York apartment and went to the Rusk Institute on East Twenty-third Street, where he made remarkable progress. The patient and my wife, Alice, got along wonderfully for three or four weeks. I could not believe how charming he was. Alice, already a daddy's girl, fell for him completely. I could not help wondering, somewhat ruefully, why he never turned on some of that charm for my mother. I was forgetting his resolution as he came off the operating table. He was now a former son of a bitch. In Arlington Avenue days, my mother had to deal with the real thing.

In Jersey City, it was politics as usual, minus Frank Hague. One day, in a moment of utter naiveté, I suggested my father might go down to City Hall and visit some old friends, such as Billy Black, who had made the transition to the new regime. He looked at me as if I were six years old. "You don't do that when you're not a big shot anymore," he said.

Only one of the old crowd from the Sixth Ward visited him regularly—the union leader, Johnny Smith. Some people, such as Aunt Mae, took a dark view of the "no-goods" who had enjoyed my father's favor and now deserted him. But I never heard a word of reproach from him. He understood that those on the lower rungs of the political ladder had to make peace with the new regime or starve. He also understood that the emphasis on loyalty or else had not ended with the Hague regime. The city still swarmed with would-be informers, and anyone seen visiting Teddy Fleming would soon be suspected of plotting dark deeds against the new rulers. Even Johnny Duff, who in later years told me how much he hated to do it, stopped seeing my father.

When I expressed my gratitude to Smitty for sticking with Teddy Fleming, he brushed it aside. "Your old man is the straightest, most on-the-level guy I ever met. I consider it a privilege to be his friend," he said.

The connection to the advice my father had written in my grammar school autograph book was uncanny. Johnny Smith became the embodiment of that primary wisdom, born in the harsh ghetto world of the downtown Jersey City Irish.

> *There are plenty of fair weather friends*
> *You can find them hereabouts*
> *But here's to the friend who will stick by me*
> *When he knows I'm "down and out."*

Johnny was another hell of a guy.

# 31

# The Last Lesson

Over in New York, I was acquiring another father figure. I went from a year of newspapering on the *Yonkers Herald-Statesman* to working as assistant to Fulton Oursler, a writer and editor who had thirty-seven books on his escutcheon, many of them best-sellers. He had also written a hit play, *The Spider*, in the late twenties and during the 1930s edited *Liberty*, the second biggest weekly in the country, where he became friendly with numerous celebrities, including several presidents.

When I joined Oursler in 1951, his book *The Greatest Story Ever Told* had been number one on the best-seller list for almost two years. Witty, wry, sophisticated, he was far from the stereotype of the religious writer. For most of his life he had been a freethinker, typified by his 1933 book *A Skeptic in the Holy Land*, which undertook to demolish the divinity of Jesus.

Oursler became a convert to Catholicism after twenty years of marriage to his Catholic-born wife, Grace Perkins, and a long debate with himself and several Jesuits. In many ways he remained a Protestant. He hated to kneel and kiss a bishop's ring. Usually he barely dipped his knee and gave the jewelry a passing smack. Later he would complain to me that it was the most stupid custom the Catholic Church retained from its nostalgia for the Middle Ages.

I was soon toiling fourteen hours a day for "FO," as everyone called him, giving satisfaction as far as I could tell, until one evening when we were relaxing prior to my departure for home. "By the way, what does your father do for a living?" FO casually asked.

"Until recently, he was leader of the Sixth Ward under Frank Hague in Jersey City," I said.

"That's the first bad thing I've heard about you," FO said.

FO, I rapidly discovered, was a very convinced Republican. During the thirties, he had been close to Franklin Roosevelt but grew disillusioned with him as FDR drifted to the left in the New Deal's unsuccessful attempts to solve the Great Depression. At first I thought it was going to be a replay in more sophisticated terms of "No Irish Need Apply." But FO was a fair-minded man, who was not about to judge me by my father. I later discovered a strong personal reason for this attitude. His own father had not been a model of respectability. He was a gambler-cum-con-man who spent a lot of his time fleecing the rubes in Atlantic City. FO's novel *The Great Jasper* was a ruefully affectionate portrait of this lovable scoundrel.

Over in New Jersey, John V. Kenny and Frank Hague's other political enemies, who were numerous after the big fellow's thirty-four bruising years in power, triggered various investigations of the old regime. They pretended to outrage over the three percent of their salaries all the Democrats on the public payroll were required to pay the Organization, although for decades they had coughed it up—and ordered others to do likewise—without any questions. Sweetheart deals with unions, contractors, and the like, the backbone of party politics, were also probed with marvelous righteousness. A congressional committee held hearings in Newark for a while. Unfortunately for them, they had no subpoena power. This was a signal to everyone who was compos mentis that they could be defied or evaded with impunity.

These federal gumshoes must have made at least two dozen calls to my father. I took a couple while I was visiting him. It was like a timetrip to my boyhood. There was Teddy Fleming in the living room, reading the newspaper. "I'm sorry," I would say. "Sheriff Fleming isn't here. He's out of town."

"How long will he be gone?"

"That's hard to say."

Sometimes my father took these calls. The performance was

worth taping. He would go into one of his ethnic acts. He was a very good mimic and could do Polish and Italian and black English. This was not really surprising; he had spent half his life listening to them in the Sixth Ward's clubhouse and saloons.

"Sorry, d'sharif he no here," he would say. "My name Pilsiduski, I pant the house."

"Pant?"

"Pant, you know? Wizzi brash? Swish swish. I dunno where d'sharif be. He gone long time now."

And so forth. Sometimes they got an Italian who was replacing the plumbing. Sometimes it was a Czech who was putting in storm windows. After paragraphs of incomprehension, none of them ever knew where Sheriff Fleming was. Surprise surprise, the sheriff never testified before the committee.

For a while, Fulton Oursler and I got along by avoiding politics. Instead, by way of rewarding me for my fourteen-hour days, he gave me an off-the-cuff course in the art of writing that was worth two years of earnest matriculation at any graduate school MFA program. But politics slumbered ominously beneath the surface of our relationship.

I was still a passionate Democrat, dismayed by the job the newspapers began doing on Harry S. Truman in the declining months of his presidency. Looming as the likely Republican candidate was General Dwight D. Eisenhower. His potential opponent was the brilliant, witty, intellectual governor of Illinois, Adlai Stevenson, a man I instinctively admired.

Early in 1952, FO began discussing an article he planned to write for *Reader's Digest*. He was a senior editor of this magazine, which was at the height of its power and influence, with a circulation of 18 million. The publisher, DeWitt Wallace, was a personal friend, who often visited Oursler in New York. The article was an attack on William O'Dwyer, former mayor of New York, who was currently ambassador to Mexico thanks to Mr. Truman. FO told me it was part of a three-pronged offensive the *Digest* was launching, with similar demolitions aimed at a leading Democrat in Illinois and another one in California. The goal was to blow big holes in Democratic majorities in these swing states.

I soon found myself working day and night on the O'Dwyer article. Most of the dirt was being leaked to FO by a Brooklyn judge who had presided over several Mafia trials while O'Dwyer had been district attorney. I had to collate and occasionally check out the judge's rather random recollections. The portrait that emerged was devastating. O'Dwyer, far from trying to put the mobsters in jail, was their covert partner in obfuscation and evasion. The story included the murder of at least one key witness, Abe "Kid" Reles, who mysteriously plunged from a Brooklyn hotel room while two cops were supposedly monitoring his every move.

As a Democrat, I was outraged by the whole operation. The judge was leaking confidential grand jury testimony, which was supposedly sealed by law. Like any good journalist, Oursler was delighted to take advantage of the judge's desire to destroy O'Dwyer. I thought it stank but I kept my mouth shut, and by early March the article was ready for publication in the May issue of the *Digest*.

As I was preparing to take the finished product to the *Digest*'s New York office for delivery to Pleasantville, the telephone rang. "Is Mr. Oursler free for Cardinal Spellman?" asked a male voice.

Oursler motioned to me to stay on my phone—a precaution he occasionally took when he thought a call might be controversial. This one more than filled that description. Cardinal Spellman was calling to beg FO not to destroy the reputation of a fellow Catholic, William O'Dwyer. Someone at the *Digest* must have leaked the general content of the article to O'Dwyer or one of his allies. The ex-mayor had reached out to His Eminence for an ultimate favor.

Here, as they say in that Gilbert and Sullivan operetta, was a howdy-do. I had to admit FO handled it beautifully. He told Cardinal Spellman he did not think religion had anything to do with what he was writing about Mr. O'Dwyer. He was simply stating facts—admittedly damaging facts—that he thought the country ought to know. His Eminence demurred, but FO politely—very politely—said he did not intend to change a line. If the article was wrong about anything, Mr. O'Dwyer had the freedom to reply in some other magazine.

By the time Cardinal Spellman hung up, FO was pouring sweat. The call had put a terrific strain on him. He fell back in his leather chair in the corner of his study and said, "How do you like that? How do you like that?" He was learning things about the Catholic Church that many Irish-Americans knew before they were old enough to vote.

FO would have been even more upset if he had known that his trusted assistant didn't like it at all. For me the clerical power play was proof that my fellow Democrat, Bill O'Dwyer, was fighting desperately for his political survival. I left with the article under my arm but I did not hail a taxi to whisk me to the *Digest*'s New York offices. Instead, I walked around and around the block for almost an hour, wondering if I should take the article to the headquarters of the New York Democratic Party. They would welcome me as a brother and immediately launch a public counterattack against this Republican smear. I seriously considered doing this—knowing that the consequences would be the obliteration of my job and my relationship with Fulton Oursler.

Gradually I calmed down and sorted it out. Was I required to be loyal to the national Democratic Party? My answer was no. The national Democrats had played no small part in destroying the Hague Organization by inflicting Woodrow Wilson II, aka Governor Charles Edison, on the state party. My party loyalty began and ended where my father's began and ended, in Jersey City.

Was I required to be loyal to William O'Dwyer? Again, my answer was no. He had never done anything for me or anyone in my family. For another thing, Bill was awfully cozy with the Mafia, no matter what Cardinal Spellman said. For a third thing, I was the son of a politician, not a politician myself. I was into a new dimension, a career as a journalist-novelist-historian, and my loyalty belonged to the man who was giving me a chance to learn a tremendous amount about the publishing business at a breakneck pace.

Whew! I hailed a cab, and in an hour the O'Dwyer demolition was on its way to publication. It probably helped Eisenhower carry New York. But at best (or worst) it was no more than a snowball in the Eisenhower avalanche, as the general buried my hero Adlai Stevenson 442 electoral votes to 89.

On the other side of the Hudson, my father followed the politics of Jersey City as it degenerated into an every-man-for-himself melee. Johnny Kenny had neither the energy nor the desire to control the political scene in Hague's domineering style. He reverted to the "Easy Boss" role of Robert "Little Bob" Davis. This eventually led the little guy to a heavy involvement with the Mafia and a sentence to a federal penitentiary.

My father amused himself by interfering in various political dust-ups on the telephone, using a variety of accents. He took a dislike to a black lawyer we shall call Leroy McClusky, who was always sounding off about racial injustice, with which I hasten to admit Jersey City was rampant. My father began calling him at two in the morning. Through friends in City Hall he knew all the crooked deals Leroy was trying to pull.

The ex-sheriff always used the same name, Aloysius K. Brown. "McCluskey," he'd say, "this yo' old friend and neighbor Aloysius K. Brown callin'. I got the dope on you, McClusky. I know you tryin' to make off with that widow's money. And when you gonna stop diddlin' yo secretary? I'm gonna tell yo pastor, McClusky. Ah'm surprised you show yo face in that church on Sunday."

"Brown," McCluskey would rave, "I'm gonna trace this call. I'm gonna find you and remove you from the earth."

Johnny Smith and I had more than one laugh about these midnight go-rounds with McClusky. One Saturday morning Smitty stopped by the house at 10 A.M. The front door was unlocked. He walked in and found Teddy Fleming still asleep. Smitty realized that the sheriff was leaving the front door open all night. Because of his missing leg, it was a lot of trouble to get out of bed and into his wheelchair to answer the bell.

Smitty decided to teach the war hero a lesson. Standing at the end of the bed, he intoned, "Aloysius K. Brown, yo' last moment on earth has come!"

Instantly, with a speed that seemed preternatural, Teddy Fleming was sitting up in bed with his big black army .45 in his hand. Smitty dove for the floor and stayed there, yelling, "It's me! It's me!"

"Don't ever do that again," my father said. Smitty never did.

During these retirement years, I tried to turn my father into a reader. I gave him novels and history books. He returned them unread. In desperation I found a book entitled *Famous Criminals of Our Time*. He expressed some interest in this offering.

On my next visit, he gestured to the book. "What a phony piece of work," he said. "I never met one of those guys." This gave me a frustratingly brief glimpse of the people that Teddy Fleming associated with in his pre–World War I slugger days and perhaps in the early 1920s, before he married his uptown beauty and became more or less respectable.

One day I tried to tell Teddy why I thought his kind of politician was important. Night after night, for thirty years, he had dealt with the thousand and one details of the Sixth Ward's voters' lives—solving quarrels between ambitious committeemen; sweet-talking dissatisfied Poles, Greeks, or Italians; getting jobs for chronic alcoholics, paroles for stickup men. I told Teddy how much I admired his patience, his steadfastness, how vital I thought it was to have men like him practicing politics on a local scale, giving the average man and woman the feeling that someone in the power structure cared about them.

My father grew more and more uncomfortable during this monologue. By the time it ended, he was looking at me as if I had gone nuts. "But Teddy," he said. "You've got to listen to an awful lot of bullshit."

With my eyes already focused on a literary career, I was naturally interested in learning as much as possible about the Hague Organization. My father declined to tell me anything even faintly revelatory. He was not about to become a snitch, even for his son the writer. But in our chats about the old days, he told me a fair amount in an informal way.

One of the shocks was the totality of Hague's power. In the Western Union office in Journal Square, a police lieutenant read every telegram that came in and out of the city each day. Anyone who deposited more than $7,000 in a local bank was liable to be invited to City Hall to explain where he got the money. Phones were, of course, tapped whenever the mayor considered it necessary. Along with fear there was the constant use of favor. If a critic could not be intimidated, his loyalty could often be purchased with a good job.

Maybe Johnny Kenny had a point with his Freedom Ticket, I thought. What a pity that the little guy had no integrity to go with the slogan.

One night in 1956, my father and I were watching the Jackie

Gleason television show. "You know the best thing you ever said to me?" he growled.

"What?" I said.

"You were proud of me for sticking with the old crowd."

"I still am," I said.

That night he gave me the ring Frank Hague had given him when he became sheriff, with the inscription from the mayor on its inner rim. I sensed layers of meaning in the gift. He was bonding me to him, to sonship, and also saying he was no longer bonded to the old crowd. He had outlived that loyalty.

At the same time he was saying he wanted me to understand the whole thing, being born Irish-American and poor, winning a commission in the U.S. Army, making good as the Sixth Ward leader, becoming chairman of the Board of Chosen Freeholders, judge of the Second Criminal Court, sheriff of Hudson County. It was a pretty good run for a guy who barely made it out of the eighth grade.

Over the next year, my father slipped inexorably toward death. He stopped using his artificial leg. "What's the point?" he said to me one day. "I don't go anywhere." Confined to the wheelchair, his body developed bladder, bowel, and stomach problems. His heart, badly damaged in the post-amputation attack, was a mess. His doctor remarked to me that he was baffled that the sheriff was still alive. His arteriosclerosis worsened steadily, exposing him to the likelihood of a stroke. Later, in a poem, I compared him to a doomed guerrilla being hunted by a main force army in a mountainous landscape, fighting from peak to peak, knowing how it was going to end.

By this time I was a married man with a growing family and a job as a magazine editor in New York. I visited Arlington Avenue at least once and often twice a week and fretted about not coming more often. One night in early November 1957, I sensed the end was near. His male nurse, a mild-mannered Englishman named Al Turnbull, told me Teddy seldom got out of bed. His appetite was dwindling. He was losing interest in politics. Aloysius K. Brown was no longer enraging Leroy McClusky.

Johnny Smith continued his almost daily visits, and Mae Fleming Gallagher, living less than a block away, came even more often. A young priest from St. Patrick's parish called every other week. One day I met him as he was leaving the house and confessed I was a little worried about my father's state of soul. He never said anything even faintly religious to me or anyone else, as far as I knew. "I'm not worried about him. Not in the least," the priest said.

The priest was an Irish-American, about my age. He hesitated for a moment and said, "He's one of the most extraordinary men I've ever met!" He too had become a captive of the force that Teddy Fleming emanated. I was tempted to tell him about the guy in the glass. I decided maybe he already knew about him in a subconscious way.

Then came a call from Al Turnbull with sad news: my father had suffered a stroke and was in very bad shape. Al had called the doctor, who visited and confirmed his diagnosis. I rushed to Jersey City and met my brother, Gene, at the door of our house. Al had summoned him too. Gene was working as a magazine writer and doing very well.

Teddy Fleming was in bed in what had been our dining room. He was surprisingly alert, and greeted me and Gene by name. We sat with him for a while and chatted about our kids. By this time I had a daughter and three sons, and Gene had the first of his two daughters.

After dinner with Al Turnbull and Gene, I glanced in at my father. He seemed to be dozing. I put on my overcoat and headed for the front door.

"Teddy—don't leave yet," Teddy Fleming called. "Stay and see me go."

I tore off my overcoat and rushed to the bed. "Shake hands," my father said. I obeyed the order, remembering the hundreds of times I had performed the ritual throughout my life. Every time I had heard those primary words, *Shake hands like a man.*

His grip was still a handshake. But it was not hard enough to hurt. I was stronger now. I could have hurt him. His hand had grown soft and old. It had lost its leathery redness. There was no doubt that he was dying. His breathing became more and more labored. His eyes closed. But he continued to clutch my hand. Gene came to the other side of the bed and took his left hand.

Gene and I stood there, weeping. He squeezed our hands again and again. The pressure dwindled little by little—and finally stopped.

With one last shuddering sigh, he was gone. I bent down and kissed his forehead. My brother Gene did the same thing.

*Stay and see me go.* I realized he was telling me and Gene the final thing he wanted us to learn as his sons. Death was just another fear a man faced. It was no big deal. It was as simple as opening and closing a door. A man with nerve walked through it without flinching.

Shake hands like a man. Live like a man, according to a code of conduct you kept no matter what. Love like a man, without your heart on your sleeve—but fiercely, firmly, stubbornly. Die like a man. For someone with no education worth mentioning, Teddy Fleming had learned a lot—and he knew how to teach it to his sons.

# 32

# Hail and Farewell

A few weeks after I returned from France with the ring on my finger once more, I dreamt about my father. He was in his wheelchair and I was pushing him up a steep winding path. The chair was incredibly heavy. Sweat poured down my face and neck. At one point I almost lost control of him. The chair started to roll back on top of me. But I gritted my teeth and continued the ascent. The going became easier, the wheelchair seemed to grow lighter.

I was trying to get my father to the top of the mountain to enjoy the magnificent view. About halfway up I saw a small half-moon-shaped plateau off the path. It reminded me of the sites marked "scenic view" on the road above the Delaware Water Gap, one of the favorite destinations of our Sunday car rides in the 1930s. I decided to stop at this gravel-covered little refuge. I guided the wheelchair into it and turned my father around to face the view.

"I bet we can see just as much from here as we can at the top," I said.

We couldn't see a thing. Everything below us was engulfed in fog. I was tremendously disappointed. "I'll be fine here," my father said. "Stop worrying about me."

He gave me a handshake—a tough squeeze. I sensed we were saying good-bye again, this time with a new finality. When I awoke, I instantly understood the dream. It was part of my unfulfilled yearning to share with my father my ideas and insights into history and religion and literature. I had never made him into a reader or a thinker.

So what? I thought, brushing away tears. *So what?*

The next morning, my brother Gene called me from Michigan, where he was completing a successful career as a speechwriter in the automobile business. I told him about the dream. Not for the first time, Gene grew impatient with big brother's pretensions to being an intellectual. He responded with his favorite memory of Teddy Fleming.

We were crabbing on the Manasquan River in our outboard motorboat, *Sandy*. The weather suddenly turned foul and we headed home in a steady drizzle. Soon we were wet and cold. My father sat in the bow. I handled the three-horsepower motor on the stern. Gene sat in the middle seat. We putt-putted slowly down the river against the tide.

"I looked at the father, huddled in the bow," Gene said. "I saw how miserable he was. Somehow that made me love him tremendously. In the city Teddy Fleming was a big deal. Here he was in this dinky boat, sharing the crummy weather with us, taking it with no complaints. He didn't say anything or do anything. He was just there. I loved him for it."

I gazed at the Argonne ring on my finger.

*My Buddy.*
*The Guy in the Glass.*
*You're all I've got.*

# Index

Note: Page numbers in *italic* type refer to photographs. The first name Teddy throughout the index refers to the author's father.